HELLENIC
PRESENCE IN AMERICA

STEPHANOS ZOTOS

Hellenic Presence In America

PILGRIMAGE, Wheaton, Ill., 1976

In English:

By the same author:

GREECE: THE STRUGGLE FOR FREEDOM
New York: Thomas Y. Crowell, 1967.

THE GREEKS: DILEMMA OF PAST AND PRESENT
New York: Funk and Wagnalls, 1969.

In Greek:

TO TAXIDI STI GALLIA (Voyage to France)
Athens: Dimitratou S.A., 1944.

KYNIGONDAS SKIES, Short Stories (Chasing Shadows)
Athens: Dimitratou S.A., 1946.

I AMERIKI ENANTION TIS AMERIKIS (America vs. America)
Athens: Kedros, 1973.

This book is dedicated to
the blessed memory of His All Holiness
the Ecumenical Patriarch Athenagoras
whose radiant personality and
unrelented effort succeeded in uniting the
Greek Orthodox Communities in the
Western Hemisphere into one
strong Archdiocese.

Contents

9 Introduction

13 Early Presence

17 Immigration

24 The Greek Spirit of Adventure

30 Explorers and Adventurers

40 In St. Augustine, North America's Oldest City

44 American Interest in the Greek War of Independence

57 Outstanding Greeks in America

65 American Diplomatic Representation in Greece

73 Greece of the Immigrants

85 Pressure Upon Greek Youth to Emigrate

89 First Days of Mass Greek Immigration

93 Exploitation, Injustice, Even Tyranny

100 Greek-American Community Life

105 Tarpon Springs—a North American "Greek Town"

108 The closing Gates of the "Promised Land"

112 The Social System and the So-Called "Melting Pot"

119 Advandages and Disadvantages of Greek Immigration

127 Adjustment Problems

133 The Greek-American "Social Class" and Social Classifications

154 New Orleans—Birthplace of a New Organized Orthodoxy

162 Greek Numerical Strength in America

167 The Political Problems of Greece "Transplanted"

171 The Second Greek-American Generation

174 The Greek Language Press

185 The Relationship Between the Greek-Americans and Greece

187 The Urge for Repatriation

195 The Contribution of the Greek-Americans to the Arts

200 The Greek Orthodox Church of North and South America

208 The Greek Orthodox Church in America and the Ecumenical Movement

110 The Problem of Greek Education in the Hands of the Greek Orthodox Church

216 The Need for a New Orientation
219 Needs and Demands of the New Greek-American Generation—
     American Orthodoxy
222 The Ecumenical Patriarchate and the Greek Orthodox Church
     of America
226 The Establishment of an Autocephalous Russian Orthodox
     Church in America
230 The 20th Clergy-Laity Congress of the Greek Orthodox
     Archdiocese of North and South America
236 Some Closing Remarks

Introduction

THE initial Hellenic presence and involvement in early American life can be traced, though not in any sizable and easily identifiable quantity, long before the end of the nineteenth century when the first Greek immigrants started arriving in the United States. The exact date of the original appearance of the Greeks in the New World cannot be determined with accuracy. The distant past is a labyrinth of conjectures in which one has to move with great caution and even some hesitation. Moreover, it is indeed very difficult to recreate with the utmost exactitude one single aspect of America's history at a moment when the country, in search of its identity and its future place in the world community, was going through constant developments. It is rather easy to reconstruct certain features of the past using the titles of kings and wars, victories and defeats that provide precise dates and ample material. But when trying to establish the facts related to the activities of one or more persons or even a group of people in the early days of the formation of a country of immigrants, one has to plunge deep into the obscurity of time. This is particularly true—though to a different extent, in connection with the later arrival and presence of the Greeks in America when the country was receiving millions of heterogeneous elements from almost all over the world. Here again, one must search into the realm of anonymity for which records are rare and incomplete. Their initial numbers being insignificant, no statistical attention was paid to the Greeks and there existed no statistics in Greece when they left their motherland. Moreover, the first Greek immigrants were frequently confused with other foreigners coming to the United States—usually with the Turks and people of Slavonic origin. The Records of the Commissioner General of Immigration make no reference to them until 1824, when the Greeks were already fighting their war of independence against the Ottoman Empire.

Ancient Greece had always been a source of inspiration and admiration for the Americans since the first moments of the spiritual growth of their land. There were prominent Americans who had advocated that the United States should adopt Greek as the official language of the new nation, but little was actually known by the American people about their Greek contemporaries. During the dark days of the four hundred years of Turkish domination, the Hellenes had been almost forgotten. This seems to have been the feeling of President James Monroe, when he said in his annual message, on December 3, 1822:

> The mention of Greece fills the mind with the utmost exalted sentiments and arouses in our bosoms the best feelings of which our nature is susceptible. Superior skill and refinement in the arts —heroic gallantry in action, disinterested patriotism, enthusiastic zeal and devotion in favor of public and personal liberty are associated with our recollections of ancient Greece. That such a country should have been overwhelmed and so long hidden, as it was, from the world under the gloomy despotism, has been a cause of increasing and deep regret for ages past. It is natural, therefore, that the reappearance of these people in their original character, contending in favor of their liberties, should produce that great excitement and sympathy in their favor, which have been so signally displayed throughout the United States.

Almost one year later, on October 31, 1823, Thomas Jefferson wrote Adamandios Korais, the famous Greek patriot and scholar residing in Paris: "Whatever service Americans might render the cause of revolutionary Greece must be considered a tribute to the splendid constellation of sages and heroes whose blood is still flowing in your veins, and whose merits are still resting, as a heavy debt, on the shoulders of the living, and the future races of men." (H.A. Washington, Editor, *Writings of Thomas Jefferson*, Vol. VII.)

However, in spite of official statements of admiration and sympathy for the Greek cause and though the American people as a whole had indeed embarked upon an ardent campaign on behalf of the hard-fighting Greeks, the United States Government observed a strict neutrality in the conflict between Greeks and Turks. In the nineteenth century the Ottoman Empire was powerful and only the outcome of the 1821 Greek War of Independence was to dictate a change in the official American attitude. The revolution was an event that stirred the American imagination and aroused respect of the American people for the Greeks. Further, Greece was a Christian nation fighting for liberty and emancipation from a Moslem rule. Above all, the Greeks were the recipients of a great legacy.

In February 1823, Andreas Luriotis, a representative of the Greek revolutionary Government delivered to the American minister in London, Richard Rush, an appeal for the establishment of diplomatic relations between Greece and the United States. But recognition of Greece by the United States came later than recognition by Russia, one of the parties of the despised Holy Alliance. (Strictly defined, the Holy Alliance was the agreement among the Emperors of Russia, Austria and the king of Prussia. It was quite distinct from the Quadruple—Quintuple after the admission of France—of Great Britain, Russia, Austria and Prussia, arrived at first in 1824, and revived in 1825.) It is only in 1833, after the war had been fought and won by the Greeks, that the United States acknowledged the sovereignty of the Kingdom of Greece, and three years later the Greek-American diplomatic treaty was signed.

In an article entitled "Early American policy concerning Ottoman minorities," (*Political Science Quarterly*, XLII, 1927) Edward Mead Earle wrote:

> Americans might have held farther aloof from the Greek cause had it not been for a variety of American interests in the Mediterranean region during the period of the Greek War of Independence ... The continuous presence in the Mediterranean of American vessels had made necessary furthermore, the maintenance in those waters of an American naval squadron, which commanded attention and respect by reason of its exploits earlier in the century at the expense of the Barbary pirates ... This squadron —in 1824—was an alert and interested observer of everything that transpired in Ottoman waters from the initial outbreak in the Morea in 1821, until after the battle of Navarino. (Naval battle in 1827, resulting from the intervention of the European powers in the Greek War of Independence. England, France and Russia had demanded an armistice in the Greek-Turkish fighting, which was rejected by the Turks. The three powers sent their fleets to stop Egyptian reinforcements from landing in Greece to offer help to the Turks. The Egyptian fleet was completely destroyed during the engagement.)

Edward Mead Earle concludes that:

> ... a study of American official policy toward nationalistic minorities of the Ottoman Empire reveals no important departure from the precepts which John Quincy Adams enunciated ... it is not true that the Government of the United States signed a treaty guaranteeing the rights of minorities in the Turkish

dominions; it is not true that it has taken an active part, diplomatic or military, in the emancipation of Christian people of the Near East from Moslem rule.

Confirming certain negative attitudes of Americans toward the Greeks, John Quincy Adams, (6th President of the United States), wrote in his Diary in 1828: "Rodgers (Commodore John Rodgers) himself and all the commanders of our armed vessels in the Mediterranean have great abhorrence and contempt for the Greeks." (John Quincy Adams, *Memoirs,* Vol. XII, p. 463).

In 1827, Elnathan Gridley, an American missionary, travelled in the Morea and the Ionian Islands to consider the services which American Protestant Christianity might offer to Greek Orthodox Christianity. Modern Greek was the first language many American missionaries undertook to learn, and the spiritual welfare of the Greek populations of Asia-Minor was one of their primary concerns. However, the United States had, not so long ago, signed a treaty with an Islamic power stipulating that:

> . . . As the Government of the United States is not in any sense founded on the Christian religion; as it has in itself no character of enmity against the laws, religion or tranquility of Musselmen . . . it is declared by the parties that no pretext arising from religious opinions shall ever produce an interruption of the harmony existing between the two countries. (Article XI of the Treaty of 1796, with Tripoli; W.M. Malloy, *Treaties-Conventions.* International Sets of American and other powers).

Obviously, this treaty prevented the United States, which was following a tradiitional policy of isolation, to show substantial interest—much less to interfere—in favor of the Greeks, who were fighting a Moslem occupant. It was not the first time—nor the last —that the policy of a great nation was to be dictated rather by what its leaders thought was its best interest, than by the feelings of its people.

Early Presence

A NUMBER of views have been expressed on the subject of the early presence of the Greeks in America. Theories have even been advanced that Christopher Columbus was a Greek. Should one day this assumption be historically confirmed and substantiated by documented evidence then, of course, not only would the Greeks be credited with having discovered America, but automatically their initial presence in the New World would be established in 1492, thirty-nine years after the fall of Constantinople to the Turks. Some historians have insisted that actually the discovery of America was, so to speak, an immediate result of the collapse of Byzantium. Whether this claim adds more credence to the allegation that Columbus was a Greek is another, debatable question. With Constantinople under Turkish domination a great many Greek scholars found refuge in various parts of the world and are known to have contributed their wisdom and talents to the evolution of the Renaissance movement, but there is no evidence that any of them came to Amrica at the moment it was discovered or immediately after.

Following some controversy, it has been finally ascertained that Juan de Fuca, whose name was given to the straits separating Vancouver from the state of Washington, was a Greek pilot, Apostolos Valerianos, alias Ioannis Phokas, working for Spain, who came to America in 1599. It has also been determined that a large group of Greeks, whose numbers are given variously by different sources, were brought to Florida in 1766—then under English rule—by an Englishman, a Scot, Andrew Turnbull, who founded the colony of New Smyrna, after the birthplace of his Greek wife, Gracia Dura Bin Turnbull. These were Greeks, some from Mani, in the Peloponnesos, and others from the island of Corsica where their families had sought asylum fleeing the island of Crete, which in 1669 had been conquered by the Turks, after a long war against the Venetians. Some had also settled in Tuscany, Italy. The first settlers in Florida were to be identified as Minorcans, because Turnbull had picked them up, along with some Italians and other foreigners, from the island of Minorca, the rendez-vous place for the departure to the New World. When the colony of New Smyrna was disbanded, some of the Greek colonists settled in St. Augustine, Florida. Still other young boys, mostly orphans, were brought to the United States by Americans who had fought in the 1821 Greek War of Independence, and can be considered among the first settlers in America of Hellenic descent.

The names of many Greeks have been mentioned in connection with the early Hellenic presence in America and indeed some of these names can be found in the Cyclopaedias and Directories of American Biography. Yet, others also figure in certain narratives, but there is little documented evidence leading to a conclusive identification of their origin or their activities. One of them is referred to as Count Theodore Caesar Logothetis, from the island of Zante, who was supposed to have been one of Lafayette's aides during the American War of Independence, but his name was not to be found in official records. The name of Demetrios Ypsilanti—like his brother Alexander, a leader and hero of the 1821 Greek War of Independence—also has been mentioned in connection with the American War of Independence. He is said to have participated in the battle of Monmouth, on June 8, 1778 against the English. Actually, there is no evidence of Ypsilanti having set foot on American soil, and the legend seems to stem out of the fact that in 1824, judge Augustus Brevoot Woodward gave the name of Ypsilanti to the "land of the Wolverine state," in honor of the leader of the Greek uprising in 1821. Ypsilanti is today a city of Michigan, on the Huron river. On the other hand, many Greeks certainly fought in the American Civil War, siding either with the North or the South, and still others fought in the Mexican-American and Spanish-American wars. Finally, an intensive research in the Cyclopaedias of American Biography (National Archives, Washington, D.C.) revealed that quite a number of Greek Americans of half-blood (their mothers were Greek), played an important early role in American education and other aspects of public life in the country.

In trying to establish historical facts related to the early presence of the Greeks in America, one must avoid wishful thinking that might be dictated by the nationalistic feelings of the Greek researcher. Emotion is not conducive to objectivity and could be detrimental even when one is gathering material. Historical narratives must be supported by evidence if they are not to fall into the domain of tales—regardless of how colorful those tales may be.

One must have always in mind that history is only what happened, and only a small proportion of all things that happen leaves a permanent record. History, whether rich or poor, kind or unkind to a subject under exploration should reflect only facts. Its purpose is to present these facts on the basis of evidence, which could withstand any investigation and dispel any eventual doubts about its genuiness. To embark upon an emotional, guessing adventure instead of offering an irrefutable conclusion is a flagrant deviation from any serious endeavor to reconstruct the past.

With some commendable exceptions, the Greeks who attempted to describe the life of the Hellenes in America, have permitted themselves a number of daring identifications, which cannot always sustain a thorough examination of their accuracy. Moreover, they seem to have seen only certain aspects of the activities of the Greeks in America and have indulged in monotonous eulogies. Thus, they have failed to record history as such, and most certainly have not rendered any service to the Greek-Americans who, after all, are entitled to know all about themselves.

This observation should not be misconstrued as a conclusion that the Greek immigrants in America deserved only criticism, which was intentionally omitted and avoided by other Greeks who wrote about them. This is not so. As a whole, the immigration of the Greeks in America is a long, fascinating story of endless and painful efforts against impossible odds, and in the final analysis a triumph. This observation is merely a reminder and a warning that in recording history related to a particular ethnic group, which grows in a foreign, at times hostile, enviroment, one is bound to come to some unfavorable findings he has no right to ignore. Recording history is not a mission of patriotic myopia, but the discharge of a duty to objectivity and to the ethnic group whose story is revived and narrated.

As a whole, mainly because of their glorious past but also because of their immeasurable pride, the Greeks have always been eager and willing to accept eulogies but very reluctant to take any criticism. Because of this inability to stand adverse judgment or opinions about themselves, the Greeks have developed a curious sense of superiority—curious indeed because when the occasion arises they are not in the habit of sparing their own compatriots their accusations and charges.

The Greek-Americans, and more particularly the first immigrants —since the new Greek-American generations represent an entirely separate and different aspect of Hellenic presence in America—are no exception to the rule. They have carried and felt the heavy burden of the glorious legacy that seems to have convinced them that they, too, have earned the privilege of a permanent and exclusive praise. Yet, like any other individuals on this earth they have qualities but also shortcomings and they have met not only success, but failure.

Through the years the dramatic story of the Greek immigrant in America, which naturally begins in Greece itself, unfolds in the impressive, often frightening but prosperous vastness of the United States and in innumerable instances ends in Greece. Only then is the historical cycle closed. Thus, the story of the first immigrant is to a certain extent the urge of the individual to return one day to the initial source of his expatriation. Not all first immigrants return to Greece. Some die before the voyage is undertaken; others decide not to leave their adopted country; some die on their way to the old country, unable to bear the weight of the emotion; still others go to Greece, only to come back to America after finding it difficult, or too late, to adjust to the requirements of what is, in fact, a new immigration. For those who stay in Greece till the end, the image of America is ever present in their thoughts. For the second time in their life they become victims of nostalgia.

There is something passionate, at times pathetic, about this strong, imperative obsession, which has persisted during the original period of ordeal the first immigrant had to face, but which did not decrease even when many of the innumerable problems were eventually met. The first immigrants have remained inexorably attached to the idea of repatriation as though pulled by a mysterious force, and even though many knew they would not find in Greece the serenity they were looking for as an ultimate reward for the long absence.

The Greeks emigrated to a land of immigrants and were among the last people to come to the United States; they also were among the last people to hang on desperately to their religion, traditions and customs. This accounts for the inalienable, sacrosanct attachment to their country of birth.

Immigration

IMMIGRATION is a sort of perpetual revolution; it is mankind in continuous motion. It has the distinctive traits of a powerful social movement of historical significance and consequences. It will never cease as long as different degrees of liberties and restrictions, different patterns of civilization will prevail in every country. The occurence of the phenomenon will not be interrupted since the individual will always yield and obey the impulse that forces him to change his physical environment. During certain periods of history—and in some instances—the impulse appears to be stronger than the individual's allegiance to the country of his birth. These are moments when immigration provides for him an outlet.

The word immigrant is a rather new acquisition of the English vocabulary. The historians trace it back to 1817. Prior to this date, and namely in the seventeenth and eighteenth century, the settler was identified as an "emigrant." The implication was, according to M.L. Hansen, that ". . . he migrated out of something. By 1817, he was migrating into something. That something was the new nation (America), which had come into being." (M.L. Hansen, *The Immigrant in American History*, Cambridge: Harvard University Press, 1940). Thus, the word immigrant, as opposed to emigrant, was adopted and established for the first time as the final and proper identification of the settlers arriving in America.

In the 19th and 20th century there was a vast influx of European immigrants into the Americas, especially into the United States, which received between 1820 and 1930, 38,000,000 settlers. One of the early important strains was the Scotch-Irish. Just before the middle of the 19th century, Irish and German immigrants were the predominant people. A little later, the Scandinavian nations supplied many settlers. After the American Civil War, the immigrants came mainly from the nations of South and East Europe: from Italy, Greece, Asia-Minor (mostly Greeks), Russia and the part of Poland then in Russia, and the variegated peoples of Austria-Hungary and the Balkans. This impressive addition to the United

States population over a period of one century marks a new era in American History which can be considered hardly less significant than the foregoing two centuries of colonization. By 1880, the United States was in the middle of a great industrial expansion. The desire for quantities of cheap, unskilled labor plus the efforts of transportation companies to promote the very profitable immigration were factors in the movement, which coincided with a large population expansion in the entire world and improved conditions and methods of transportation. Despite strong opposition, a literacy test was imposed on all immigrants in 1917. In 1921, the quota system was established for European countries limiting the number of immigrants received from a country in any year to 3 per cent of the number of their natives residing in the United States in 1910.

The percentage of Greek elements included in this wave of European immigration to America was relatively small but substantial in proportion to the total population of Greece. Between 1821 and 1934, 488,824 Greeks arrived in the United States—"almost one tenth of the entire population of Greece during the same period of time." (Vassilios Valaoras, *The Hellenism of the United States*, Athens, 1937). The statistics for the years 1881-1946, reveal that 431,650 Greek immigrated to America. To this number, however, must be added the proportion of the immigrants arriving from European and Asiatic Turkey, also from Egypt, Albania, Rumania, Bulgaria, Russia and Austria. The Report of the Commissioner General of Immigration, United States Department of Labor, 1932, permits the conclusion that approximately 500,000 Greeks had reached the United States prior to the Second World War. In the official records of the United States Immigration Service one finds the information that 431,650 Greeks arrived in America between 1881 and 1946, but this figure comprises only the Greeks arriving exclusively from Greece.

The exact number of Greeks who came to America will never be accurately established. Greece did not keep any records of the departures, and even those kept in more recent times are far from complete. If an average figure were to be drawn out of the approximate estimates of various sources, one would be led to believe that very probably over 800,000 Greeks came to America—and many more are still coming.

The story of Greek mass immigration to America begins in Greece. It is in Greece, therefore, that one must seek the reasons of their exodus. Knowing the Greeks deep love for their motherland one must come to the conclusion that economic conditions in the country must have been, indeed, extremely precarious for them to decide to leave and search elsewhere for a better future. In contrast to other ethnic groups, the Greeks never left home on account of political or religious persecutions. A false picture of America offered to them at the moment of their decision to depart, was another reason for the mass immigration of the Greeks to the United States. In enslaved Greece the causes of immigration were different. There, there was constant Turkish pressure, systematic persecution of the Christian Orthodox and finally compulsory service in the Turkish army. Yet, it would be a mistake to attribute the Greek immigration to America, or for that matter, anywhere in the world, to one cause. The Greek imagination has always been haunted by the desire for adventure. The Greeks from ancient times have been venturesome, seafaring, bold colonizers, who, however, were the first to relinquish their colonies. Very probably many Greeks left for the New World under the urge to face the unknown. Every Greek is another Ulysses and each one of his perilous experiences another Odyssey. However, the modern Ulysses, on his way to a foreign land had a definite advantage over Homer's hero. Wherever he went he carried a very religious feeling and an unshaken devotion to his Church which has always been the rallying point of the expatriated Greeks. It was the Greek Church that kept alive the spark of patriotism and education, and the modern Greek has never forgotten his incalculable debt to the Greek Orthodox Church. One of the primary concerns of the first immigrants in America was to build churches, to gather around them and form their communities.

In his book *Our Greek Immigrants*, Rev. Thomas J. Lacey wrote: "(The Greek's) care is to make provisions for religious services." Another writer, Rev. Thomas Burgess, in *Greeks in America* comes to the conclusion that ". . . Greeks are above all else Orthodox and patriots . . . Nor have social inequality or class hatred ever been motives for emigration of the democratic Greek." The Church holds a place of supreme importance in the life of the Greeks. Among no other people is the identity of church and the state more strongly rooted. In turn, the Church accepted gradually the heavy responsibility of offering instruction in the Greek language to the immigrants and of continuing tradition. However, there were years when the Greek Orthodox Church in America felt the direct impact of the tragic political divisions prevailing in Greece and, unfortunately, succumbed itself to the microbe of dissent. Indeed, these years were the most obscure and the most deplorable in the life of the Greek immigrants in the United States. It took time, patience, perseverence and initiative to restore the great damage suffered by the Greek name. Today, the Greek Orthodox Church in America —one of the major faiths in the country—stands as never before, well organized, viable and respected.

Between the end of the nineteenth century and the beginning of the twentieth century the Greeks came by the thousands to America to look for a more promising life. Their arrival coincided with the moment when antiforeignism and racial prejudice were at their peak in the country. For the greatest part the first Greek immigrants were uneducated, ignorant people—shepherds and laborers mostly from the Peloponnesos—who did not know how to read or write. Their country had been freed from the Turkish yoke only a few decades earlier and this accounted for their state of ignorance as well as for the economic conditions existing in Greece at that time. Prior to the crossing of the mysterious and dangerous Atlantic Ocean, most of these peasants had never seen even Athens or Piraeus or, for that matter, any town besides their own remote, primitive village.

The departure from Greece was not a happy occasion for the immigrants and for their relatives staying behind. There was no fanfare like in some other countries on similar occasions. In Germany, for example, the departing immigrants were serenaded by noisy crowds; parades were held and words of encouragement spoken to them. In Ireland, there were processions in honor of the prospective Americans and the church bells were set in motion. In Greece, as the future immigrants—destitute people among other destitute—were getting ready to sail only silence prevailed, broken now and then by sobbing.

The arrival of the Greek immigrants on the American shores was not a joyful event either. The fear that had possessed them at the very last moment of the departure, only to increase during the exhausting sea-voyage, had not faded away. Some of them cursed Columbus that he had discovered a new continent to tempt them away from their peaceful villages. As a rule, there was no one to meet them at the docks. They did not understand a word of English and their own Greek vocabulary was limited. After (in most cases) passing the strange "test," the Greek immigrants, who had been screened in Garden Castle, later on Ellis Island or elsewhere, were literally turned loose in the then unfriendly streets of the American cities. Tags, with their names or only a serial number attached to a piece of string and passed around their necks, hung on their chests. These tags were their only identification in this foreign land where they had come to live, work and eventually die. In most instances they had little money, or none at all. Very few had already a relative or an acquaintance, somewhere in the cold immensity of America. They were hungry; the battle of survival, which they believed they had lost back in Greece was, in reality, about to begin in America. It was to be a long, difficult battle, which, however, they finally won.

The newcomers to America brought with them no institutions except those of religion and family and an instinctive and strong pride for their glorious heritage. They also brought a rich but difficult language, which was to be an obstacle to their association with people of their kind, but of different nationalities. The Greeks differed in certain ways from the other minority groups which had either preceded them, or had come at the same time with them, to populate America. "True the problem of adjustment was common to all minorities," writes Burgess, "but the Greek—an individualist even when ignorant—had more difficulties than other immigrants." The Greeks were the recipients of the highest western culture, yet those landing in America were among the most ignorant of all immigrants. They combined a curious state of mind influenced by the blighting effects of four hundred years of slavery under the Turks combined with an ever-present consciousness of their illustrious ancestry. How was this to affect their activities and their eventual participation in the American experiment under way?

In his book *The Immigrant in American History*, Professor Hansen writes: "Was the American soil fertile or barren? It is certain that what many immigrants hoped and many native American feared, would happen, did not happen. There is today an American society which, in spite of local and temporary variations, is rather uniform —too uniform critics say, there are standards of collective conduct, forms of community activities considered American."

The structure of a nation of immigrants is molded by the influence of the foreign elements that populate the country, but only to the extent of their numbers and the proportion of their conrtibution and involvement to the collective effort. The first Greek immigrants did little to shape the American character and structure. Things have changed since. "The Greek immigrant makes a precious contribution to America's greatness and is to be counted a valuable asset to American life," writes Rev. Thomas J. Lacey.

The Greeks in America have lived and struggled away from their own geographical environment in a hospitable country, which, however, had not always been friendly to them and where they were often exploited by Americans and other Greeks, who had preceded them in "the land of the free." Moreover, it cannot be said that they were consistently held in the highest esteem among other ethnic groups. The necessity for self-defense prevented, perhaps, a different, earlier, deeper involvement in American life.

When was it that the Americans, as a whole, thought in more favorable terms about their fellow-citizens the Greeks? The turning point seems to be the Second World War and more particularly the 1940 Greek victories over the Italians in Albania. Yet, many Greeks had fought in the American Army during the First World War. During the 1944-46 civil war in Greece, American feelings towards the Greeks again changed. Too many Americans confused the issues at stake and the forces involved in the civil war. Some complained they were tired of too much "politicking" in Greece, because they failed at that time to recognize the nature and the real causes of the conflict. Later, not only did the United States reverse its position, but it helped Greece with economic and military assistance, to overcome the communist threat.

The fact that the first Greek immigrants lived outside their national frontiers permits to conclude that they were, and still are, different from what they would have been had they remained in Greece. This conclusion is important because it might help us understand better what they did or did not do in America, as well as many of the motives behind their various achievements and failures.

There is no doubt, whatsoever, that as a whole the first Greek immigrants secured in the United States a kind of life they would not have enjoyed had they not crossed the Atlantic Ocean to come to the New World. This can be easily ascertained through a comparison between their achievements in Amrica and the conditions under which the majority of their close relatives live today in Greece. The living conditions of these relatives—parents, brothers, sisters and cousins—who stayed behind would have been even worse were it not for the financial assistance they have been steadily receiving for years from their beloved ones in the United States. Needless to say that the constant flow of remittance from Greek-Americans has always been one of the major sources of national income for Greece.

The young shepherd or laborer, who half a century ago, and even earlier, left the meadows of the Peloponnesos or the mountain ranges of Epirus or Thessaly, is today somebody in America. He has a social standing; a profession or a job; he has money and, above all, his sons and daughters have become an inherent part of the American mainstream of progress. Back in Greece, most of his relatives have hardly improved their living standards and some of them, though no longer young, still work in the fields, and live in lodgements which lack the most elementary conveniences.

Some observers have contended that the first Greek immigrants would have been much better off and happier had they stayed in Greece, instead of being today—as they say—a strange, ugly combination of half-Greeks and half-Americans, who vacillate between a past that no longer exists and a present to which they have never really been adjusted. The contention is cruel and wicked and, moreover, seems to ignore the fact that any group of first immigrants— especially in the American environment—gradually develops into a very particular pattern of citizens who display a "mixture" of the characteristics of both the country of their birth and that of their adoption. The blend is not necessarily always harmonious. This particularity does not pertain exclusively to the Greek-Americans; it is a much more general phenomenon which affects most of the minority groups.

Those who speak with some superficiality and haste about the loss to Greece of the future Greek-American generations fail to take into consideration America's attitude towards its citizens whose parents belong to various ethnic groups. After all, America fought its own war of independence and ceased to be a colony to attain nationhood. Why should America encourage and permit the establishment of small foreign "colonies" on its soil? The United States has offered hospitality, freedom, opportunities and prosperity in order to achieve one day a genuine, uniform national entity. It also fought a costly civil war for almost the same purpose. Efforts or tendencies at preventing eventually this natural phenomenon cannot be expected to be tolerated by the American nation. The new Greek-American generations cannot and should not become a separate entity within the United States.

The Greek Spirit of Adventure

THE GREEK settlers and immigrants who came to the New World were heirs of the ancient Hellenes and of the passionate revolutionaries who had liberated Greece from the Turkish yoke in 1821, in spite of intestine quarrels which led even to armed clashes among them and threatened the victorious outcome of the national uprising.

How far back into the immensity of time can this heritage be traced, and who is actually a Greek? Archaeological remains prove that Hellenism had a long prehistory from at least the New Stone Age. By the Bronze Age important cultures had developed. The Aegean civilization had several phases, two of the most influential being the Minoan and the Mycenaean civilizations. These cultures disappeared by 1,100 B.C. As to the origin of the Hellenic race, Isocrates (436-338 B.C.), perhaps the greatest teacher in Greek History, ventured to say that "A Greek is a person who received Greek education." The National Geographic Atlas of the United States, on the other hand, gives a rather hasty and debatable description of the Greeks whom it defines as "Descendants of the Slavs, Turks and early Greek tribes."

When Constantinople fell to the Turks in 1453, the last remnants of Greek nationality were expected to vanish. For centuries the frequent barbarian invasions had driven what had survived of Hellenic culture within the walls of the capital of Byzantium. Now the metropolis of culture had collapsed and what it had harbored, cultivated and developed faced the mortal danger of disintegration. However, contrary to fears and pessimistic predictions the fall of the last bastion of Hellenic civilization produced the opposite result. Neither Greek nationality nor Hellenic consciousness were extinguished. Following the occupation of Constantinople by the Turks the Greek scholars who fled the city and settled in other parts of the world contributed to the revival of Hellenism.

In his book *The War of Greek Independence: 1821-1833* (Smith, Elder and Co., London) W. Alison Philips wrote that:

No nation . . . has ever been so tenacious of its individuality. Conquered again and again, Hellenism, vanquished in arms, ever retaliated by a bloodless victory over its conquerors. Macedonians and Romans in turn, themselves submitted to the empire of Hellenic culture; and though with the decay of the ancient civilization, this culture gradually faded away, all the evidence tends to prove that the Greeks, more than any other nation of modern Europe, have succeeded in assimilating these numerous foreign elements which must, in confusion of troubled centuries, have become intermingled with them.

In a study published in 1960, and entitled *The Origins of the Greeks: An Ethnogenetic Study,* Professor Aris Poulianos reaches the conclusion that the actual population of Greece is indigenous and that all types belong to the Eastern Mediterranean branch of the European population. He writes that "modern Greeks are the descendants of ancient peoples who assimilated Greek language and civilization." Professor Poulianos does not exclude other influences when he says that "anthropological types from Asia-Minor, the Balkans and Central Europe played a significant part in shaping the Greek nation." The racial uniformity of the Greeks from the Neolithic period was established by Professor Poulianos after a systematic anthropological study of thousands of men and women whom he divided into six categories: Southern Central, Epirus, Thrace, Northern Greece, West Macedonia and Aegean. Speaking about the features of the people, Professor Poulianos says that: "The Southern Central type has fairly dark eyes, smooth or curly hair and a straight or hooked nose. The Epirus type has lighter eyes, fewer hair with hooked nose, rarely straight hair and a characteristic skull formation. The Thrace type has mainly black eyes but there is a large percentage of mixed hues. Hair types are straight or curly, rare hair growth, thin face and straight or hooked nose. The West Macedonian type is rather a mixture of Thrace Pelasgic and Illyric, and there are no cut and dry boundaries of distinction. Hair growth is rare but beard is denser, eye shade mixed and the nose straight but low. This type has the lightest color in Greece and the percentage of dark to light eyes is almost equal. The Aegean is the tallest with medium hairgrowth or curly, a rather dense beard, and large forehead."

The origin of the Greeks has become, at various periods of time, the subject of discussions, but the eventual conclusions which might be drawn out of any debate would have little bearing on the nationality of the Greeks who came to America. Nationality in the United

States is not based on races but on the principle of the soil. All children born in the United States are U.S. citizens (children of diplomats excepted) irrespective of the origin of their parents. Thus, a Greek in America fits perhaps the description given by the prominent Greek statesman Eleftherios Venizelos, who said during a debate at the 1919 Versailles Peace Conference, while arguing in support of the Hellenism of Greek minorities under Turkish rule, "A Greek is a person who wants to be a Greek, feels he is a Greek and says he is a Greek." Greek consciousness being rather an instinct than a deliberate conviction, Venizelos may have given the perfect definition of what any Greek has always been and still is.

Regardless of how far back in history one can trace the origins of the Hellenic race, many centuries before the word immigration was devised the Greeks were—so to speak—international immigrants always intrigued and attracted by distant lands. Moreover, fully aware that the initial source of any knowledge is the unknown, the Greeks endeavored to reach the unexplored, and the predominant factor which prompted their extraordinary peregrinations was an influence of mythical origin coupled with the enticement of the unknown.

At practically every stage of its historical evolution Greek civilization is revealed, at one and the same time, as both amazingly modern and surprisingly ancient. During the various periods of their cultural attainments the Greeks were enamored with a noble past, which had endowed them with a rich heritage or innumerable and thrilling myths. In ancient Greece, the enlightenment of man began with the telling of myths, which were the basis of all education. Plato wanted the future citizens of his ideal republic to begin their learning with the telling of myths rather than with mere facts and Aristotle, this other master of pure reason, insisted that the friend of wisdom is also a friend of myth. In our days excavations almost all over the arid land of Greece have established the historical reality of certain legends and have also encouraged the Greeks to feel additional faith in the factual confirmation of various aspects of myth.

In their constant quest for the unknown the Greeks wrote history without realizing it. Because of their urge to explore the "ultima Thule"—the most distant goal of human pursuit or a land remote beyond all reckoning—they spread their influence wherever they settled. Thus, one is tempted to dispute the argument that in ancient times the Greeks sailed to foreign lands only to bring their own brand of civilization, and instead support the idea that it was also, and perhaps above all, their impulse for adventure that made them the intrepid colonizers they were. Greek colonies, probably before 1,000 B.C., flourished in Asia-Minor. In the 8th, 7th and 6th century B.C., the Greeks sent out colonies from the Black Sea, where Byzantium was founded, to Sicily, South Italy, Mediterranean France, the northern shores of Africa and Spain. Odessa, in Russia, was an early, prosperous Greek community, and Alexandria, in Egypt, was founded late in 332 B.C. by Alexander the Great, the conqueror of much of Asia. In 310 B.C., Pytheas, a Greek dreamer from Marseilles, decided to reach the most distant parts of the world and is said to have discovered an "island" variously identified with Jutland, Iceland and Norway. Not many historians are willing, however, to credit Pytheas with his alleged achievement.

Naturally, the wide dispersion of the Greeks all over the ancient world cannot be compared to the immigration of the Hellenes of more recent days. The only similarity lies in the fact that unlike people from other countries who sought freedom from persecution outside of their own native surroundings, at no time in history did the Hellenes leave Greece only on account of adverse conditions existing at the moment of their exodus. Moreover, wherever they went, neither in sorrow nor in happiness have they ever forgotten their native land. It seems as though deep inside the Greek mind, whether one, two or three thousand years ago or yesterday or today, the basic motive that instigated exploration, colonization or immigration—or for that matter, any form of expatriation—might very well have been the same thirst for the unknown, which is a characteristic trait of the Hellenic race. If this is so, then it is not perhaps unreasonable to believe that many Greeks came to America under its impact. True, the precarious economic conditions prevailing in their country at the end of the 19th century dictated their departure, but it cannot be excluded all together that it could have provided at the same time, an excuse for some of them to yield to the innate attraction for adventure. Whatever was their origin and their intellectual capacity at the moment of their arrival in America they gradually affected—to a certain extent—American life. Speaking about these early arrivals of the Greeks, Rev. Thomas J. Lacey wrote that "Their ancestral culture tempers our rudeness."

The rebirth of the Balkan nationalities was a salient sign of the nineteenth century. Greece, Serbia and Bulgaria, after so many centuries in complete obscurity and oblivion resumed their continuity as independent nations. Some historians have asserted that the Greeks suffered much less than other Christian subjects of the Turks, but what is certain is that the Greeks displayed constant restlessness while under Turkish rule, which culminated in the 1821 national uprising, for which they paid a heavy price. It is true that through the Ecumenical Patriarchate, the Greeks enjoyed a real hegemony over the other Christian minorities of the Ottoman Empire. But it could not have been otherwise; the Greeks were the recipients of a great heritage of culture and valor, which created for them a sort of responsibility toward history and the tradition of freedom. It was a matter of time for these feelings to materialize and transform the Greeks from conquered people into fighting forces.

In the Danubian principalities (Walachia and Moldavia) under Turkish suzerainty, there were Greek Princes, and in Constantinople the Greeks held key positions in the Turkish administration, often dictating the foreign policy of the country. However, it was these prominent Greeks, along with others residing outside of occupied Greece, who fomented the 1821 Revolution.

Following the victorious termination of the Greek War of Independence, Greece obtained recognition of its complete independence by the European powers and a northward extension of its borders. In 1832, Arta and Volos, including the district of Lamia, became the northern frontiers of the newly created Hellenic kingdom. The Greeks received the Cyclades but not the Ionian Islands (the British had occupied these islands in 1809, and in 1815 the Treaty of Paris established a British protectorate over them), which were restored to them only in 1864. Thus, the poorest portion of Hellenism was returned to Greece while the richest remained in Turkish hands. The revolution had prevailed, but because of powerful foreign influence and pressure the Greeks did not receive the entirety of what had been, from ages past, the Hellenic world. The Turks were still a mighty nation and, moreover, some Western countries preconized the well known axiom that the balance of power in any part of the world was essential to their predominance.

In this historically and geographically unjust partition of the Hellenic world lies the principal cause for the difficult economic situation existing in Greece at the moment when the first Greek immigrants crossed the Atlantic Ocean to come to America in search of a better future. It must also be stated that with the re-emergence of Greece as an independent nation the mutual attraction between Greece and the United States deepened.

When the Greek War of Independence came to an end and the Greeks regained a freedom for which they always longed, the national characteristics of their strong individualism—the same individualistic temper that had provoked dissent among them during the revolution—became more apparent through the radical differences between highlanders and islanders, continentals and unredeemed, aristocrats and democratic peasants, seafarers and agrarians. The first Greek immigrants who set foot on American soil at the end of the nineteenth century to become part of the melting pot were themselves the product of another crucible. There existed sharp differences among them originating from the diversified habits and customs of the particular regions of Greece from which they came, and which they never forgot even in their new environment.

If the individualism of the Greek was so pronounced as to permit the perpetuation of differences among themselves even during the years of their struggle for survival on a foreign soil, how could they have been expected to surrender easily and eagerly to the process of assimilation? The initial reaction of any first immigrant—irrespective of the reasons which forced him to abandon his native land —was to resist, consciously or unconsciously, the loss of national identity with his country of origin. The willingness and the possibility for adjustment to the new requirements was a matter of time but, in some instances, it was also a question of national pride. The first Greek immigrants fought desperately against Americanization through their devotion to their Church and through it to Greece and the Greek language.

The Greek War of Independence was the cause of the cross; now the cross and the identification with the country they had left, became the weapon of protection of the Greeks. In the mind of the Greek the spirit of adventure remains alive and conducive to new perilous peregrinations, and is also receptive to certain adjustments, but only as long as it is not demanded of him to deny his religious and historical heritage.

Explorers and Adventurers

T HE NAMES of certain Greeks who are supposed to have set foot in America, as early as 1527 or 1528, are mentioned in some rather unreliable Spanish documents of that time. Mention is made only of their first names and very little, if anything, was known of them except that they had followed some daring Spaniards in their sailing expeditions to America. Neither their full names nor the place from which they came can be checked or confirmed. They seem to have faded into oblivion—into the deep mystery that surrounded practically everything in those distant days of vague and always dangerous adventures. History did not reserve a place for them—a place sustained by unchallenged facts. They were probably part of a beginning for which there has been no recorded ending. Thus, they disappeared as they had come and were only incidentally mentioned.

The case of Juan de Fuca—or Apostolos Valerianos, a Greek from the island of Cephalonia—is something entirely different though the account he himself gave of his achievements was for a long time doubted and discredited. Apostolos Valerianos discovered and gave his name to the Juan de Fuca Strait, an inlet of the Pacific, 100 miles long and 15 to 20 miles wide between Vancouver Island and the Washington State. Some encyclopedias write that "It was discovered by Captain Charles William Barkley in 1787," but that "the name of the strait derives from that of a sailor, Juan de Fuca, who legend says, discovered it for Spain in 1592."

In this connection the *North American Review* (January 1839) has this to say:

> There is good English authority for believing another important fact; that is, the truth of the alleged discovery of the strait of Juan de Fuca, in 1599, by a Greek pilot of that name, in the service of Spain.

The only printed account of the voyage of the Greek pilot is credited to Samuel Purchas, an English historian who gives it as he received it from Juan de Fuca himself, through Mr. Michael Lok, English

Consul of Aleppo (*Pilgrims*, Vol. III). This account, according to various documents kept in the Washington National Archives,

> was for a long time doubted or discredited, owing to the want of knowledge of facts. But the researchers of Gray, Meares, Vancouver, Malespina and others, having shown that there is a broad strait in the place indicated by Juan de Fuca, answering all essential particulars to his description; and the description itself, as given by Purchas, being so minute and exact as to negative altogether the supposition of its being fabricated, or derived from any other source than actual observation, the general sense of modern geographers has admitted the claim of the Greek pilot to the honor of the discovery of the strait, and has bestowed upon it his name, which it now universally bears.

Here is the account of Purchas, as it appears in his *Pilgrims* (Vol. III, page 849) (I have kept the actual spelling of words as used in Purchas' account):

> When I was at Venice, in April 1596, happily arrived there an old man about threscore yeares of age, called commonly Juan de Fuca, but named Apostolos Valerianos, of Nation a Greeke born in the island of Cefalonia, of profession a mariner; and an ancient pilot of Shippes.

It is further said that,

> He (Valerianos, alias de Fuca) became Pilot of a Venetian Ship, named Ragasone for England; they both came to Venice. This Greeke pilot declared in the Italian and Spanish languages . . . that he went on Land in divers places and that he saw some people on Land, clad in Beast skins; and that the Land is very fruitful, and rich in Gold, Silver, Pearle, and other things . . . He was greatly welcomed in Spain at the king's Court. He did not get a reward . . . He returned to California, since the British could not pay his voyage to England.

In regard to the persistent, erroneous allegations of some historians to the effect that Juan de Fuca actually did not exist as a "historical personality," Alex. S. Taylor (*Hutchings' California Magazine*, September and October 1859) thinks that if no data were found about Juan de Fuca in the National Archives of Spain or Mexico, this should be attributed to political reasons.

However, for Greece and the Greek-Americans, New Smyrna, named by Andrew Turnbull after the birthplace of his wife Maria Gracia —the daughter of a merchant from Smyrna, in Asia-Minor—is considered the starting point of Greek collective presence in America.

The location, which was the first known location where the first Greeks lived with their families in America, was also the first place where a Greek settlement died.

It is important to remember that:

> New Smyrna had not been established for philanthropic or religious purposes as had many contemporary settlements in the English colonies of America. New Smyrna's purpose had been repeatedly stated as being "the Cultivation of Cochineal, Indigo rubber, Rice, Hemp and many other useful Articles of Commerce Especially Cotton, silk, wine" and the "Culture of Articles now purchased from foreign nations." It was a financial enterprise, having as sole purpose the materialization of profit, which had attracted the interest of its distinguished founders." (*New Smyrna, An Eighteenth Century Odyssey*, by E. P. Panagopoulos, University of Florida Press Gainesville, 1966).

In fact, it is the idea of a successful commercial enterprise that induced Andrew Turnbull in 1763, when Florida became an English colony, to bring some farmers from the Peloponnesos in southern Greece, then under Turkish domination, the mild climate of which was very similar to the clime of Florida.

However, Andrew Turnbull, the founder of New Smyrna, was not the first who thought of bringing Greek farmers and laborers to Florida. William Knox—who was under-Secretary of State for American affairs from 1770 to 1782, had made the suggestion when Florida had been transferred to the British. He insisted that the Greeks were needed there more than any other people in the world because a special kind of settlers was necessary. He had said:

> These are the Greeks or any other inhabitants of the Archipelago who profess the Christian religion. I am well assured that great numbers of these people might be induced to become our subjects if their mode of worship is tolerated and the expense of their transportation defrayed; their priests who are the proper persons to employ might be easily brought to persuade them to emigrate and our Island or Minorca could be a convenient place for them to rendez-vous at." (*The Florida Historical Quarterly*, XXXV, No. 2, October, 1956).

The idea of bringing Greek farmers and laborers to the English colonies in America had entered into the mind of the English much earlier. There had been a proposal in 1675, to settle Greeks in Virginia. A suggestion to that effect was made to Secretary Sir Joseph Williamson setting forth the misery of the Mainoti (Maniates) "the inhabitants of the famous Morea who are greatly persecuted by the Turks, who endeavor to drive them out of their country; the numbers that have left in consequence and the great advantage may service to encourage these 'very laborious' people to inhabit Virginia, Jamaica etc." (*The Virginia Magazine of History and Biography*, Vol. I, January 12, 1912). However, "the said proposal being discoursed of was laid aside as a thing of charge." (*Virginia Seventeenth Century Records.*)

Another description of the "qualities" of the Greeks of that time is given by a Scottish pamphleteer, Archibald Menzies (*Small Pamphlet*, October 1763). He writes: "The Greeks of the Levant are accustomed to a hot climate, and bred to the culture of the vine, olive, cotton, tobacco, nadder etc. These people are sober and industrious; and being reduced by their severe masters to the greatest misery would be easily persuaded to fly from slavery to the protection of our Government."

In reality, the Greek farmers and laborers living in Morea under the Turkish yoke were about to exchange one form of slavery for another. What awaited them in New Smyrna in those days of ruthless exploitation was not very different from the treatment they were receiving at the hands of the Turks—with one difference: the psychological effect of being at least theoretically free under "the protection of a great civilized country."

Besides using the Greek priests to convince the Greek laborers to leave their enslaved country and come to America, Andrew Turnbull thought it expedient to use these Greeks, who lived under British Rule in Port Mahon, Minorca. The Greek priests were induced to tell their compatriots of the mainland "how happier they would be under His Majesty's Government than any other whatsoever."

Andrew Turnbull had served as a British Consul in Smyrna (Turkey) and his son Nicholas was born there. He married the beautiful and elegant Gracia Dura Bin, the daughter of a Greek merchant from Smyrna. In June 1766, Turnbull and his wife sailed from England to St. Augustine (north-east of Florida on a narrow peninsula between the Matanzas and San Sebastian rivers and separated from the Atlantic by Anastasia Island. The oldest city in the United States, it was founded in September 1565 by Pedro Menendez de Aviles). He arrived there in November 1766 and selected his land which was granted through orders from the King—10,000 acres near Mosquito Inlet, about seventy miles south of St. Augustine. It is there that the first Greek immigrants in America were to meet insurmountable difficulties and face unbelievable hardships. Next year, in 1767, Andrew Turnbull left for Europe to bring back his settlers. He had, in the meantime, submitted a petition to the Board of Trade which had approved it and had decided to pay "forty shillings per head to the first five hundred Greeks (children excepted) that shall be imported and actually settled in that province.

Recruiting Greeks under Turkish domination and strict supervision was not an easy task, though Andrew Turnbull had decided to bribe the occupants—something he is said to have done in many instances. In every port where he harbored in occupied Greece, in every place he passed, Turnbull found the Turks on guard and preventing him from recruiting settlers. On the island of Milos, however, Turnbull recruited one of his first settlers—a man by the name of Anastassios Mavromatis.

Andrew Turnbull had heard of the sufferings of the people of Greece and "how they had managed to defy the strength of the Ottoman Empire; about the heavy price they paid for freedom, losing great numbers in their continuous fight with the Turks; and he was probably informed about the frequent migrations from Mani, during the past hundred years, to the Ionian Islands, Italy and Corsica, where they had gone to escape . . ." (Anastasios Goudas, *Vioi Paralliloi ton andron tis Epanastaseos*, Athens, 1875). When Turnbull arrived the atmosphere was grave, full of anxiety and despair. Plagues lasting for several years had only recently ended.

Andrew Turnbull gave his own description of what he found in Greece while trying to recruit his settlers for Florida: ". . . these Greeks are ruled by chiefs called captains, to whom they pay small tribute yearly to enable them to provide warlike ammunition to defend them against the Turks. This, however, is frequently consumed in civil wars among themselves. It was cruel tyranny and the most pinching poverty that made them wish to fly from such complicated distress; otherwise they would not have emigrated. For there is not a nation on earth more prejudiced in favour of their own country than the Greeks, and indeed with reason." (P. Lee Phillips, *The Greek Revolution*, p. 107).

The Scottish doctor visited also the island of Crete, from which came at least one settler by the name of Demetrios Fundulakis (as happened with most Greek names of the colonists of New Smyrna, his name appears in the various records and censuses hispanisized and corrupt: Fudelachi, Tudelachi, Pedulachi). The Spanish census mentions that "he is of the Greek Church, which constitues a unique exception among the known compatriots of his who, by that time, had become converted Roman Catholics." However, there is no evidence to sustain the allegations of the Spanish records and it is well known that the Greek sticks to his religion with stubbornness.

Andrew Turnbull stopped also at the volcanic island of Santorin from which came the only known Greek woman, Maria Parta. From there, Turnbull returned to Smyrna. The only man known to come from Smyrna, however, was Gaspar Papi, whose descendants carried his name in Florida into the middle of the twentieth century. Finally, Turnbull, left mainland Greece—where he had returned to try to find additional settlers, and on February 3, 1768, he entered the "deep water" of Port Mahon, Minorca, where his settlers were waiting for him. It was a crowd that had been gathered from many places: from Italy, Greece, Southern France and Corsica. Those who had come from Corsica had Greek names: Nicholas Stephanopoli, Georgios Stephanopoulos, Andonios Stephanopoulos, Petros Drimarochis, Petros Corsifachos, Michael Costas, and others.

On April 30, 1768, seven crowded ships left Minorca for Florida with more than 1,400 people aboard. All evidence at that time pointed out that these first settlers were going to Florida as "tenants," who should divide the products of their land equally with Andrew Turnbull "between five and a maximum of six years." It turned out to be an entirely different story.

However, the tragedy of the first Greek settlers—their numbers are given between 400 and 500—started with the crossing of the Atlantic. Indeed, ever since and especially during the first years of mass immigration to the new world, the ordeal of every immigrant would begin as soon as he was setting foot on the ship, which was supposed to bring him to the land where all his problems would be automatically solved.

The Greeks, the third major group of Turnbull's recruits, living in Minorca at that time were unhappy people who had already experienced many a tragedy. Most of them had come from the island of Corsica, where they had settled as a result of an agreement with the Genoese occupants. The Greeks became a target of the Corsicans who fought to liberate themselves from the Genoese domination.

Actually the Odyssey of these Greeks had started in 1668, when the island of Crete fell to the Turks, ending a very long war between the Ottoman Empire and the Venetians. The Greeks had naturally sided with the Venetians against the common enemy but were abandoned by their allies when Crete was conquered. As a result of the loss of the island of Crete, Turkish persecutions and massacres on the Greek mainland and more particularly in the Morea area became unbearable and the Greeks did not see any other alternative than to escape to another country.

The first migration of the Maniotes took place when a number of families left the Peloponnesos and established themselves in Tuscany, Italy (Archives of Florence and Venice, published in Italian by Professor Spyridon P. Lambros). They officially settled in Minorca in 1745, when the British, who wanted to use them in their war against the French, permitted them to form their own colony to avoid extermination at the hands of the Turks. These Greeks in Minorca were mostly sailors and merchants and at the beginning of the eighteenth century numbered approximately 2,000 members in a community composed of British and other foreigners.

The fanatically catholic local population felt nothing but deep, violent religious hatred for the Greeks stubbornly attached to Orthodoxy. Thus, once again, the Greeks on Minorca had to face another wave of pressures, persecutions and humiliations they believed they had earned the right to forget. Andrew Turnbull, the realistic Scottish doctor, was to take immediate advantage of the psychological state of mind of the Greeks who at his arrival in the island were ready to go anywhere and risk anything to escape their new ordeal. Turnbull had little difficulty in convincing Greeks, but also Italians and Corsicans, that a better life was waiting for them in the new world and more precisely in Florida and its sunny beaches where the climate was as mild as that of the Mediterranean. The big adventure was under way and the first Greek settlers in America were about to attempt the unknown and much dreaded crossing of the Atlantic.

By the end of March 1768, approximately 1,300 future inhabitants of America, distributed in six ships left for Gibraltar, which was to be the first port of call before the crossing of the unfriendly ocean. The number of the departing was impressive. It was the first time that such a massive collective enterprise was undertaken. In a letter sent later—July 20, 1768—to Lord Hillsborough the British Secretary for the colonies, Governor Grant of Florida, wrote: "This, My Lord I believe is the largest Importation of White Inhabitants that was ever brought into America at a time."

The exact numbers of these first Greek settlers who sailed to the new world at that time has never been accurately established. Estimates of the numbers differ slightly according to the sources of information. The exact number of those recruited by Andrew Turnbull from Greece itself is not known either. However, it is safe to come to the conclusion that five hundred Greeks, men, women and even newly born babies, were among the Minorcans that Turnbull took with him to Florida to start his daring experiment.

While the voyage in the Mediterranean waters, between Minorca and Gibraltar, could be compared to an enjoyable cruise, things changed considerably as soon as the ships carrying the settlers to America sailed into the Atlantic. There were frequent storms but sickness also spread among the passengers. It is said that during the voyage 148 of them died and were buried in the "deep Atlantic." It is not known how many Greeks perished during the crossing. On June 26, the "human cargoes" arrived at St. Augustine. There was still a distance of some seventy miles to cover before reaching the ultimate destination—New Smyrna, the settlement owned by Andrew Turnbull. Some of the settlers covered the distance on foot, others continued on ship.

No adequate preparations had been made to receive the Minorcans and while the landscape was indeed beautiful the conditions of life were not what had been expected. As a matter of fact, at that time the location was part of the immense wilderness of America —a fascinating but also frightening sight. Food was scarce and under the supervision of tough noncommissioned British officers the work undertaken by the new settlers was exhausting. Moreover, the area had not been named by the Spaniards "The Mosquitoes" for nothing. This part of Florida was infested by millions of vicious mosquitoes, which continually attacked the unfortunate, newly arrived adventurers. The mosquitoes brought malaria—an additional calamity.

Life in New Smyrna had taken the form and the proportions of real slavery. Greeks and Italians revolted against the mistreatment at the hands of their ruthless supervisors and all sorts of privations to which they were subjected. The leader of the insurrection was an Italian, Carlo Forni, who directed an armed attack against the installations and their guards. Very soon the rebels increased to 300 and Turnbull asked for military help to quell the insurrection. In January 1769, the British had the situation under control but Turnbull's experiment had come to a tragic end. New Smyrna was about to be abandoned. The leaders of the revolution were arrested and tried. Some of them were sentenced to death. A Greek from Corsica, Elia Medici (probably Elias Iatrou or Iatropoulos) was also condemned to death for killing a cow. In those days the British law stipulated that killing a cow called for capital punishment, but the life of Elias Medici was spared. According to a British practice he was to be given the right to live under the condition that he would execute two others of his co-confederates who had been also sentenced to death.

Bernard Romans, a Dutch surveyor, who supposedly witnessed the incident had this to write:

> On this occasion I saw one of the most moving scenes I ever experienced; long and obstinate was the struggle of this man's mind (Elias Medici) who repeatedly called out, that he chose to die rather than to be executioner of his friends in distress: this not a little perplexed Mr. Woolridge, the sheriff, till at last the entreaties of the victims themselves, put an end to the conflict in his breast, by encouraging him to act. Now we beheld a man thus compelled to mount the ladder, take leave of his friends in the most moving manner, kissing them the moment before he commited them to an ignominious death. (In Phillips, *op. cit.,* p. 106).

When the revolt was put down Governor Grant reported officially that the losses for 1767 were "Men and women 300. Children 150. Total dead for 1767: 450." Here again the number of Greeks who died from the time they left Gibraltar to the end of the New Smyrna revolt is not known.

New Smyrna had survived the uprising of the exploited and mistreated settlers whom Turnbull had brought to America, but by 1775 a series of events and the rumor that workers were living under much better conditions in St. Augustine sealed the fate of New Smyrna and ended Andrew Turnbull's dream. By August 1777, almost all of the settlers who had come to New Smyrna with Turnbull were already in St. Augustine.

In his book *New Smyrna—an Eighteenth Century Greek Odyssey,* E. P. Panagopoulos has this to say about the end of New Smyrna:

> In a short time, however, the situation changed, and New Smyrna entered its last dramatic phase. No one knows exactly how things happened, but for more than 150 years an account about it has been transmitted orally and unchanged from generation to generation among the descendants of these settlers, an account re-

peated also by all contemporary authors who delt with the story of the colony.

On July 17, 1777, and on the basis of a decision reached by the courts, Doctor Andrew Turnbull's attorneys had no other choice than to set all the colonists free. Another phase of their long Odyssey was about to begin.

Thus the colony which the well known French historian Guillaume Thomas François Abbe Raynal (1713-96, author of the *Histoires philosophiques et politiques des établissements et du commerce des Européens dans les deux Indes*) had hailed as a possible new Athens or Lacedaemon in America, which could have been "the residence of politeness, of the fine arts and of elegance" disappeared because of the perennial cruelty and exploitation of man by man. When finally in 1781, Andrew Turnbull and his beautiful wife, after whose birthplace he had named his now extinct colony, left Florida, New Smyrna no longer existed.

The frustrated dreams of the first Greek settlers who had come to New Smyrna only to suffer a new ordeal were revived in St. Augustine, where they brought the will—and the experience of a long and painful adventure—to build a better life for themselves within the American entourage.

In St. Augustine, North America's Oldest City

FROM AN historical point of view the destiny of these first Greek settlers in the new world is as curious as it is dramatic. It is indeed extremely interesting and most significant to remember that they—and their fathers and mothers—had been subjected to frequent changes of civic identity and had lived in different geographical environments. They had left their own country—Greece, then under the yoke of the Ottoman Empire, as Turkish subjects, to go to Corsica and Minorca under another foreign rule. They arrived in America as Minorcans in the middle of an agonizing revolution which was to alter the national identity of the country of their adoption. They settled in Florida, which was then a British colony but was later transferred to the Spanish.

Each time since the early days of the endless journey to the unknown these Greeks met a new ruler, lived within a different landscape and had to abide by new habits and customs only to discover that regardless of their nationality people are ruthless and cruel. However, in spite of so many hardships and so many unremitting pressures and continuous humiliations, the Greeks never entirely lost their national identity. There is something inexplicable, perhaps unique, in this profound, irrevocable attachment of the Greek—any Greek, to Greece, that the change of a geographical location or a different civic identity, or moments of joy or distress might modify but could not extinguish.

The Minorcans from the now defunct New Smyrna did not solve their problems upon their arrival in St. Augustine. At that time St. Augustine, the "little town of the deep" as it was then called, was overcrowded with all sorts of people who had fled there to escape the effects of the Revolution. Food was again scarce and the improvised shelters toward the city gates did not offer any conveniences or even protection against the seasonal rains. The destitute, hungry, unfortunate people who had come from New Smyrna, put an heroic fight against privations but many lost their lives. The British Governor, Patrick Tonyn, in his report to his superiors in London wrote that from May to December of 1777, 53 men and women, and 16 children had died. Thirty-four of them were Greeks.

The "Greek Settlement" as the British called the area where the Greek settlers had tried to establish themselves

> extended approximately from Hypolita Street north to the city gates, and from St. George Street to the San Sebastian River. Within these boundaries those who survived from among the former settlers of New Smyrna built their homes, cultivated small plots of land, and after some time opened their small business enterprises. When Father Padro Camps came to St. Augustine from New Smyrna in November, 1777, he established a Roman Catholic church on the second floor of a house on St. George Street, next to a building subsequently called the "Spanish Inn." It was also known as "the Greek Church," or "the Church of the Mahonese," and sometimes "the Minorcan chapel." (E. P. Panagopoulos, *New Smyrna—an Eighteenth Century Greek Odyssey.*)

It is in this "building" with so many different names that the Greeks worshipped. They did not have their own Orthodox Church. Nor did they have any Orthodox priest. Dr. Andrew Turnbull had requested the king of England to permit that an Orthodox priest be invited to come to Florida in order to meet the religious needs of the Greeks, but no answer was ever received in this connection.

In September 1763, and as a result of a treaty signed between Spain and England, St. Augustine, and the entire province of Florida, was transferred to the Spanish. Once again the Greeks had to make a new decision. However, most of them, if not all of them, were physically and spiritually exchausted from their previous "evacuations" and they decided that this time they would not leave. They stayed on and even signed a sort of memorial stating they were happy to remain under the Spanish rule.

This is probably the moment when the Greeks—the first settlers in America, seem to have at least theoretically, forgotten their religious identity. It must be said that the memorial submitted to the new Spanish Governor of St. Augustine, and signed by Italians but also 29 Greeks stated that "as Catholics and natural born Spanish subjects we rejoice in finding ourselves restored to the dominion of our legitimate lord and sovereign." The memorial was signed by Greeks whose names had been hispanized, such as Martin Arnadis, Juan Yuanedas (probably Ioannis Ioannidis), Juan Colominas and Marcos Andres (obviously Ioannis Kalominas and Markos

Andreas).

There is no doubt that the intermarriages between the Greeks, the Italians and the Minorcans in St. Augustine that had taken place in the meantime had to some extent influenced the Greeks in signing such a document which in fact was a denial of their national identity and of their religious beliefs. However, it must be repeated that this allegiance to the Spanish was rather theoretical than real. Though the Spanish rule, especially when compared to the way the British had governed the province of Florida, brought welcome changes in the lives of the Minorcans, the Greeks were uncertain about their own fate under the new regime. For one thing, they feared that the Spanish would not permit them to keep the land that had been allotted to them by the British Governor.

A number of Greeks played a distinct role in the life of the hellenic community of St. Augustine: Gaspar Papi, from Smyrna Asia-Minor, who introduced new farming methods, Ioannis Giannopoulos, from Mani, who founded the first Greek school in the area, and many others whose contribution to the life of the Greek settlers is less known and has fallen into oblivion after two hundred years that brought drastic changes to St. Augustine and the surrounding region.

The first building that the visitor sees today in St. Augustine as he enters from the City Gates is the "Oldest Wooden Schoolhouse in the United States." Until a few years ago a sign hanging outside the house read: "Giannopolis School." Giannopoulos was a carpenter by profession but he distinguished himself as an "educator," another profession very much needed at that time among the ignorant settlers. There was also a Michael Costa, who in 1783, was known as a "Medical Doctor." There is no record of Costa's having graduated from any medical school.

What happened to the descendants of the first Greek settlers of St. Augustine generally referred to as the Minorcans? Panagopoulos has this to say:

> When in the narrow lanes of St. Augustine the stranger meets the dark eyes and expressive Mediterranean faces of these descendants, his mind travels back almost 200 years to the first New Smyrna colonists who came from cosmopolitan Smyrna and the white islands of the Aegean, from the rocky shoulders of Mani and the mild Italian valleys, from manly Corsica and charming Minorca, all places strung like beads in a rosary stretched from one end to the other of the blue Mediterranean.

And one feels, on reading the verses written by Stephen Vincent Benet, himself a descendant of this Minorcan generation:

> They came here, they toiled here
> They broke their hearts afar
>
> ....
>
> It was not so to be
> Let us still remember them
> Men from oversea
>
> ....
>
> They lived here, and died here
> They left singing names.

(Rosemary and Stephen Vincent Benet, *A Book of Americans*, New York: Farrar and Rinehart, Inc. 1933).

The question arising from a close study of the descendants of the first Greek colonists of New Smyrna and St. Augustine is this: could they be regarded as an example of how hellenism will evolve in America? In other words will the descendants of the first Greek immigrants who came in great numbers to the new world much later (mostly between the end of the 19th century and the beginning of the 20th) be absorbed by the American environment to a point which will force them to forget or deny their Greek consciousness?

The question will be answered in length elsewhere in this book. But one thing must be said here: since New Smyrna and St. Augustine, the Greek Orthodox Church of North and South America has entered the scene and through its religious influence, its educational programs and other activities has assumed the role of the protector of hellenic perpetuation in America.

The battle for the survival of hellenism in America is under way. One has to follow very carefully the outcome.

American Interest in the Greek
War of Independence

I N REGARD to the presence, the growth and the activities of
the Greeks in America, there seems to be a deep historical vacuum between the tragic end of the New Smyrna experiment and
the mass immigration from Greece, which started at the end of the
19th century and continued through the early part of the 20th
century. We know only of a few arrivals of Greeks and of the
unavoidable addition of offspring to the Greek families that had
settled in St. Augustine.

The largest element to emigrate to the United States after the War
of 1812, consisted of men and women of the British Isles and
British North America. Great Britain and Ireland sent a population,
as the census compilers say "for a kingdom," as it amounted to
approximately two and three quarter millions. Next was the immigration from Germany and Russia: over 1,500,000. The third
largest immigration at that time came from France: some 250,000
citizens "lost to America" as their chauvinistic compatriots thought.

The number of immigrants from smaller European countries who
came to America during this early period was, with some exceptions,
too small to have been either officially recorded or to have any
marked influence upon the American environment.

From October 1819 to 1860, the following immigrants entered the
United States:

Ireland	967,366
England, Scotland and Wales	55,825
Germany	1,486,044
Germany (Prussia included)	1,546,476
France	208,063

(Eight Census, 1860. The Statistics of the Population).

There is no mention of any either consistent or substantial number
of Greeks having entered the United States during the same period
of time. Yet, this was the moment when a restless, young America
was moving towards an amazing future. This was the moment of

the California Gold Rush of 1849. "This was the moment of restless growing America. It had the eye of the world" (Karl Sandburg, *Abraham Lincoln: The Prairie Years and the War Years,* New York: Harcourt, Brace and World Inc.). At that time the State Department reported that from San Francisco—which had become a world port, the Irish immigrants alone had in three years sent back home to their relatives $15,000,000. But not one Greek name is mentioned among the many new immigrants who had rushed to California to make a fortune.

Then something happened which seems to have stirred up the interest of America in Greece—and vice versa—and which moreover, opened the gates of the new world to a number of young Greek orphans: the 1821 Greek War of Independence.

In a series of articles published in the *American Historical Review,* Vol. XXXIII (October 1927 to July 1928) Edward Mead Earle had this to write about the American interest in the Greek cause:

> When the Greeks of the Morea rose in 1821, to throw off the Ottoman rule of four centuries, their cause promptly claimed the sympathy of Americans. With their own revolution fresh in mind, Americans were not indifferent to the fate of another people struggling for emancipation from an oppressive imperialism. The clergy were shocked by the execution of the venerable Greek Patriarch Gregorios, who was hanged in his sacred robes on Easter Sunday, 1821, and whose body was delivered to the Jews to be dragged through the streets of Constantinople and un-ceremoniously thrown into the Bosporus.

In April 1822, American public opinion was again horrified when it finally learned of the devastation of the island of Chios, where the Turks massacred approximately 30,000 Greeks and sold many more thousands to slavery.

The Americans saw in the fighting Greeks of 1821, the descendants of the glorious, ancient Hellenes and believed that as such the modern Greeks were entitled to the immediate assistance of the Western world which owed so much to ancient Hellas. Philhellenism spread in the United States—mostly among the people, but failed to impress the United States Government beyond official words of sympathy.

It was only natural that the fighting Greeks had turned to the Americans for help. It was even flattering for the democratically-minded people of the United States. However, during the years 1821 and 1822, nothing much was done to answer the appeal of the desperate Greeks. A meeting was held in Albany, New York for the purpose of soliciting funds for the Greek War of Independence. George Jarvis, a New Yorker, then residing abroad, joined the Greek revolutionaries and he "became the vanguard of a small group of American Philhellenes who were to serve with distinction throughout the Greek War of Independence. Jarvis became a lieutenant-general in the Greek forces," (Edward Mead Earle, *Ibid.*).

For a moment, during 1823, there was a sharp decline in American interest in the Greek War of Independence. News had reached America that the leaders of the Greek Revolution were at odds with one another. Then at the end of the same year Lord Byron embraced the Greek cause and arrived at Missolonghi. And Earle again concludes that: "Henceforth there could be little question of the strength of Philhellenism in the United States; in America as elsewhere else. Byron's dramatic sacrifice rendered the cause of Greek Independence services which can never be repaid." The high point of Philhellenism in America was reached between the years 1823-1824.

Edward Everett (1794-1865), a professor of Greek literature, wrote in the *North American Review* (1823) that the Greeks had established their right to independence. Everett became Secretary of the Committee of the Philhellenes in Boston. By December 1823, a spirited campaign on behalf of the fighting Greeks was under way.

Everett and his friend General Theodore Lyman had visited Greece in 1819. His impressions on the voyage, which was to play an important role in his future attitude towards the Greeks, are contained in a handwritten manuscript (Archives of the Massachusetts Historical Society). His desire to visit Greece was prompted by the reading of *Itinéraire de Paris à Jerusalem* by Chateaubriand and Byron's *Childe Harold's Pilgrimage*. In a letter written after his own journey to Greece he wrote Chateaubriand: "Votre Itinéraire, il y a plusieurs ans m'a donné l'idée d'aller voyager dans ce pays: et je garderai toujours une association bien agréable des noms de la Grèce et de Chateaubriand." (François René, vicomte de Chateaubriand (1768-1848), French writer and diplomat, had visited Greece in 1806.)

On January 6, 1824, the *New York Commercial Advertiser* reported:

We cannot keep the record of the numerous meetings called in every part of the country to procure aid for the Greeks' cause. It is sufficient to say that the feeling is universal. Meetings are called in every considerable village, and country clergymen are taking up collections to augment the fund.

At the Universities and Colleges throughout America the students were enthusiastic about the Greek cause. Special benefit performances were given at the theaters; special sermons were preached at almost every Church. Merchants were persuaded to assign to Greek relief a percentage of their profits; valuable objects were offered at public auction to help the fighting Hellenes. It is said that even at schools children donated their savings. In 1824, American companies shipped to Greece "a collection of muskets, rifles, swords, small cannon and medical supplies."

The United States press had embarked on a pro-philhellene campaign and in response to an appeal from Lord Byron, American literary men wrote in defense of the Greeks.

In the spring of 1824, several young Americans left the United States to fight with the Greek revolutionaries and were incorporated in the Greek forces. Among these American idealists was Dr. Samuel Gridley Howe (1801-1876). He spent six years in Greece as surgeon-general of the Greek army. The troubles in the island of Crete (1866-1867) took him again to Greece "toward the end of a long life spent in the service of others."

Other Americans who joined the Greek forces were: Jonathan Miller from Randolph, Vermont; George Wilson, Providence, Rhodes Island; James Williams, a heroic negro from Baltimore; Captain John M. Allen, a close friend of Lafayette. There was also William T. Washington, from Washington D.C., who falsely described himself as a nephew of the great general and who was killed in 1827, in a battle between feuding Greek factions.

The Greek War of Independence had restored faith in the Greek spirit and confidence in the cause of the fighting modern Hellenes. Previous to the national uprising of the Greeks they were hardly known:

> It will be remembered that after four centuries of Turkish rule, or rather misrule, Greece had sunk to so low a level that she excited no interest abroad beyond the pitiful belief that the Hellenic spirit had expired in dust and ashes, affording no hope of future resurrection. (*Magazine of American History*, Vol. XVIII, July-December 1887, article signed by Charles K. Tuckerman, Florence, Italy, and edited by Mrs. Martha J. Lamb, New York, New York).

And Tuckerman adds:

Had the popular wish alone been consulted (in America) the model for Greece to adopt would have been the Republic of the United States.

In the House of Representatives of the United States, Daniel Webster —an ardent friend of the fighting Greeks, moved the following resolution:

Resolved, that provision ought to be made by law for defraying the expense incident to the appointment of an agent or commission to Greece, when the President shall deem it expedient to make such an appointment.

It was not until 1867, however, that the establishment of a full mission in Athens was decided upon. The Greeks who by then had acquired their independence did not wait for the arrival of the American representative to appoint and send their own Minister to Washington. They did this mainly to try to neutralize the continuing influence of the Ottoman minister in the American capital. The man sent to Washington as the first Greek Minister was Alexandros Rizos Rangabes—one of the most distinguished of Greek diplomats—an erudite man of letters.

On August 18, 1823, John Quincy Adams—then a Secretary of State, answering demands for recognition of the fighting Greeks had stated: "If, in the progress of events, the Greeks should be enabled to establish and organize themselves as an independent nation, the United States will be among the first to welcome them in that capacity into the general family, to establish diplomatic and commercial relations with them suited to the mutual interests, and to recognize with special satisfaction their constituted states in the character of a sister Republic, etc."

Yet annual messages of the President of the United States to the Congress included strong expressions of sympathy and support for the Greek struggle for independence. Here is a list of these messages, which, however, failed to prompt a concrete action on the part of the United States Government:

Message of President James Monroe, dated December 3, 1822 (*House Journal*, 17th Congress, 2nd session, p. 16).

Message of President James Monroe, dated December 2, 1823 (*Ibid.*, 18th Congress, 1st session, p. 21).

Message of President James Monroe, dated December 7, 1824 (*Ibid.,* 18th Congress, 2nd session, p. 21).

Message of President John Quincy Adams, dated December 6, 1825 (*Ibid.*, 19th Congress, 1st session, p. 19).

Message of President John Quincy Adams, dated December 4, 1827 (*Ibid.*, 20th Congress, 1st session, p. 16).

Other printed Congressional documents that deal with the Greek War of Independence:

The record of the debate in the House of Representatives on December 24, 1822, consequent upon the presentation by Representative Henry Williams Dwight (of Massachusetts), of a memorial from more than 100 citizens of Washington and Georgetown "to appropriate two or three millions, in provisions, and whatever may be necessary to the Greeks . . ." (*Annals of Congress*, 17th Congress, 2nd session, vol. 3, pp. 457-460).

The record of the debate in the House of Representatives on Webster's resolution (*Annals of Congress*, 18th Congress, 1st session, vol. 1: Dec. 8, 1823, pp. 805, 806; Jan. 19, 1824, pp. 1084-1099; Jan. 20, 1824, pp. 1104-1126; Jan. 21, 1824, pp. 1127-1144; Jan. 22, 1824, pp. 1146-1163; Jan. 23, 1824, pp. 1166-1178; Jan. 24, 1824, pp. 1182-1202; Jan. 26, 1824, pp. 1204-1214).

Resolution submitted on December 18, 1823, by Representative Lewis Williams, of North Carolina:

Resolved, That the President of the United States be requested to lay before this House any information he may have received, and which he may not deem it improper to communicate, relating to the present condition and future prospects of the Greeks. (*House Journal*, 18th Congress, 1st session, p. 76.)

The House adopted this resolution on December 19, 1823, *Ibid.*, p. 79.

Memorial of a "Committee appointed at a public meeting of the citizens of New York to take into consideration the situation of the Greeks" (*Annals of Congress*, 18th Congress, 1st session, vol. 2, Appendix, pp. 3104-3107). The House tabled this memorial; it had been presented by Rep. John J. Morgan on December 29, 1823. Message to the House from President James Monroe, transmitting a report of the Secretary of State upon the "present condition and future prospects of the Greeks" (House Document 14, 18th Congress, 1st session, Dec. 31, 1823, 25pp. Also printed in the *Annals of Congress*, 18th Congress, 1st session, vol. 2, Appendix, pp. 2917-2935). Resolutions, passed in December 1823, by the Legislature of South Carolina, and communicated to the U.S. Senate by Senator Robert Y. Hayne:

Resolved, That the State of South Carolina regards with deep interest the noble and patriotic struggle of the modern Greeks to rescue from the foot of the infidel and the barbarian the hallowed land of Leonidas and Socrates; and would hail with pleasure the recognition, by the American Government, of the independence of Greece . . . (*Annals of Congress*, 18th Congress, 1st session, vol. 1, p. 80).

The Senate tabled the memorial, *Ibid.*

Memorial "of the inhabitants of Boston, on the subject of the Greeks," presented on January 5, 1824, by Representative Daniel Webster (*Annals of Congress*, 18th Congress, 1st session, vol. 2, Appendix, pp. 3107-3109). This memorial was also tabled. Resolution submitted on January 2, 1827, by Edward Livingston, of Louisiana, directing the Committee on Ways and Means to bring in a bill to appropriate $50,000 for the "purchase and transportation of provisions for the suffering inhabitants of Greece" (House Journal, 19th Congress, 2nd session, p. 114). The House initially tabled the resolution and, on January 11, 1827, refused to consider it (*Ibid.*, pp. 146-147).

The record of debate on Livingston's resolution: *Register of Debates in Congress*, 19th Congress, 2nd session, vol. 3, Jan. 2, 1827, pp. 578-580.

Message from E. Sissiny, President of the Third National Assembly of Greece, to President John Quincy Adams, dated May 5, 1827, expressing the gratitude of Greece for "the signal testimonies of the philanthropic sentiments of the people of North America, as well as its generous assistance" (Senate Document 1, 20th Congress, 1st session, December 4, 1827, p. 23).

Among the Congressional records housed in the National Archives are the following unpublished documents:

Memorial (see item 6, *supra*) from sundry inhabitants of the city of Washington, "praying that aid may be sent to the Greeks . . ." (10 pp.). Representative Henry W. Dwight presented the memorial to the House on December 24, 1822; it was then tabled (*House Journal*, 17th Congress, 2nd session, p. 73).

Memorial, presented to the House on January 19, 1824, by Representative Daniel Webster, from a committee which had been "appointed at a numerous meeting of the inhabitants of the City of Washington" on behalf of the Greek people, 4 pp. The memorial was referred to the Committee of the Whole House on the State of the Union (*House Journal*, 18th Congress, 1st session, p. 156).

It is obvious that there was a flagrant contrast between the feelings of sympathy and admiration of the American people as a whole to the Greek cause and the official attitude of their Government. There were undoubtedly other considerations which compelled Washington to avoid taking a strong attitude in favor of the hard-fighting Greeks. The United States could, however, have adopted a more severe stand against the Turkish oppressors. After all, Greece was a Christian nation struggling against ruthless Moslem rule and above all the Greeks were possessed of a great name which favorably impressed the entire American nation. Moreover, the occasion of the outbreak of the 1821 Greek War of Independence required of the United States to define its policy toward the minorities residing within the Turkish dominions. Yet this policy was never clearly defined. At that time financial, naval and even diplomatic factors had to be taken into account.

Rivalry in those days between the United States and other powers in Europe was non-existent. Thus, it is rather Russia than America that offered help and assistance to the Greek revolutionaries to regain a freedom they had lost for four centuries.

> The War of Greek Independence was, in fact, from the first a people's war, a revolt of peasants and *Klephts* against an intolerable subjection; and it succeeded only because of this irresistible popular impulse, and in spite of the general corruption and incapacity of its so-called leaders. It began, characteristically enough, with isolated acts of violence." (W. Alison Phillips, *The War of Greek Independence*, London: Smith, Elder and Co., 1897).

It is true that the 1821 Greek War of Independence was fought mostly by peasants and laborers from the rugged mountains of Greece, but it is equally true that it was inspired and directed by Greek aristocrats residing abroad at the time of the uprising. One of the leaders of the Revolution, and later the first Prime Minister of liberated Greece, was Count Capodistria, a Greek from the island of Corfu and Russia's Foreign Minister in 1820. Another leader of the Revolution was Prince Alexander Ypsilantis, the scion of an ancient Phanariot family which boasted its descent from the Byzantine Caesars, who was a general in the Russian army. Moreover, almost all those Greeks who founded the famous secret Society (*Philiki Etairia*) to prepare and head the uprising were highly educated people.

There is no doubt that the success of the American Revolution, followed by that of the French (though the latter was different in character and purpose) stimulated the Greeks to attempt to recover their liberty. On the other hand, what animated the feelings of the Greeks in 1821, was their profound attachment—a double tie of faith and national sentiment—to their religion and to the head of the religion, to which alone they owed allegiance. These feelings prevailed during the 1821 War of Independence and are still manifest among today's Greeks.

During and after the war a number of young Greeks—mostly orphans—were brought to America to be educated. They had been saved by American missionaries from Turkish persecutions and massacre.

The part that the American missionaries played—though rather indirectly, in the 1821 Greek War of Independence by trying to alleviate as much as possible the suffering of the oppressed Greeks, deserves special attention. They must also be credited with bringing Greek boys to the new world, who put down the roots of hellenism in America. These missionaries, who toured Greece under Turkish domination and even went deep into Asia-Minor to fulfil their philanthropic mission, were inspired by the idea of "what service Christianity might render to Orthodox Christianity." They seem to have had an innate inclination and love for Greece. Modern Greek was the first language the American missionaries undertook to learn and the "spiritual welfare of the Greek population of Asia-Minor was one of their primary concerns."

Very little attention has been given to the fact that the American missionaries helped in establishing on the island of Malta a printing press which during the ten years of its existence (between 1822 to 1832) distributed some 350,000 volumes to an astonished Near East. Of these volumes a considerable proportion consisted of Bibles, Grammars and other educational books written in the modern Greek language—the language that Adamandios Korais had created during the War of Independence.

The young Greek orphans brought to America by the missionaries originated from the islands of the Aegean and more particularly from Chios, which had been sacked by the Turks in 1822.

The names of a number of Greek orphans who were brought over to America by the missionaries are mentioned in practically all books which dealt with the hellenic presence in the United States. The most outstanding of the first Greek immigrants or rather "settlers" in the new world are, I believe, the Perdikaris'. Gregorios Perdikaris, who taught Greek for several years, was finally appointed United States Consul in Athens, in 1845. Upon his return to the States he wrote a book *The Greece of the Greeks*. His son, John Perdikaris, was known as the "Greek-American." He too wrote a book: *American Claims and the Protection of Native Subjects in Morocco, by a Resident*, which was published in London in 1886. However, John Perdikaris became famous when he was abducted in 1904, by the bandit Raissuli.

Perdikaris told his adventure in an article which was published in the magazine *Leslie's Monthly* under the title "In Raissuli's Hands: The Story of My Captivity and Deliverance, May 18 to June 26, 1904." Ahmed ben Mahamed Raissuli (1875-1925) was a Berber bandit and tribal leader in Morocco. His kidnapping of foreigners created international incidents embarrassing to the Moroccan Government. Defeated by the Spanish in 1919, he joined them later against Abd-el-Krim, who captured him.

> In the United States even school-children (were) familiar with the picturesque demand made by President Theodore Roosevelt on the Sultan of Morocco: "Either John Perdikaris alive or Raissuli dead." (George C. Vournas in the Congressional Record "Greeks in America," Proceedings and debates of the 86th Congress Second session.)

Some of these Greek orphans who had come to America during the period of the 1821 Greek War of Independence, found themselves involved in the American Civil War on both the Union and the Confederate sides.

In his book *Greeks in America* Reverend Thomas Burgess mentions three Greeks who became officers of the United States Navy during the Civil War. George Musalas Calvokoressis is the best known of the three. The others are Photius Kavasales (Fisk) and George Sirian (or Sirianis), a resident of Virginia.

Ella Lonn, in her book *Foreigners in the Union Army and Navy* (1951) maintains that Calvokoressis was an extremely interesting person. Biographical sketches of the same officer are found in *The Dictionary of American Biography, The National Cyclopaedia of American Biography, Appleton's Cyclopaedia of American Biography* and the *Washington Historical Quarterly*.

According to these sketches Calvokoressis was captured by the Turks during the sack of Chios, in 1822. He was taken to Smyrna, where he was ransomed by his family and was put on board a ship sailing to America. He landed in Baltimore. The young boy was enrolled in the military Academy of Norwich, Connecticut and finally received in 1832 a warrant of Midshipman in the United States Navy.

The *National Cyclopaedia of American Biography* has this to say about the role that Calvokoressis played during the Civil War:

At the outbreak of the Civil War he was commissioned commander and with the U.S. ship *Supply* captured the blockade runner *Stephen Hart*, which was carrying ammunition supplies to the Confederacy. In 1863, he was transferred to the *Saratoga* under Rear Adm. Dahlgren, and assigned to duty off the South Carolina and Georgia coasts. He trained his crew for landing expeditions and made several sorties in August, 1864, destroying bridges and encampments, capturing enemy troops, guns and ammunition and freeing slaves. These achievements won two citations in general orders by Adm. Dahlgren and commendation by Secretary Gilden Welles.

Calvokoressis himself narrated some of his experiences in the South Seas and the Antarctic (1838-1842) in a book titled *Four Years in the Government Exploring Expedition*.

In his later years, Calvokoressis, endowed with a quick mind and with a pleasing personality, often gave lectures on his voyages and on topics of natural history. Ironically, the retired officer met a violent and civilian death; on June 3, 1872, he was shot and killed by footpads (thieves) on a street in Bridgeport, Connecticut, while on a business trip from his home in Litchfield, Connecticut. (George Perros, *Officers of Greek Descent in the Union Navy 1861-1865*, Washington, D.C.: National Paragon Press.)

Nothing particularly impressive is known about George Sirian (or Sirianis). Thomas Burgess says that the Greek seafarer married the daughter of George Marshal, a Greek himself, who "published probably the first manual of naval gunnery in our service."

In a letter published in the Portsmouth, *Virginia Star* of May 2, 1923, Rear Admiral George Partridge Calvokoressis, the son of Captain George M. Calvokoressis wrote that:

George Sirian was the native of another island that was raided by the Turks; his mother fled with him to the beach and placing him in the bottom of an empty boat, shoved it from the shore. She awaited a dreadful fate while her boy drifted out to sea and was finally picked up by men of the U.S.S. *Macedonia*, then cruising the Mediterranean waters. The boy was received with great kindness, adopted by the crew, became a sailor and by intelligence and good conduct in time was given the warrant of Gunner. He served with credit, was much respected and died at a good old age.

Sirian died in Portsmouth, Virginia, his home town, on December 21, 1891, at the age of 73.

Photius Kavasales (Fisk), according to the information provided in *Appleton's Annual Cyclopaedia and Register of Important Events of the Year 1890*, was also born on one of the Aegean islands. During an outbreak of the plague in 1814, "he was found crying in the streets of Smyrna; he had apparently lost his entire family from the pestilence. American missionaries took Kavasales and another boy named Anastasios to Malta." The two boys were later put aboard an American brig and arrived in Salem, Massachusetts on February 21, 1823.

In his comprehensive account of the presence of Greeks in the American Navy during the Civil War, George Perros writes:

> After having attended Amherst College, Kavasales sailed to the Mediterranean Sea as a representative of the Board of Foreign Mission to deliver a cargo of provisions for the relief of destitute Greeks, then fighting for independence from Turkey; but, upon finding himself unable to help their struggle, he returned to the United States. In 1828, he became a communicant of the Congregational Church, and began to study for the ministry. He graduated from the Auburn (New York) Theological Seminary, was ordained at Halifax Vermont, and then discharged his ministerial duties in New England.

He was later appointed by President John Tyler a chaplain in the United States Navy. "His appointment to the Navy Chaplaincy in 1842, was chiefly owing to the action of John Quincy Adams, then in the House of Representatives. While Kavasales' linguistic abilities and his Greek birth and history were special elements in his favor, giving him, in the eyes of a classical scholar like Mr. Adams, a great advantage over several other candidates, Joshua Giddings and Gerrit Smith were also influential in his interest" (George Perros' findings).

Kavasales was instrumental in the abolition of flogging on American men-of-war following his report on the treatment of sailors and marines in the United States Navy.

Actually Kavasales (Fisk) did not see active service in the Civil War. The Navy Registers covering the years 1861 to 1865 reveal that he was in the status of "Waiting Orders." His religious views led him to contemplate resigning; but he was finally persuaded to withdraw his application.

Kavasales died in Boston, Massachusetts, on February 7, 1890 "a zealous believer in, and worker for, Calvinistic Congregationalism, but in his later years, he lapsed from the faith." He fell in love with the daughter of Gerrit Smith, and when she refused to marry him he vowed a life of celibacy.

The name of another officer in the United States Navy during the Civil War is found in the Navy's Registers: He is Leonidas D. Rodocanachi, also known as Leonidas Rody. On November 2, 1861, he enlisted, at Boston, as landsman in the Navy for "three years of war" and served on the receiving ship U.S.S. *Ohio*.

George Perros concludes that "In short, there were, at least, two commissioned, and two warrant officers of Greek birth in the United States Navy during the Civil War. Three of them saw active service throughout the conflict, and the fourth, apparently because of religious convictions, saw no duty, though he was on the active list of officers until July 18, 1864, the date of retirement from the Navy."

There is no doubt that other Greeks served with the forces, either of the North or the South, during the Civil War.

A research in Washington (National Archives and Records Services) disclosed the existence of an "unofficial memorandum" in Record Group 109 which mentions "Greek Company A," Louisiana Militia, 1861, and lists the following officers:

Touloubief, Nicholas	Captain
Laxareado, Alex	1st Lieutenant
Gregori, D.	2d Lieutenant
Brazoroff, N.	2d Lieutenant
Coratosas, Constantino	2d Lieutenant

There are no rolls on file in the War Department collection of Confederate records for this organization.

Moreover, in Chapter VIII (RG 109), Volume 157, page 288, is the following order.

Orders No. 478   Head Quarters Lª Mª

Col. J. T. Winnimore, Qʳ Mʳ Genˡ Lª Army will issue to Capt. Nicholas Touloubief of the Greek Cʸ A of One Capt., three Lieutenants, eight non-commissioned officers and Twenty privates, Qʳ Mʳ and Subsistence stores on requisisions made.

By Order Tho. O. Moore, Govʳ and Comm-in-Chief
M. GRIVOT Adj. and Insp. Genl.

Outstanding Greeks in America

T HERE can be no chronological order in the presentation of persons of Hellenic descent which distinguished themselves in the early years of the formation of America. Neither is it possible to be certain that any account of their activities in various fields of endeavor has indeed included all of them. For one thing, not all of them reached the degree of prominence which usually secures official recognition. Moreover, what might be considered an outstanding achievement in one country might be overlooked or even belittled in another. On the other hand, there are no official records or sources that have kept such a chronological order and, besides, some prominent people of Greek origin have been identified in the *Dictionaries of American Biography* or the *National Encyclopaedia of American Biography* under the American names of their fathers — their mothers being Greek.

Therefore, it is rather with caution that one is compelled to speak about the exact numbers of the first Greeks who participated in American life and achieved some degree of success, since it is rather at random that one has come across their names while leafing the Dictionaries and the various Encyclopaedias at the Washington National Archives.

However, details about the achievements and the activities of some of these "first" Greeks can be found in more than one reference book—an indication of the extent of their prominence.

Sophocles Evangelinos Apostolides (1805-1883) was a classicist and neo-hellenist, one of the most picturesque figures in American education. He was born between 1800 and 1808 (he always refused to give the exact date of his birth) in Thessaly, Greece, near Mt. Pelion. Even the original form of his names is uncertain and disputed. According to one report he was christened Sophocles, to which he affixed his grandfather's patronymic Evangelinos (after his father) and finally the surname.

It is believed that Apostolides was educated in Cairo. He returned to Greece only to decide to emigrate to the United States. He wrote a *Greek Grammar* for the use of the learners, *Greek Exercises, Greek Lessons,* all of them marked by a perfect clarity and also a striking originality. In 1860, he was elected to the unique position of Professor of Ancient, Byzantium and Modern Greek at Harvard University.

The following description of Apostolides is found in the Encyclopaedias, at the Washington National Archives:

> His small body was surmounted by an Olympian head covered with a shock of white hair; his dark eyes gleamed almost ferociously. But under a brusqueness, which terrified the stranger, he cherished a tender sympathy for his intimate friends. With securing parsimony he saved money to build a bridge and waterworks for his native village (Tsangarada, in Thessaly, Greece) and he left large sums to friends and to the Harvard library. His dignity, courtesy and frugality suggested the Greek peasant.

It is said that he was disappointed in the results of the Greek Revolution (The 1821 Greek War of Independence); he thought that "a Bavarian Greece had not been his ideal of a liberated Greece."

John Celivergos Zachos (1820-1898) was an educator, unitarian clergyman, an author and an inventor. He was born in Constantinople—from parents who were natives of Athens.

Zachos was brought to American by Dr. Samuel Gridley Howe. In 1849, he married Harriet Tomkins Canfield. They had six children. At the beginning of the Civil War, Zachos joined the Union Army as assistant-surgeon. He was stationed at Parris Island, Port Royal, in South Carolina. He is said to have been practically the Governor of the island. Zachos demonstrated that Negroes were capable of benefiting by instruction (Private sources: *New York Times,* March 21, 1898).

A writer of literary distinction and of Hellenic descent—of the half blood since only his mother was Greek—was Lafcadio Hearn (1850-1904). He is described by the *Columbia Encyclopaedia* as a multinational author of works in English. Born Leucadio, in the Ionian Islands, of Irish-Greek parentage, he was educated in Ireland, England and France. He was the son of Charles Bush Hearn, surgeon-major in the British Army. There was indeed English, Irish and a touch of Gypsy blood in the Dorset family of his father who was ordered to duty on a Greek island of the Aegean.

There he met a lovely Greek girl, Rosa Tessina, whose family probably had a strain of Arab and Moorish blood. Lafcadio Hearn lost his left eye in an accident and as a result developed a complex which was to shadow him during all his life. He arrived in New York in 1869, "friendless, half-blind, shy, grotesquely unfitted to cope with a strange environment." He started earning some money by waiting in a cheap restaurant. Later, he did some articles for the *Sunday Cincinnati Enquirer* (1873).

From his Greek mother Hearn had inherited a love for the beautiful and, possibly, "his marked lubricity." He spoke excellent French and translated Theophile Gautier's *Avatar*. He had been enormously influenced by Charles Baudelaire and, strangely enough, like Baudelaire, was in love and lived with a mulatto woman. He settled in New Orleans where he wrote a series of short stories entitled *Fantastics.*

He was a restless man, always persecuted by the complex developed as a result of his having lost one eye. He returned for a while to New York from where he left for Martinique. Once again he returned to New York only to leave, this time for Japan, where he settled in Matsu and married a Japanese girl. He became a Japanese citizen and took the name of Koizumi Yakumo. According to the Japanese law he had to adopt a Japanese name in order to marry a Japanese and settle in the country. It is worth mentioning that he wrote twelve books about a country (Japan) whose language he had never learned.

Another curious, but hardly literary career was that of Thomas Telemachus Timayenis. The *Mississippi Valley Historical Review* (June 1950 to March 1957) has this to say about him:

> ... The dubious honor of inaugurating race-thinking anti-semitism in America belongs to a middle-class Greek immigrant, Telemachus Timayenis. While establishing himself in New York City as a language teacher, Timayenis developed a varied literary career. He produced fifteen books altogether, including popular history, romantic novels, and three works on the 'Jewish Question.' An unprincipled schemer, he evidently hoped to be the advance agent of an organized anti-Semitic movement. To that end he formed a publishing house and tried to launch a monthly magazine. The first of his books in this vein was *The Original Mr. Jacobs, a Standing Expose*, appeared in 1888, two years after Edmond Drumont opened the floodgates of French anti-Semitism. Timayenis copied Drumont's ideas. According

to Timayenis and Drumont, European history reveals an elemental conflict between the noble Aryan and the plotting Jew; the latter intrigues incessantly to overthrow the Aryan order of things through financial monopoly on the one hand and the revolution on the other . . .

Thomas Telemachus Timayenis wrote also *Greece in the Times of Homer* (An account of the life and customs and habits of the Greeks during the Homeric period). Also *A History of Greece from the Earliest Time to the Present, with Maps and Illustrations, Judas Iscariot,* and finally *The Modern Greek.*

Michael Anagnos (or Anagnostopoulos) born in 1837, in the village Papingu, Epirus, was perhaps the most outstanding of all other prominent persons of Hellenic descent who distinguished themselves in one way or another, in America. He was a protege of Dr. Samuel G. Howe, whose daughter, Julia Romana, he married in 1876. Dr. Howe met Anagnos during one of his voyages to Greece and was highly impressed by his "burning desire for learning" but also for Greek independence and social betterment (Anagnos left a will providing that his entire estate should be used for the establishment of schools in Greece). Anagnos was a fervent Democrat, and while in Greece was sent to jail because of the articles he had written against the antiliberal regime of Otto I—the first king of the Hellenes. Upon Dr. Howe's death, Anagnos became the director of the Perkins Institution for the blind. One of his first concerns was the collection of the sum of one hundred thousand dollars for the establishment of a printing office and the publication of books for the blind. With the help of his wife he founded in Jamaica Plain, Mass., a kindergarten for blind children. Helen Keller is said to have been one of Anagnos' "pupils."

In 1906, Anagnos travelled to Athens, Turkey, Serbia and Rumania. He died while abroad as a result of an illness, the nature of which went unrecorded. He was buried at his birthplace—the village Papingu, in Epirus. Anagnos devoted all his life to the service of the handicapped and his contribution to the assistance and welfare of the blind and deaf-mute is considered invaluable. It is appropriate to say that Michael Anagnos' name belongs to Greece but that his fame belongs to America.

Again we owe to the Dictionaries of American Biography the name of Pol. Nicholas Coryllos—another outstanding American of Hellenic origin. He came rather late to the United States—

in 1923—from Patras, Greece, where he was born. He became professor of clinical surgery at Cornell Medical College and held many posts in the United States hospitals. A pioneer in the surgical treatment of tuberculosis and pneumonia, he was the author of medical books and numerous articles in Greek, French and American periodicals. "Possessing a most unusual mind, he retained an elastic originality of thought." Coryllos died in New York, in 1938.

The *Congressional Record* on February 25, 1963, published an article written by United States Senate Chaplain Dr. Frederick Brown Harris and printed originally in the *Washington Star* under the title "Walls that Speak." The article is supposed to tell the story of Constantine Brumidi "who is most appropriately acclaimed as the Michelangelo of the United States Capitol." Chaplain Brown Harris accepts—in his article, the assertion of Dr. Myrtle Cheney Murdock, who wrote the only comprehensive biography of Brumidi, whom he called "an Italian refugee" that the latter is said to have stated once: "My daily prayer is that I may live long enough to make beautiful the Capitol of the one country in the world in which there is liberty." The remarkable painter who embellished the United States Capitol was born in Rome, in 1806 but was a Greek—the son of a Latin mother and a Greek father.

In a research made by Dr. Harry Lagoudakis, of the State Department, it is assumed that "in all probability Brumidi's father had fled his homeland then dominated by the Turks and sought refuge in Italy. At that time many Greeks engaged in underground activities aimed at preparing the upsurge of Greece against the Sultan, were compelled to leave their country to escape persecution." According to Mr. Lagoudakis "Brumidi was not only aware of his Greek family background but freely talked of his Greek origin." And Mr. Lagoudakis points out the following facts:

There is evidence (of the Greek origin of Brumidi) in the Memoirs of the first Greek envoy to the United States, who met the U.S. Capitol artist . . . He mentioned the artist twice in the third volume of his Journal. The Greek envoy (Rangabes) writes that "the Central Hall (of the Capitol) . . . is covered by a very high dome which holds in its center a beautiful fresco worked out by a Greek artist." Rangabes did not mention the name of the artist on this occasion but must have gathered from those who accompanied him at the Capitol that the artist of the "Apotheosis of Washington" was the El Greco of America: Constantine Brumidi. Later in another of his books Rangabes notes "the domed corridor," between the House and the Senate rooms, and describes its decorator as the Greek Brumidi, reared in Rome, "whose acquaintance I made with great interest."

Brumidi died in Washington in 1878 or 1879, a forgotten and unrecognized master and was buried in an unmarked grave in some cemetery of the capital city of the United States. It is said that shortly after his death a prophecy was pronounced by an admirer who was overwhelmed at the sight of the heroic art of Brumidi: "One day this man will be crowned by the gratitude of succeeding generations." "Unfortunately, this prophecy has not yet come true in its deserved full extent, nearly a century after the completion of his grandiose work. It is therefore only fair that the millions of Americans who are visiting the Capitol in Washintgon learn that it was a Greek painter, a dedicated citizen of this country, who has created the magnificent frescoes which are so impressively adorning the venerable building." (Panos Peclaris, *The Hellenic Review,* April 1963.)

It is now known that Brumidi left Rome as an exile, in 1852 having been in jail for one year for his revolutionary activities on behalf of the Italian national unity and indepedence. He emigrated to the United States before Italy was liberated.

Another outstanding American of Hellenic descent was Lucas Miltiades Miller. The following biographical sketch of Rep. Miller —member of the U.S. House of Representatives in the 52nd Congress, December 7, 1891 to March 3, 1893—is included in the *Congressional Directory*, 52nd Congress, 2nd session (p. 111):

Lucas M. Miller, of Oshkosch, was born in Levadia, Greece in 1824; is the son of a Greek chieftain, who was killed by the Turks during the Greek revolution, soon after his mother died, and was cared for for a short time by a woman who claimed she found him in an abandoned town soon after the battle had taken place within its streets; subsequently she applied to Colonel J.P. Miller for assistance; the colonel was an American who joined the Greek Army at the beginning of the revolution; was commissioned as Colonel and distinguished himself as an efficient officer . . . and rendered very material service to the Greeks by securing the donation of several vessels laden with provisions and clothing by the citizens of his country for the benefit of the destitute people of Greece; the colonel learning the history of the orphan boy concluded to adopt him . . . While in Congress, Representative Miller played an active role in the debate of various issues.

Other Greeks who had come either by themselves to America in those days or were brought to the United States by American misionaries were destined to play some role in the intellectual and educational life of America. Among them were noted writers and educators. One finds in the National Archives in Washington the names of George and Ioannis Griegos, Petros Margarites, Ioannis Kapotas—known as "John Cabot," Andrew Karavitos, Andrew Ninos, Ioannis Rivas, Elias Batelos, Alexander Dimitry (or Dimitris) about whom there will be more to say in a special chapter on New Orleans and the activities of the Greek-American community in that city in the early days of Greek immigration to the United States. Dr. Demetrios Callimachos, an ordained priest and a confirmed Hellenist who was editor-in-chief of the *National Herald* for many years was one of the most outstanding Greek-Americans. More about his own activities will be found in a special chapter about the Greek-American Press and its role in the United States. Another prominent Greek, who was brought to America by Dr. Samuel Gridley Howe and John R. Suyvesant, was Christopher Kastanis. He studied at the Mount Pleasant Classical Institute in Amherst, and worked for a while as a printer in Boston. Later— having visited Greece, he gave a series of lectures on the situation prevailing there (1837) and on the immediate needs of the Greek people. He wrote *The Greek Exile,* a sort of autobiography. It is Kastanis who mentions in his book that during the 1821 Greek War of Independence the American missionaries brought to America approximately forty young Greek boys who studied in various American colleges. Most of them returned to Greece after graduation. Another well-known Greek was Vasilios Argyros (Argyras), who graduated in 1840 from Yale University and returned to Greece where he got involved in various uprisings against the Government. He finally settled in America, where he died in 1866.

In his book *Greeks of America* (*Oi Ellines tis Amerikis,* New York) Babis Malafouris, who wrote one of the most extensive and comprehensive accounts of the history of the Greek-Americans, says that during the middle of the last century a few Greeks came to the United States, who embraced Protestantism and worked as missionaries or representatives of misionaries. One of them was Michael Kalapothakis who studied at the Union Theological Seminary and, later, founded the Evangelical Church in Athens, Greece (1874). Another young Greek who studied to be a priest was George Constandinou. He became United States Consul to Greece from 1864 to 1874. Malafouris writes that some other Theologians were George Papadakis (Paterson), Andreas Xenos, Ioannis Rodokanakis and Christos Ap. Derevis.

There is no doubt that over the years many other Greeks have distinguished themselves in America but no one can be sure of their exact number and in what specific fields they excelled.

American Diplomatic Representation in Greece

BEFORE one deals in length with the mass immigration of the Greeks to the United States, between the end of the nineteenth century and the beginning of the twentieth century, and the causes that provoked it, it is perhaps necessary to give a brief account of the duties and the activities of the American diplomats in Greece at that time.

Early in the Revolutionary War the Continental Congress began to send diplomatic agents on missions to various European courts. With the appointment of Benjamin Franklin, on September 14, 1778, as Minister Plenipotentiary to France, the United States had its first resident of permanent diplomatic representation. (From the list of Foreign Service Post Records, National Archives, Washington, D.C.).

In the same records one comes across the information that the first American diplomatic representation to Greece was established in 1837. American consuls were appointed to Athens, to Canea, Crete, Corfu, Kalamata, Mitylene, Patras, Piraeus, Salonika, Syros and Zante (Geographical List of American Consular Posts and Agencies, National Archives, Washington, D.C.).

A study of the United States consular correspondence proved to be very informative in connection with the situation that prevailed in Greece during these years. In its letter of December 23, 1871, to the State Department the Legation of the United States in Athens writes: "Brigandage is the great evil in Greece. It prevents inter-communications, retards enterprise and paralyses business . . . The American Mission schools in Athens are doing an excellent job... Another report from the same source, in Athens, mentions that there (National Archives, Washington, D.C.). It should be added that under the auspices of the Protestant Episcopal Church of the United States, the first American school in Greece was established in July 1831.

In another letter of the United States Legation in Athens to the State Department (February 3, 1872) it is said that: ". . . a party of

Americans made an excursion to Marathon. They were accompanied by a cavalry escort furnished by the Government . . . Small squads of infantry were placed at several points where an ambuscade by the brigands would be possible but for the precaution . . ."

Another report from the same source, in Athens, mentions that there were riots in the Greek capital when the Bible was translated into demotic Greek. Six people were killed and 32 wounded.

Further information from the United States Legation in Athens (Letter of June 29, 1872, to the State Department) reveals some rather strange occurences. It says: "There appeared in the semi-weekly of the *New York Times* of the 28 ultimo an article copied from the *Ancona* (Italian) *Journal* stating that nine Greek criminals of the worst description had been liberated by the Greek Minister of Justice from the penal colony of Corfu, on condition of their emigrating to the United States and that they were taken in chains from Corfu stone quarries on board the Italian bark *Agamemnon*, bound for New Orleans. The names of the alledged criminals were given."

However, the statement was considered "false" and was attributed by the Greek Government to the "circulation of rumors."

Again the United States Legation in Athens informed the State Department (in 1903) that "It seems that about two monts ago quite a large number of Greeks left Megara, Thebes and Corinth for Boston, New York, St. Louis and other American cities. Most of these immigrants were passed satisfactorily, but a number of them —notably those whose destination was St. Louis, were stopped and sent back . . ."

On July 2, 1906, the State Department was informed that ". . . The immigration of Greeks to the United States is more or less of recent date. The number exceeded 1,000 for the first time in 1890. Since that year the emigration has been of more importance, the increase being fairly regular."

However, according to recently published statistics, more than 14,000 Greeks left for the United States, while in 1904, less than 10,000 are said to have gone. The number of departures for 1902 is given as 15,510.

The American diplomatic representatives in Greece, at that time, thought that no "especial reason" seemed to exist for the emigration, as it was certainly not due to the lack of work, for most of the men come from the Peloponnesos, where agricultural laborers "are always in demand."

The U.S. Legation in Athens, comes to the conclusion that "The Greek has always gone abroad to make money, and education is making the peasant more or less dissatisfied with his lot. It is practically impossible to ascertain how much money these men send home, but it is certain that there has been a rapid increase in the amount (which is one of the causes of the increasing expensiveness of life in Greece)." However, this account does not seem to be in accord with reports from other sources that the main reason for the mass Greek immigration to the United States was the unbelievable rate of unemployment—or to be more precise to the almost total lack of work.

It should be added that the American Legation in Athens appointed a Commission to study the question of emigration which made a report to the Greek Chamber of Commerce stating that Greece having no statistics, the emigration of Greeks to the United States "is increasing in' enormous proportion" compared to other countries. The report concluded that Greece, however, was by no means depopulated, as "the regions which furnish the largest number of emigrants are also the most prolific part of the country." Furthermore, the Commission thought the Greeks did not generally emigrate, in the usual sense of the word, but after a longer or shorter absence returned to settle in Greece. They remain in constant communication with their families at home—as is shown by the amount of money they sent back.

In 1906, the money orders alone reached the sum of $6,000,000. The Commission came up with a severe recommendation. It asked that the State Department ought to protest such an important source of wealth, and insisted upon a strict suspension of the agents of emigration companies, who should be obliged to have a special authorization. It recommended also the establishment of an office for the sanitary inspection, and measures to decide upon the foreign ports where emigrants should embark for America.

Other letters sent by the American Legation in Athens to the State Department give a picturesque account of Greek life. In March 1875, the American Charge d'Affaires wrote to Washington:

A magnificent ball took place at the palace on the 3d instant. On that occasion the American Minister had the honor to be selected to lead a contra-dance with the Queen. The spacious salons were filled at half past nine and the festivities continued until half past five in the morning. The arrangements throughout were of the most admirable character. An elaborate supper for

800 guests as laid in the royal salle à manger and in the two large adjoining rooms, while the ministers of state and the diplomatic corps were entertained by the king and queen in the beautiful private apartments of their majesties . . . The ample entrances (of the royal palace) and stately corridors are adorned with rare plants and flowers. The crimson carpets bring into brilliant relief the white marble floors. On either hand a double row of attendants display the spendor of the national costume. The two principal ball-rooms are of vast size. Their highly decorated walls and lofty ceilings stand revealed in the soft rays of two thousand wax candles. The hall of Greek portraits and historic pictures is likewise invested with a special interest, when one sees walking therein not only the descendants of heroes, but sometimes even a hero himself, like the venerable and illustrious Admiral Canaris. The names of Mavrocordato, Kolokotronis, Botzaris, Capo d'Istria and many more which long ago became household words in America, have now in Greece living illustrations in the second and third generations. These representatives of a glorious past pace today beneath the paintings which tell in a graphic way their ancestors' heroic story. Truly, the near and the remote history of this nation team with such examples of lofty patriotism and enduring courage that will beget confidence in their present condition and inspire hope for their future progress.

However, the "splendor" of the Royal Palace was in striking contrast to the situation prevailing in Greece itself. Obviously the American envoy—as all other early American diplomatic envoys in foreign countries, was impressed both by the glory of Greece and the luxury of the Royal Palace. Yet, the political and financial situation (which prompted the mass immigration of the Greeks to the United States) at that time was far from satisfactory. Thus, as stated in the Washington Archives: ". . . The public business was in consequence entirely suspended. The finance measures, on which the credit of the country depends, could not be passed, and the spectacle presented to the friends and well-wishers of Greece was indeed a most melancholy one." (Foreign Relations, National Archives, Washington, D.C.).

In regard to the financial situation of Greece, the United States Legation in Athens sent later some alarming reports. Their conclusion was that three radical defects impede the nation's march and check its healthy growth:

1) The lack of proper means of transit within the kingdom, and the absence of easy daily lines of communication with the outer world.

2) The land tax, and

3) The instability arising from the constant change of ministers.

One of these reports concluded that: "In America we are taught to regard Greece as part of Europe. The truth is that she is nominally in it without being of it. She has nothing in common with the European system, nor does she come into immediate contact with the rest of mankind. She does not possess even the advantages of an island, for an island can be approached from all sides. The busy currents of life and trade sweep past her interesting shores touching them only incidentally at two or three widely-separated spots. Athens is an exclamation point, for every traveller arriving from the farther East, including even Constantinople, finds at the Grecian capital abundant evidences of European taste and culture, which present a remarkable contrast to the under life of the remoter Orient."

The Americans in Greece at that time came to the ultimate conclusion that whoever attempted to judge Greece by her capital (Athens) would be guilty of a "folly."

Another official report states that within twenty miles of the Acropolis and the Parthenon modern civilization vanished like a dream, carrying with it all modern improvements. "It is entirely safe"—the report added—"that the agricultural life of Greece, which engages more than one half of the entire population is an existence of primitive simplicity. It is an existence compatible with honor and honesty, frugality and economy, hospitality and kindest dealings with strangers. But it is lacking in many of the elements which today seem absolutely necessary for the welfare of mankind . . ."

In regard to the political situation in Greece, the official reports of the United States Legation, in Athens, were rather gloomy. One report says that: ". . . the unwholesome political agitation in Greece grows out of the detached condition of each handful of people and out of the want of variety and extent of industrial and commercial pursuits . . ." And the following description is offered about life in Athens: ". . . donkeys take the place of steam, and produce reaches the market on their backs . . . the mountains frequently are denuded of forests by the large population of wandering shepherds, who burn the trees for the purpose of getting grass and cut them to give food to their goats . . ." The report adds: "If goat-raising could be stopped, the living in tents and the habits which so largely prevail would entirely disappear. The wounds consist principally from irresponsible foreigners, coming, in many instances, from Turkey, who hire for a season, sometimes for several years, the mountain pastures, paying the rent, a merely nominal sum, in advance. Nomadic pasturage has discouraged agriculture . . ."

The American officials in Athens urged for the removal of crushing land tax—"a barbarious relic of Turkish rule—it drags today from the unhappy farmer forty percent of his earnings."

A study of the United States consular correspondence brings to light other very interesting factors connected with the immigration of the Greeks to America.

One of the problems created by the Greek immigration to the United States, and which affected to some extent, and during certain periods, the relations between Washington and Athens, was the question of the citizenship of the immigrants. Greece considered them "Greeks" and as a matter of fact still maintains, that Greeks naturalized Americans are Greeks and that therefore cannot be exempt from certain obligations towards Greece—namely the military service in the Greek armed forces. In reality, Greeks naturalized as Americans have two citizenships for the rest of their lives—unless they renounce the American one.

Thus, when some Greek immigrants, who had become naturalized Americans returned to Greece, they found out that they were eligible for military service in the Greek army. The United States protested, but to no avail.

The United States Legation, in Athens, in a letter to the State Department dated March 1, 1900, wrote that ". . . Economopoulos (Louis Economopoulos) emigrated to the United States (New York) in his 16th year, January 1893, and was duly naturalized August 23, 1899, being then over 21 years of age. Economopoulos left New York September 2, 1899, for a brief visit to Laraphon, a village in Laconia. He was arrested and taken to Sparta where in spite of his United States citizenship he was made to take the military oath." (Foreign Relations. Consular correspondence— Washington National Archives).

Other Greeks United States citizens who had returned for a while in Greece, were arrested and forced to discharge their military "obligations." Many other Greeks who became U.S.

70

citizens and later asked the State Department if they could go to Greece, were told they would do so at their own risk. Greece had rejected an American offer to sign a convention by which the Greeks naturalized Americans were no longer responsible to the Greek law and regulations. The right of expatriation was not recognized by the Greek Constitution.

In a letter of 1870 to the American Minister in Athens, A.S. Hardy, the Greek Foreign Minister, A. Romanos, said: ". . . to my regret I cannot conclude a convention which would accord American citizenship to Greek subjects in conformity with the terms of similar conventions with other European countries. The American citizenship of Greek emigrants cannot be recognized in Greece unless they have requested and obtained the prescribed permission of the Government and discharged their military obligations to the country of their origin."

There was also another problem created in the process of immigration to the United States: the illegal entry of Greeks into America.

On December 12, 1908, the Secretary of State, E. Root, wrote to the Foreign Minister of Greece:

"I am sending . . . copy of a report made to the Bureau of Immigration and Naturalization of the Department of Commerce and Labor, by Miltiades M. Constantinides, an interpreter employed in the Immigration Service at Boston, Mass., in relation to the practice of certain Greeks who enter the United States, as alleged priests of the Greek Church, but who are in reality either imposters or ordained monks incompetent to perform validly the functions of the priesthood. In view of that these persons are performing sacerdotal acts, which are legally invalid, as the celebration of marriage and the like, and the abuse is one which no less affects your Government than our own, it is proposed to instruct the American Minister at Athens to confer with the Government in view of adopting regulations and some form of certification which should effectively prevent the abuse . . ."

Under the Immigration law prevailing at that time priests of all denominations landing in the United States were entering America under the "exempt classes." Most of those entering illegally the United States were "only Greek monks who had run away from their old country monastery for one reason or another. By their actions and their behaviour they only bring trouble and discord and scandal into a peaceful Greek Church and its congregation." They were entering the United States in the role of a priest when they had no right to do so, and there were rumors that a few of these alleged priests were not even monks but plain outlaws who had come to America disguised as priests in violation of the law. Any subterfuge would be used in those days to enter the United States—and illegal entry to America has not stopped, even to this day, in spite of severe restrictions and measures taken by the Immigration Office.

Greece of the Immigrants

WHEN the flow of emigration from western and northern Europe had already brought millions of foreigners to the new world—from the Atlantic to the Pacific, and was declining, Greek mass immigration to America was about to begin. The Greeks were indeed the last immigrants on the American continent.

The immigration of the Greeks to the United States is not a unique phenomenon and therefore should not be examined as such. Immigration from Greece has always existed in one form or another though naturally the numbers of the immigrants varied according to the situation prevailing in Greece at the time of their exodus and to the needs and demands of the countries to which they emigrated. America, however, was a distant goal for an immigrant, as Burgess states: "The Greek emigrant had sought as the haven of the wanderlust Rumania, Bulgaria, Russia, England— and elsewhere over the nearer parts of the world. America was out of range of his thinking." (Thomas Burgess, *Greeks in America.*)

According to the Annual Reports of the Commissioner General of Immigration in 1848, there arrived in New York, 91,061 Irish, 51,973 Germans and only one Greek. In 1858, there were two Greeks among the immigrants. From 1847 to 1864, the total number of Greeks entering New York port was 77.

It must be stated here that no two different sources—whether official or semi-official—agree either on the exact numbers of the Greeks arriving in the United States or on the precise dates of these arrivals. This is obviously due to the lack of statistics in Greece and to the fact that during the early days of Greek immigration to America those emigrating from unredeemed parts of Greece were not "classified" as Greeks by the Immigration services.

The movement of Greek immigration to the United States, as such, probably begins in 1882, when 125 men and one woman arrived in America. Their numbers doubled next year. In 1891, 1040 men and 65 women emigrated to the United States, and since then their numbers increased every passing year. In 1907, 36,580 Greeks—approximately 1.5 percent of the entire population of Greece, at that time, came to the new world. During the years 1911-1920, with 184,201 arrivals, one tenth of the total population of Greece had emigrated to the United States, at an average of 20,000 a year.

According to the figures of the American Office of Information, from 1821 to 1945, 432,048 Greeks emigrated to the United States from Greece proper, 156,000 from European Turkey and 205,474 from Asia-Minor—a total of 793,522.

During the same period of time many more thousands of Greeks come to America, who, however, were not included in the above figures of immigrants of Greek descent because they had come from unredeemed parts of Greece. Before the Balkan War of 1912-13, almost half of what Greece is today was part of the Ottoman Empire. Many regions of Northern Greece, the Dodecanese, Cyprus (an independent island today) and even Crete, were under foreign domination. One is led to conclude that as a matter of fact more Greeks came to the new world from areas which were not within the frontiers of the then Greek state.

The systematic Greek immigration to the United States covers a period of approximately thirty years (1891-1921). During these thirty years almost half a million Greek immigrants from Greece proper came to the new world and spread throughout the vastness of the United States.

George C. Vournas (Congressional Record Proceedings and Debates of the 86th Congress, Second Session) writes that:

> Greek immigration to the United States, as the term is commonly understood, did not begin until late in the 19th century. In 1889, 158 immigrants arrived from Greece; in 1896, 2,175 —the number reaching 36,580 for the year 1907. The statistics: 1820-80: 398; 1881-1946: 431,650. To this number, however, must be added a great proportion of the immigrants arriving from European Turkey, statistically given for the period as 156,000, plus proportional numbers of those from Egypt, Albania, Rumania (total for the period 157,345), Bulgaria (66,026), Russia (3,340,611), Austria, Hungary (4,444,556) and Asiatic Turkey (205,473). Thus, on the basis of these statistics it would not be an exaggeration to state that immigrants to the United

States up to 1946, meeting the Venizelos's definition of a "Greek" (Eleftherios Venizelos, the great Greek statesman, said during a debate at the 1919, Versailles Peace Conference that "A Greek is a person who wants to be a Greek, feels he is a Greek and says he is a Greek")—without its political connotation—would number between 750,000 and 800,000 (Cyprus, Dodecanese Islands, no statistics available).

In his book *Greek Immigration in the United States,* Henry Pratt Fairchild writes that: "Up to the last decade of the nineteenth century Greek immigration into the United States was not of sufficient volume to be called a movement. Not until 1891, did the figure reach 1,000." He adds that: "The men were wanted and needed—quality was not of essence, quantity was the great desiratum ... Whether the literacy or illiteracy of a group of immigrants is a matter of importance or not depends on one's conception of the immigrant in the United States. If we adopt the idea, which is probably the prevailing one in the United States, that the business of the immigrant is to do the hard and menial work of the country, which is beneath the dignity of a native American, then perhaps the more dull, stolid and devoid of ambition or culture the foreigners are, the better it will be, provided only they have sturdy bodies and humble spirits."

The Greek immigrants fall into the "image" that the Americans had about the kind of immigrants they needed to build their new country—yet they only approximated this image. The Greeks were ignorant, humble people destined to do "the hard and menial work" expected of them. But being the descendants of a high culture and civilization they were not deprived of ambition. This they proved over the years that followed the date of their first arrival to the United States.

Originally, the Greek Immigration to America was not in any sense an immigration of families but almost entirely of unmarried men or of men with families left behind. This is why there was such a high proportion of men and young boys among the first Greek immigrants to the new world.

Reverend Thomas J. Lacey, in his book *Our Greek Immigrants* says that "Greeks are a comparatively recent addition to the complex stream of American life. In 1848, only one Greek arrived in New York. Three years later there were two. At the close of the civil war there were less than 100 Greeks in the United States. In 1886, the United States Consul in Greece reported that there was no emigration from Greece. In 1900, the total number of Greeks amongst (us) was about equal to the number that Xenophon led in his famous *Anabasis*. In a decade this number increased ten-fold..." Lacey further writes: "...the Greek immigrant makes a precious contribution to America's greatness and is to be counted a valuable asset to American life . . . their (the Greeks') ancestral culture tempers our rudeness..."

Modern Greek immigration started from the early days of the establishment of the new Greek state (after the Greeks won their 1821 War of Independence against the Turks).

Professor Vasilios Valaoras (*O Ellinismos ton Inomenon Polition-Hellenism of the United States*, Athens, 1937) writes:

> Already in 1824, when the struggle for independence had reached its peak, five Greeks are reported to have abandoned the soil of their motherland to come and settle in the United States. In 1826, another four followed; in 1827, another seven, and the flow of Greek immigrants to the United States continued the following years and reached its largest percentage during the first two decades of the present century . . . later, and because of immigration restrictions in the United States, immigration from Greece slowed down without, however, having entirely stopped.

During the years between 1824 to 1932—according to Valaoras, 448,015 Greeks left their homeland for the United States while during the same period of time only 40,814 Greeks emigrated to other countries. This "preference" for the United States, the promised land, explains perhaps why Hellenism in America has become the most important and most compact of all Greek colonies. Naturally, one must have in mind that over the years, other Greek colonies in some parts of the world have yielded to political pressure and persecution which resulted in the decrease of their numbers. For example, thousands of Greeks from Egypt and from Turkey (mostly Constantinople) were forced to flee to Greece.

Professor Valaoras concludes that Greek immigration to the United States before 1890 was unimportant and continued to be insignificant until 1900, when it became steady. During the first part of the 20th century, the flow of Greek immigrants to the new world reached enormous proportions. More than 300,000 are believed to have left Greece for America. The largest number of immigrants to the United States is reported for the year 1907 (36,580), the second largest one occurred during 1914 (35,832), and the third one (28,502) in 1922, after the disastrous war between Greece and Turkey in Asia-Minor (when Greece was defeated after being abandoned by her allies who had supported her presence and activities in the area as a result of a treaty which was subsequently violated).

The age and sex of the Greeks emigrating to the United States is characteristic of the particular circumstances under which Greek immigration had occurred. The main goal of the first Greek immigrants was to come to the United States for a short while and make some money before returning to the homeland and to their families. However, as time went by and the first Greek immigrants came into closer contact with American life, the original goal was abandoned. It remained in most cases a permanent but unfulfilled dream. "Moreover, once in America shame and lack of money prevented the return home—and they had to find the original conditions are as unimaginable—shame prevents to write the truth at home . . ." (Thomas Burgess, *Greeks in America*). Gradually Greek women came either to meet their immigrant husbands or to get married to Greek bachelors who had sent for them.

It is interesting to remember that in 1900, there were 11 women for every one hundred Greek immigrants; in 1910, 14 to every hundred; in 1920, 23, and in 1930, only 35 to every hundred. The ideal analogy would have been one hundred women to one hundred men. This figure has not been reached even today though the proportion of Greek women coming to the United States increased from 10 percent, at the beginning of this century, to 61 percent. This is perhaps one reason, among others, why many Greek immigrants married women of a different nationality and of another religion. It also explains, in some cases, why a certain percentage of first Greek immigrants remained unmarried.

It should also be added here that 90 percent of the immigrants who came from Greece to America, were men between the age of 25 and 65, while the Americans of Greek descent born in the United States—during the period of the first mass immigration—were youngsters depending entirely on the work of the first "classification." This is another reason why there has been—especially during the first years of the presence of the Greek immigrants in America, a difficult "rapport" between them and the first American generation, their offspring, of hellenic ancestry. The problem will be examined in another part of this study.

The causes of Greek immigration to America were not religious or political, but mainly economic or social (lack of education for one thing). However, the reason of immigration from enslaved Greece were quite different from those in the case of the free kingdom. There, the principal cause, if not the only one, was Turkish pressure and persecution of the Christian and more especially of the Greek Orthodox. Moreover, the service of Greek young men in the Turkish army was compulsory, and as Burgess explains, in the army "neither their religion nor their morality was safeguarded . . . (which) drove many to leave the country for the 'land of the free'."

It has already been said that in the historically and geographically unjust partition of the Hellenic world in 1821, after the victorious Greek War of Independence against the Turks, lies the principal cause for the difficult economic situation existing in Greece when the first Greek immigrants crossed the Atlantic Ocean to come to America in search of a better life. Yet, some writers have disputed —or at least have minimized, the fact that the economic situation in Greece at the time of the rebirth of the country was indeed so precarious as to provoke a wave of expatriation.

The truth is that the Greeks emigrated to the United States, and as a matter of fact elsewhere, because Greece was poor at the moment of their mass departure, but also because of their perennial thirst for the unknown. Whether ignorant or sophisticated the Greek is always tempted by adventure. Moreover, the era of mass immigration coincided with a new period of mutual admiration between Greece and the United States prompted by American interest and participation in the war that had liberated modern Greeks from the Turkish yoke.

There seems to be little doubt that the mass immigration of the Greeks to the new world began because of dissatisfaction and discomfort in the homeland, which caused large bodies of people to leave. However, the real extent of poverty existing then in Greece offers the opportunity both for negative and positive arguments. Poverty as every other condition in life, is relative; what is bearable to some is unbearable to others.

In reality many factors contributed in exaggerating the precariousness of the economic conditions in Greece, on one hand, and the magic of the new life that was awaiting the Greek immigrants in the new world, on the other. Exploitation of the destitute is a perennial evil and the exaggeration of certain situations is another.

Four centuries of slavery, of pillages and looting on the part of the Turkish occupants had kept the Greek people in a state of real stagnation. There was no progress, or economic development. Greek families did not perhaps starve; however, under the constant pressure and persecution of the Turks, the Greeks had little opportunity to acquire the economic assets that bring security and dignity to human beings. Moreover, when political antagonism among the big powers closed the "outlets" towards Russia, the Balkans, the Middle East, and Africa, the Greeks joined the large movement of immigration to America.

Economic difficulties in Greece, around 1890, coincided with the industrial revolution in the United States. There are historical, though contrasting coincidences that change the fate of people—or at least of a certain percentage of people. The demand for workers in America was known in Greece as the Greek governments were facing one crisis after another. There was no trade or industry in the country at that time. The population of Greece almost in its entirety was agricultural. However, the poor farmers were the victims of userers protected by the law and were sent to jail whenever they could not pay their debts—which was often.

Between 1882 and 1883, the stock exchange suffered a serious setback, the harvest was bad, the drop in the price of raisins—the principal income for the Peloponnesos and the Ionian Islands, led to an economic deadlock. The resulting situation helped in increasing the immigration trend which, moreover, the government was encouraging. Almost at the same time Turkey passed a law according to which military service was compulsory for all Christian minorities. This provoked the exodus of Greek Orthodox from most parts of Asia-Minor, who came to the United States—as we have already seen—as "foreign subjects."

Professor Vassilios Valaoras (*Hellenism of the United States*) writes that "It is known that since the beginning of her history Greece is constantly losing part of her population because of immigration in foreign lands . . . This is ascribed to the narrowness of the Greek territory the limited yield of which does not permit large increase of the population."

In 1911, the Carnegie Institute of Washington, sent H. P. Fairchild to Greece to study the "phenomenon" of Greek immigration. Fairchild has described in his book *Greek Immigration to the United States* the country he visited and studied with objectivity but about which he used some caustic remarks, when he analyzed in detail the Greek character. Fairchild was convinced that Greek immigration to the United States was exclusively due to economic causes and he had come to some conclusions that obviously were taken into account later when the new immigration law was adopted, which practically prevented the Greek immigrants from coming to America.

Some of Fairchild's remarks about the Greeks are indeed mean—though not entirely inaccurate. He writes, among other things, that "a clannishness (of the Greeks), an inability to take the point of view of one's neighbor, which has extended beyond the tribal limits making it very difficult for Greeks to unite in any common enterprise . . ." Writing about the language the first Greek immigrants spoke, or tried to speak, Fairchild remarks on the ". . . isolation, which explains perhaps why they could not learn the language—at least the real spoken language, to which they have added their own dialectical abomination. Thus killing both English and Greek at the same time."

It is true, however, that even today some Greek-Americans seem to speak a sort of dialect of their own which is an ugly melange of Greek and English. When they do speak English they use a lot of "mutilated" Greek words—and vice versa.

Professor Valaoras does not seem to agree with the conclusions that Fairchild had reached in his study of the "phenomenon" of Greek immigration. He thinks that only an intensive pressure on the population which provoked a feeling of incertitude and discomfort can induce large bodies of people to expatriate. The pressure can be the result of many causes: political, religious, economic or the result of an exaggerated increase of the population. Valaoras says that "there was no political or any other persecution of the population and the economic situation of the country during the intensive immigration movement was not worse than the situation that had prevailed during other periods of time to justify the increase in immigration." Therefore, Valaoras concludes, "what has to be examined is the question of the existence or of the non-existence of the symptoms of the overpopulation of the country."

Unfortunately, no responsible answer can be given to the question asked by Mr. Valaoras, because there were no statistics in connection with the movement of the population during those days.

Psychological causes, however, seem to have prompted the increase of the immigration of the Greeks to America. And the reason was provided by those first immigrants who had already arrived—if not settled—in the United States. The first letters from the Greek immigrants to their families and friends back home were full of exaggerations and in many instances full of lies. They spoke of fabulous wages and wonderful living conditions. The Greek of the Peloponnesos—and elsewhere, who was fighting for survival, was given a false image of America, in striking contrast to the life he was living. Mass immigration was on.

Thomas Burgess (*Greeks in America*) writes that: "There were exaggerated reports sent home of the land of the marvels—and by the steam agents who soon became ubiquitous and unscrupulous." Emigration began in the Peloponnesos, but as the rumors of "success" of the first immigrants in America persisted it spread to central Greece, Epirus, Thessaly, Macedonia, Thrace, the Islands, and over the Aegean, to Smyrna and the surrounding Greek inhabitants of Turkey, in Asia. Every section of Greece had thus contributed to the emigrant stream, but "Sparta and Tripolis (are) the cradle of Greek Immigration to America" (Henry Pratt Fairchild, *Greek Immigration in the United States*).

Thomas Burgess (*Greeks in America*) writes that "in the late 90s more and more reported cases of prosperity in America made the poor Greek farmer open his eyes. Success is certain in America. But no one in Greece really knew, nor do they know now, the conditions as they actually were in America. All are doomed to bitter disillusionment, when they find hard, inevitable toil, the like of which they never dreamed at home."

The Greeks started leaving first by tens, then by hundreds and then by thousands. Nearly all of them came originally from the mountain regions of the Peloponnesos—poorly educated, or rather not educated at all since they were mostly shepherds and farmers.

The psychological effect upon the Greeks, who were now in a hurry to join those of their compatriots or relatives already in the new world, was skilfully developed and strengthened by unscrupulous operators. Numerous agencies were gradually established in Piraeus, Patras and other ports of Greece, with the purpose of exploiting the situation to the fullest. The emigration agents, a very special brand of obscure individuals, began to excite the imagination of the Greek peasants as to the "glories and the opportunities" of America. They seemed to be able to solve all problems and to ward off all hurdles. The fare for the distant voyage to the "promised land" was usually secured through mortgage, and the agents guaranteed a fast, easy journey to the new world—which was not the case. In those days the duration of the voyage was from 20 to 45 days, and sometimes even longer. The ships were sailing from Genoa, Marseilles, Le Havre and later from

Greece itself. Sailing conditions were undescribable and many immigrants regretted their fatal decision as soon as they had come aboard the ship which was to take them to America. But they had already cut themselves from Greece and most of them were ashamed to recognize their mistake. Others, however, were ready to go through any ordeal provided they would be given an opportunity to reach the American shores. Originally, New York was supposed to be their first settling place—later Chicago, Boston and a few other large cities of the United States.

In his book *Ellines tis Amerikis* (New York, 1948) Babis Malafouris mentions that Greek Professor Andreas Mih. Andreadis published a study on the causes of Greek immigration to America based on the findings and observations of some studies from various parts of Greece. These were findings of people who lived in Tripolis, Patras, Kalavryta, Tegea, Corinth, Agrinion, Trikkala, the island of Cephalonia, but also in certain areas of the island of Crete, Mytilene as well as Macedonia and Epirus. Most of the observations attribute the causes of immigration to America to the economic situation that prevailed in these particular regions of the country.

Taking into consideration that the above regions of Greece, from where the largest numbers of immigrants came, were also the most fertile, it is easy to come to the conclusion that the immigration could not have but augmented the economic plight of the country. Practically no men were left to cultivate the soil and the number of births decreased considerably.

It must be noted that from the Greeks who had come to America during the early days of the mass immigration approximately 10,000 —though no one can be sure about the accuracy of the figures— returned every year to Greece. It is believed that during the years between 1908 and 1924, 170,000 Greeks came back to their home-land—that is to say almost 50 percent of those who had originally emigrated in the new world. But many of them stayed in Greece only for a short period of time and decided, later, to sail back to America. Between 1912 and 1913, 34,892 Greeks returned to Greece to participate in the war against the Turks. The years of their sojourn in America had not extinguished their patriotic feelings for their country. To the contrary, it seems that their sentimental ties with Greece had become stronger.

Greek mass immigration to America coincided with a peculiar moment in the history of Greece—a moment which could perhaps be called an historical contrast. After having been liberated from the Turks, "the Greeks, with a passion unequaled since the days of the War of Independence, were waging vociferous crusades for the union of their 'unredeemed brothers' in Crete, Macedonia, the Aegean Islands, and other portions of the Ottoman Empire with 'Mother Greece'." (Professor Theodore Saloutos, *The Greeks in the United States,* Cambridge: Harvard University Press, 1964.)

A sort of renaissance was spreading through the country which, however, seemed to be rather theoretical or psychological than actual, though the Greek economy was showing some progress. Then in 1899, there was a sudden but steady decline in the value of the national currency—the drachma. The depreciation of the Greek currency was blamed on the war in South Africa and on speculation (Bureau of Foreign Commerce, *Commercial Relations with the United States,* Washington National Archives, 1899). There were other reasons for which the Greek economy received a serious blow: drought and crop failures. However, and this was the time when the first positive sign of Greek immigration to the United States was manifested, " the gold streaming into Greece from America, that is to say the money sent by the immigrants to their relatives in the old country, pumped fresh blood into the anemic economy of Greece" (National Archives, Washington, D.C.). One has to remember that at the time of the immigration of the Greeks to the new world, the population of Greece was 2,500,000.

This number, however, was dangerously augmented when political refugees fled to Greece from the areas still under Turkish domination. Twenty thousand persons found refuge in Thessaly and another 90,000 came to Greece after the Balkan Wars. The national economy could not sustain the new burden.

In his book *The Greeks in the United States,* Theodore Saloutos, who has written an excellent study both on the causes of the Greek immigration and the conditions prevailing in Greece at the moment of the mass exodus, concludes that:

> This . . . was the Hellas of the immigrant—a land of poverty, restlessness, unstable rule, and passionate Panhellenic aspirations. But it also was a country that seemed to be on the threshold of a national awakening. Agriculture of a primitive and impoverished kind formed the basis of the economy, and large cities were few and far between. But the middle classes were increasing in numbers and influence, and commercial ties were being forged but surely with the United States. Greece's peasants, about to become immigrants, were imbued with the same pioneering

spirit that carried the people of other nations to America. They were nurtured in a climate of individualism that was to blend admirably with the native American variety.

One should perhaps add that though Greek individualism was "nurtured in a climate of individualism" that was to blend with the American environment, it took many years of unbelievable hardships for the Greeks before they got accustomed to the strange land that America was for them.

For one thing the nature of the country from where they came and the physical environment of their new homeland were totally different. Their religion and their language were different. The moment of their arrival in the new world coincided with an exaggerated anti-foreignism. They were terribly exploited both by the native Americans and by some Greeks who had preceeded them in the promised land. The process of their adaptation to the United States began under the most dreadful living conditions. Any conclusion that they blended rather early with the American climate would be an inaccuracy. The "blend" did occur but not before the poor, ignorant Greek immigrant had gone through the most cruel experiences. It took courage, pride and physical strength to overcome all the numerous problems that the Greeks were facing from the first moment they were setting foot on American soil. During the early days of the Greek mass immigration to the new world, only a prophet could have foreseen their final success in the "land of the free," where they indeed found themselves treated like slaves. Any old immigrant who would care to comment about the early years of his adventures in America will testify to that. This is perhaps why Greek immigrants should be praised for their achievements, I mean, not because they finally adapted themselves to the American entourage or made money, but because they were capable of scoring a tremendous victory over the original hostility they met in a country where they were supposed to be happy and prosperous. Happiness and prosperity came much later—in the declining years of their superhuman efforts to win a decent place in the new world.

Pressure Upon Greek Youth to Emigrate

ONE CAN easily invoke a variety of motivations for the mass immigration of the Greeks to America—and all of them are indeed valid. Yet, the principal, leading cause, though disputed by some writers, was the economic situation prevailing in Greece at the time of the exodus to the new world. This is what Fairchild believed when he wrote in *Greek Immigration to the United States*: "Stated succinctly, Greece has always been a splendid place to go away from to make a fortune."

Constant and skillful pressure was exercised upon the ignorant youth of the country through strong exhortations like the following:

> Why remain to struggle for a piece of bread without any security for the future, without honor and independence?
> Why not open your eyes and see the good that awaits you; harden your heart and seek your fortune abroad, where so many of your countrymen already have made theirs?
> Why linger? To protect your parents? Today or tomorrow, whether their children are here or abroad, they will close their eyes forever. It will be better for you to leave home and send a little money to provide for them in their advancing years.
> Or are you waiting to cultivate the barren land with the ploughshare and dig in the fields? Have you seen how much progress you have made thus far? (Theodore Saloutos, *They Remember America*, Berkeley and Los Angeles: University of California Press, 1956.)

At the time when the general exodus from Greece was about to begin a Greek parliamentary committee which was appointed to investigate the possibilities of immigration, had this to say about the attraction of the new world for the destitute and depressed people of the world—and more particularly for the poor people of Greece:

> It is the strength of a new nation, strong, energetic, drastic, tireless, making gigantic strides forward, building large cities,

creating excellent opportunities, advancing civilization vigorously and happily. It is the strength (of a nation) with colossal capital in circulation, and capable of providing means of transportation on the ocean and into the interior which beckons the myriads of working hands.

The exhortations to the Greek youth though probably cynical were beyond any doubt highly influential and the conclusions of the parliamentary committee made publicly known were in reality a direct appeal for a prompt departure to America. Regardless of the precariousness of the prevailing situation these appeals contained the seeds of tragedy—in fact, the government was asking the people of the country to abandon it for a better life which was not in sight in their homeland. It was also a recognition of inability to cope with a difficult situation. However, these appeals played an important role in convincing thousands of disappointed youngsters that a better future was to be found only in America. It looked to them that there was no prospect for any improvement in Greece and the present was far from satisfactory.

Other reasons of lesser impact might have contributed to augment and precipitate the exodus from Greece.

In his comprehensive study *The Assimilation of Greeks in the United States* (Athens: National Centre of Social Research, 1968), Professor Evangelos C. Vlachos writes that: "Although the economic motive has been very strong in the case of the Greek immigration to the United States, we must also take into account reasons that gave rise to the motivation for emigration, such as relative overpopulation, communication, and political and religious reasons."

Mr. Vlachos insists that the "great exodus" from Greece at the turn of the century was above all the result of an economic crisis. He writes that from 1882 to 1886, the economic situation in the country was "deplorable." Treasury deficits were faced following the issuing of paper currency and heavy taxation. Finally, he comes to the conclusion that the blockade (of Greece) by the Great Powers, which had warned against hostilities with neighboring Turkey, contributed to aggravating the already shaky economy of the country.

Some other writers seem to think that there were also some political reasons that prompted young Greeks to leave their homeland; they wrote that many Greeks "in the military classes" subject to enlistment left the country to avoid fulfilling their military obligations. Knowing the innate patriotism of the Greeks one is inclined to believe that the allegation should probably have been made in relation to Greeks living in Turkey, who, as we already have seen, fled to avoid serving in the army of the Ottoman Empire of which they were the persecuted subjects.

Some historians have come to another conclusion: they have insisted that the emigration of the Greeks from ancient times was mainly due to the "narrowness" of the Greek territory. Indeed, even Plato attributed the expatriation tendencies of the Greeks to this narrowness and it is on the basis of this specific argument that he had stressed the necessity to adopt a law limiting the rate of births in the country. The issue of the explosion of population we are facing today had been foreseen by the great thinker and philosopher of ancient Greece—though in those days the problem presented itself in a much smaller scale.

Still other writers ventured to say that as a matter of fact the campaign of the Greeks against Troy had not been provoked by any moral causes or reasons of vengence as believed by Homer, but rather because the plains of Asia-Minor were known to be much more fertile than the "barren meadows" of Greece.

In his book *Apodimos Ellinismos* (Athens, 1961), Panos Pamboukis writes that: "New Greece, even after the victorious wars of 1912-1913 . . . was a country without a backbone, without an agricultural -continental population, with a narrow, poor and waterless soil, without any dense forests and deprived raw materials." He concludes that although the density of the Greek population (at the time of the mass immigration of the Greeks) was small in proportion to the geographical size of the country, it was indeed very large in relation to the soil that could be cultivated.

It should also be mentioned here that, as I point out in *Greece: the Struggle for Freedom*, "Greece's geographical position at the crossroads of international antagonism makes it a testing ground between East and West." This antagonism, which still persists in the area, had led to a sequence of wars and economic crises thereof, which had prevented the economic, social and political development of the country.

The mass Greek immigration to the United States was the direct product of the conditions that a tragic situation had created in an underdeveloped country, which had been through four hundred years of brutal foreign conquest.

It is estimated that approximately 38,000,000 people left their own countries to come to the new world. The Greeks were among them. Just how many Greeks emigrated to America will probably never be known. The figures vary between 750,000 and 800,000 "on the basis of various subjective definitions"; perhaps as many as 1,500,000 came to America "contrasted to the 377,000 reported by the 1960 Census, and tracing their parentage to Greece."

What has been established beyond any doubt is the fact that the first Greek immigrants—perhaps more than any other ethnic group in the new world, went through an unbelievable ordeal before finding a decent place within the American environment.

First Days of Mass Greek Immigration

THE arrival to the promised land so much praised and so much advertised in Greece, and which had been discovered by Columbus, whom many Greeks had cursed during the painful crossing of the Atlantic because, somehow, they considered him responsible for their new misfortune, was far from being a happy conclusion. It did not bring the end of their ordeal but perhaps only the beginning of another experience fraught with innumerable dangers and all sorts of insoluble problems. The landing in America meant for these first immigrants that they had just crossed the demarcation line between myth and reality.

Most of the first Greek immigrants were laborers, farmers and shepherds from the rocky mountains of Arcadia, the dry meadows of Corinth or from some other provincial area. They did not speak a word of English and thus were unable to seek advice or look for work. Even their knowledge of Greek was quite inadequate. Very few, if any, knew in advance where they were going or what they would be asked to do. They only knew they wanted to find something different from what they had left behind—which, except for their families, was not very much. They were longing for some sort of security—or was it an illusion, which was nonexistent in their own country.

Upon their arrival they had to overcome the first and often extremely difficult obstacle: the Immigration Service. They were compelled to pass a test originally in Garden Castle (The Battery, New York) which in their inability to identify in English they conveniently called *Kastingari*. They were also screened on Ellis Island—both a dream and a nightmare for every immigrant hoping and praying to be admitted to the United States. The test was physical and so-called intellectual; they had to meet the strict requirements for the eventual undertaking of any menial work and answer questions about their financial situation; their past, their social and political convictions or if they had any relatives or friends already residing in the United States.

Not all of the new immigrants passed the dreaded test. Many of them were told that America did not want them. Yet, not far away from the location where the examination took place stood the Statue of Liberty, about which they had so often heard and which they had seen "smiling" at them as they were entering the port of New York to find freedom, work and happiness.

The percentage of those rejected by the Immigration Service was rather small. Strong bodies were badly needed in those days to build the new country. According to official statistics in 1903, 614 Greeks were not permitted to enter the United States; 527 in 1904, 353 in 1905, 584 in 1907 and 459 in 1908. The number of rejections decreased as years went by perhaps because the later visitors had prepared themselves for the test with the help of what they had learned from letters sent to Greece by those who had been already admitted, or simply because more and more workers were needed as the demand for menial work augmented rapidly. Usually the principal reason for which they were rejected was that the Immigration Service feared they might become a public burden if they did not meet the necessary physical requirements. The negative answer was generally given after the medical examination which indicated that only able bodies were needed. A number of Greeks were not admitted to the United States during the years 1900-1908, because they "carried contagious illnesses." It must be said that the Immigration Service was not only trying to protect the population of the country from sick people, mentally or otherwise, from criminals or "undesirable" persons, but in reality was also protecting some of the immigrants themselves from the exploitation that was awaiting them at the hands of unscrupulous employers. Among the criteria used in certain cases for the admission or the rejection of an immigrant was the amount of money he carried with him. Very few of the immigrants had over 30 dollars in their pockets. Thus all of them had to try to find some kind of work as soon as they set foot on the American soil.

For those who had failed to pass the mandatory test there were not too many alternatives; if they could pay their passage back to Greece, which was seldom, if ever, they would be returning to their homeland after an unforgettable voyage and a fast glimpse at the skyscrapers of New York; those penniless or considered physically unacceptable were detained on Ellis Island, in the expectation of a miracle: their admission to America at a later date after the eventual "reconsideration" of their particular case.

Those more—or perhaps less, fortunate who had passed the examination immediately came in contact with the cold indifference of the American cities, which at that time were swept by a real storm of antiforeignism.

The battle of survival of the future American citizen would start from the first day of his arrival anywhere in the country. Usually, New York was the main port of entry; but some immigrants went to the New England states, Boston, Lowell, Chicago, Philadelphia or elsewhere. From there some of them would go to Colorado, Texas, California and even as far as Alaska.

The Greek immigrants had not been preceded by a very good reputation. Reverend Thomas J. Lacey in *Our Greek Immigrants* wrote that "the weaker side of Hellenic character manifests itself chiefly in factiousness and a love for exploitation . . . jealousies, feuds, faction rivalry or leadership and intestine quarreling in the communities, the churches and the press . . . Among Italians, crimes of violence are common, but with the Greeks, the feuds exhaust themselves in mutual vituperation."

Elsewhere in the same book, Lacey has this to say: "The mill agents at Lowell (Mass.) complain of the factiousness of their Greek employees who form small groups in constant altercation with one another."

Writing about the occupation of the first immigrants in the cities of the United States, Professor Theodore Saloutos (*The Greeks in the United States*) writes:

> The earliest arrivals were forced into the petty street trades and sold cigars, flowers, sweets and other articles; or else they kept lodging and boarding houses or small tavernas for seamen. They had no choice but to content themselves with trifling occupations. Most were honest working people. They lived on next to nothing in order to save and send money to their relatives, which they in turn would lend out at interest. A sum of two thousand dollars was a fortune; lending this out at 20 to 30 percent interest per year brought enough to make a living.

In 1904, the *Washington Post,* writing about the first attempts of Greek immigrants to make some money, had this to say: "Not everyone knows that ninety-nine of every hundred of itinerant vendors is a Greek and that every Georgios or Demetrios among them, boy or man . . . is a small capitalist, and carries anywhere from fifty to several hundred dollars concealed about his person."

However, there are no accurate statistical data on the occupations of the early Greek immigrants in the United States. According to a report from the Greek Consul General in New York (1901) there were about 1,500 "roving" Greek salesmen in the city and another 1,500 or more in Chicago.

In 1907, the then Greek Consul General in New York City, Demetrios Botassis, in his report to the Greek Foreign Ministry stated that "of the 150,000 Greeks in the United States, between 30,000 and 40,000 were working as laborers in factories and railroad construction gangs. Others were employed as bootblacks, waiters, and clerks in stores that catered to the immigrant trade."

Yet, the most ambitious out of the immigrants had already acquired their own business; grocery stores, coffee houses, bakeries, laundries, print shops, etc.

However, regardless of whether they were bootblacks, waiters, bakers, carpenters, laborers or businessmen, the first Greek immigrants had one and the same goal in mind: to save money to send to their relatives in Greece. Pride but also innate kindness characterized all their efforts to overcome the tremendous difficulties they were constantly meeting wherever they worked —and whatever type of work they were doing. One must have in mind that they had also contracted debts to undertake the voyage to America and they were eager to settle their accounts with their exploiters in Greece. They had a great sense of obligation and therefore of thrift; and this is one of the reasons why they did not participate in American life, staying away from any kind of entertainment.

Exploitation, Injustice, Even Tyranny

A NTIFOREIGNISM—a real disease which prevailed in America in those days—manifested itself in many cruel ways. The first Greek immigrants became immediately the favored target of contempt, humiliation, mockery and scorn, but above all of injustice and exploitation either by other Greeks who had come before them to the United States or by native Americans.

It was their inability to speak English, their obsolete habits but mainly their ignorance that offered the opportunity to others to attack them and to humiliate them almost constantly. Even when the time had come for them to be naturalized Americans they had not shown any "intellectual" improvement.

To illustrate the degree of ignorance of these first Greek immigrants and why they became the easy prey of all kinds of exploiters, one only has to remember that they were unable to understand the questions asked of them at the moment they were to become United States citizens. Invariably the American judge would ask the following questions:

"Do you believe in anarchy? Do you believe in polygamy?"

Though both words come from the Greek, the United States citizen-elect (a Greek) had difficulties in understanding the question and the judge had to be helpful and supply additional assistance by saying: "Do you believe in having several wives at the same time?" Unfortunately there are no records of the answers given to either questions but is is easy to come to the conclusion that they both must have been negative.

George C. Vournas (*Greeks in America,* Congressional Record Proceedings and Debates of the 86th Congress, Second Session) writes that: "Not knowing the language, customs or the laws of the territory of the country, they were the subject of continuous exploitation by the employment agencies, interpreters, and advisers. Long hours, unhygienic living conditions—it has been reported that early immigrants were sleeping as many as 10 to a room—and the eventual development of contract labor (young boys contracted by their parents to work as bootblacks for fixed terms at ridiculously low wages), a practice which, fortunately, was outlawed—accented their daily lives . . . While such was the lot of those in the city, the ones working in the mines had to contend with the excesses of the mining companies' private police, as the record testifies at Trinidad and Ludlow, Colorado, even as late as 1913."

One of the most abject forms of exploitation was imposed by what came to be known as the "padrone system" to which were subjected Italians, Bulgarians, Macedonians, Mexicans but also Greeks.

The padrone (Patron, master; applied to either the master of a trading vessel in the Mediterranean, or an Italian employer of street musicians, begging children, etc.) was the uncontested boss of these first Greek immigrants—the victims of their ignorance and of the unfriendliness of the environment. Though the padrone as a rule was a cruel man, an unscrupulous exploiter, the ignorant immigrant had no other alternative than to depend almost exclusively on him in order to survive.

On the basis of information contained in the *Abstract of the Reports of the Immigration Commission II* (Washington, 1911, 61st Congress, Third Session, Senate Document No. 747) but also in personal accounts of old immigrants "the padrone was the person in authority" and "in a dispute or an arbitration his decision was law among immigrants."

Theodore Saloutos (*The Greeks in the United States*) writes that:

> Among the Greeks, the padrone system assumed a slightly different form; it is said to have been in operation in almost every city having a population of ten thousand or more. It was confined to the shoeshining trade, to the flower, fruit, and vegetable peddlers in the larger cities, and the railroad construction workers in the Western States. As employed by the Greeks, the padrone system appears to have been a modernized version of the indentured-servant system of the late seventeenth and early eighteenth centuries.

There are no accurate reports as to the extent to which the padrone system was inflicted upon the Greeks. The antiforeign press often exaggerated its activities and its scope of operation but as Professor Saloutos writes: "The system, however, did exist, especially during the earlier years, when the immigrants were less informed about the United States and before aroused community leaders and immigration authorities sought to bring an end to the vicious practice."

The first Greek immigrants to the United States were divided into two classifications: laborers who were employed in the Western States in mines and railroad construction, and those who struggled for survival in the cities and worked in hotels, restaurants, candy shops and shoeshining places.

The idea of importing and employing young boys from Greece was conceived during the 1890s, "after the Greeks had invaded the shoeshining business." The recruiting of youngsters in Greece was an easy job—at least at the beginning. The *Abstracts of the Reports of the Immigration Commission II* (Washington, 1911) provide ample information on both the procedure followed in bringing Greek youth to the United States and on the way they were treated.

To relatives or friends in Greece, a padrone would write letters full of lies as to the opportunities he was offering to young boys who wanted to live a better, "prosperous" life. In most instances he was willing to pay for transportation. The prospect of providing "earning power" to their children was a convincing factor, which prompted most parents in Greece not only to allow but even to force their boys to leave for America. They knew that a few dollars sent back home would solve a number of their most pressing problems.

The padrone did not fail to use every possible method to induce young boys to come to the United States to work for him. In many instances he would take a trip to Greece for the single purpose of recruiting Greek youth. He would try to become a godfather or a best man in order to extend the circle of his acquaintances and augment the "warmth" of his relationship with certain families. Once this was achieved he would start working on the parents and telling them of the beautiful life their sons would lead in the United States if they only would permit them to leave.

Professor Theodore Saloutos gives a vivid picture of the early life of these youngsters (*The Greeks in the United States*):

> The work of these shoeshine boys began early in the morning and continued well into the evening, seven days a week. The shops opened between 6 and 6:30, which meant that the boys had to awake between 5 and 4:30 a.m. . . . They labored until 9 and 10 o'clock at night, and later on Saturdays and Sundays; . . . After the doors were closed, the boys generally mopped the floor, cleaned the marble stand and fixtures, and gathered up the shoeshining rags to take home, wash, dry, and have in readiness for the following day.

Because of the working hours that were imposed upon them the youngsters had no time to attend day or night school. They remained ignorant both of the English language and, generally, of the conditions of life in the United States. Actually very little change was brought into their daily lives except for the fact that they had never worked that hard in their own country . . . The padrones were paying wages ranging from $80 to $250 a year and estimates figured the income of every padrone at $100 to $200 a year for each boy working for him.

The abject exploitation of these innocent youngsters was soon to arouse the indignation of some Greek comunities in the United States but also in Greece itself, where the Foreign Office exhorted the Greeks at home to avoid helping this "dishonorable trade." Some Greek-American newspapers launched a severe campaign against what they called "flesh emporium" and a complete disgrace "on the Greek nationality." The padrone system was gradually eliminated mainly because the young boys had grown older and were, now, capable of looking for a different job or start a business of their own.

The exploitation of the first Greek immigrants—whether young boys or older men, is one of the darkest pages of the history of early Hellenism in America.

The Greek youth was not alone in being exploited and humiliated during the first moments of Greek immigration to America. The padrone system was applied even to the railroad construction workers but mostly in Omaha, Nebraska, where riots ensued that took on, on one memorable occasion, the proportions of armed uprising—and of course an armed quelling of the riots followed.

Rumors circulated widely in Greece that the Greek immigrants were exploited and mistreated in America. Some of these reports were indeed either exaggerated or in some instances false. Exploitation most certainly was not a myth but the Greek press often described America as a "living hell," in which hunger, despair, decay, idleness and fasting reigned, and the Greek immigrants dying in the streets from hunger and becoming "rag and bone pickers."

These "descriptions" were picked up by the American newspapers and the result was that Americans as a whole resented both Greece and those Greeks who had come to America to become United States citizens and share American democracy and prosperity. The moment coincided with a series of assaults against Greek communities or centers where Greeks were working. The best known and most publicized attack against Greek immigrants occured in South Omaha, Nebraska, early in 1909. Saloutos writes that:

> The colony in this suburban community consisted of about eighteen hundred, to which must be added another three thousand living in Omaha proper. It appears that this number was swelled by the seasonal workers who came into South Omaha during the winter months in search of work in the slaughter houses. Some of these men probably were strike-breakers brought in to replace striking employees at a time when jobs were scarce. At any rate, a strong feeling of resentment had been built against them by some segments of the local population.

The riots were provoked on February 19, 1909, when a Greek in the company of an unknown woman killed a police officer. The Greeks were accused of all sorts of crimes, and during a public mass meeting a resolution was adopted to "effectively rid the city of the undesirable Greeks . . ." The resolution was "implemented by a mob estimated at several thousand citizens of South Omaha. The mob destroyed all Greek property and succeeded in driving several hundred Greeks from the city."

In his report to the U.S. Congress, the President of the Foreign Relations Committee of the United States Senate said that:

> On February 21, 1909, a riot occurred in the city of South Omaha, Nebraska, which was directed against Greek subjects residing in that place. Personal injuries and property losses were inflicted on the victims of acts of violence committed by the rioters, and approximately 1,200 Greeks were driven from the city.

The report went on as follows:

> Prior to these riots, a feeling of hostility appears to have existed among the people of South Omaha against Greek subjects there resident, caused, as represented by residents of the city, by the manner of living of some of them; it being alleged that they lived in most unsanitary surroundings; by the lawlessness and offensive conduct of some of them in congregating in a certain quarter of the city and repeatedly insulting women passing along the streets; and by the fact that Greek laborers were brought into South Omaha to be employed in packing houses where they worked for less wages than those ordinary paid to residents of the city. On the night of February 19, 1909, a policeman named Edward Lowry was shot and killed by a Greek named John Masourides, whom the officer had arrested . . . After the Sunday meeting closed an attack was begun, which lasted well into the evening. Stores were broken into, property destroyed, and some

personal injuries inflicted. The attack had the effect of driving the Greeks from the city.

At the same time a number of subjects of Austria-Hungary, and of Turkey also suffered from the "fury of the mob." These persons were obviously mistaken for Greeks.

On the next day the Greek Legation in Washington sent a letter of protest to the State Department signed by L. A. Coromilas, Minister of Greece. It said:

> . . . populace was incited by several speakers, among whom were two members of the Legislature and a lawyer, conceived the plan of attaking the Greeks residing in the city. There were several tens of wounded. The Greeks found themselves constrained to fire back in self-defence. Their shops were gutted . . . a whole class of industrious, active, and temperate men is now reduced to ruin and despair.

The Greek Minister demanded further protection for the Greeks in Omaha and compensation for the suffereres.

Compensation to the Greeks of Omaha, Nebraska, was paid only in 1918. An act to authorize the payment of indemnities to the Government of Greece for injuries inflicted on its nationals in South Omaha, Nebraska, was approved August 30, 1918. The amount paid was $40,000. The Greek Government had claimed $135,533.

The Congress had acted on the following message received from the President of the United States, Woodrow Wilson, two years earlier (January 14, 1916), in which the President stressed:

> I trasmit a report from the Secretary of State etc. etc., and I recommend that, as an act of grace and without reference to the question of the liability of the United States, an appropriation be made to effect a settlement of these claims in accordance with the recommendation of the Secretary of State.

The Congress refused to appropriate compensation to nationals of Austria-Hungary and Turkey who claimed to have suffered property losses and injuries during the Omaha, Nebraska, riots.

The Congress ". . . deemed advisable, in view of the fact that this country is at war with Austria-Hungary and that the Government of Turkey has severed diplomatic relations, to eliminate from the provisions of the bill (the same bill providing indemnities for the Greeks) the payment of indemnities to the nationals of these Governments for injuries received in the riots referred to." (*Report of the President of the Committee on Foreign Relations in the Senate*, 65th

Congress, 2nd Session).

Regardless of the percentage of guilt either of the Greeks residing in Omaha, Nebraska or of the "unknown" mob which set out to destroy their property and to drive them from the city, the result was that for many years—and perhaps not until the Greek victory over the Italians at the beginning of the Second World War—the feelings of the Americans towards the Greeks in the United States were far from being friendly. It took a miracle to eliminate an unjustified attitude.

Greek-American Community Life

I T IS difficult if not impossible to examine in detail how the various groups of the first Greek immigrants organized their community life within the vastness of America. However, a certain uniform pattern seems to emerge from all accounts and also from the fact that a particular type of Greek-American conduct is still very obvious today; without any doubt it has its roots in the early days of the efforts of the Greek immigrants to build a community life of their own, as similar as possible to the one they were used to in Greece.

Writing about the geographical distribution of the Greeks in the United States, Evangelos C. Vlachos (*The Assimilation of Greeks in the United States,* Athens: National Centre of Social Research, 1968) writes that: "Arriving usually in New York, or some other Eastern port, the Greek immigrants took three main directions. One was proceeding towards the interior where they would meet other relatives, or friends from the same village or region of Greece. Another group of immigrants drifted to the New England Greek centers, such as Boston, Lowell, Mass., where they would find relatively large Greek colonies. Finally, a third direction was taken by the Greek immigrants to the big cities, such as New York, Chicago, Philadelphia, where they had a better chance of meeting other compatriots and a similar ethnic environment."

In his study *Immigration and Group Settlements,* C. A. Price offers a very interesting example of patterns of settlement of immigrants which could perhaps be used in relation to the movement of the various groups of the first Greek immigrants in the new world. There is reference to an organized settlement which comprises such cases as when a certain group left the same region together, embarked on the same ship and finally settled in the same area. Another pattern is described as "chain" settlement; it is related to immigrants who following letters received from other immigrants already settled in certain parts of a country joined those who had preceded them. The third pattern of settlement is known as the "gravitation" settlement; it concerns centers where groups of immigrants are brought together by the similar problems they face.

In the case of the first Greek immigrants one can safely conclude that the main reason for trying to "get together" and build a "Greek" community life was this powerful sense of Hellenism which is characteristic of every Greek on earth—regardless if this feeling is often apparently either forgotten or set aside because of the perennial dissidence that divides the Greeks wherever they are.

It is logical to state—at least in regard to the Greeks—that the building of a church is most certainly an evidence of the beginning of an organized community life.

Reverend Thomas J. Lacey (*Our Greek Immigrants*) writes that:

> When Greeks settle in a locality they organize a 'community' made up of all Greeks in the district with officers, executive committees and financial obligations . . . Formed primarily for the establishment of the church it functions as the representative voice of the colony . . . in spite of the dissidence among Greeks.

The first Greek Orthodox Church in America was built in New Orleans in 1886; the second in New York during 1891, and the third in Chicago during 1898. The foundations of Greek-American community life were thus established. It is around the church that the other Greek institutions were built and evolved.

Reverend Henry Pratt Fairchild (*Greek Immigration in the United States*) believed that "As soon as a few Greeks get together in some city or town in this country, one of the first things that they think of is the establishment of a palace of worship."

Besides building churches, the first Greek immigrants sponsored schools, theatrical and musical productions but the most fascinating and popular Greek institution was the coffee-house—a unique "reward" for the nostalgic immigrant.

Thus, Rev. Thomas J. Lacey (*Our Greek Immigrants*) wrote that: "The coffee-house takes the place of the saloon or beer garden. This is a distinctively Hellenic institution found all over the Near East and introduced into England in 1652, by Konopios, a Cretan."

The coffee-house plays indeed an important role in the community life of the Greek wherever he is—whether at home or away from his homeland. During the early days of Greek immigration it became a "must." There the hard-working, depressed, exploited Greeks would find an atmosphere to which they had been accustomed. At any hour you would find some Greeks "sitting around small tables," sipping what they themselves call Turkish coffee, smoking cigarettes

101

and naturally talking politics. It is at the coffee-house that the first Greek immigrants gathered to read the Greek-American newspaper through which they kept in touch with the affairs in Greece. They very seldom would indulge in an outdoor excursion. They disliked the atmosphere of the already polluted American cities and towns. Instead of the clear, invigorating air of their native villages they were forced now to breath the violated atmosphere of a store or a factory. Though the atmospere of the coffee-house was not ideal either, it nevertheless had other attractions for the sentimental immigrants.

Attendance at the coffee-house seemed to provide some relief to the deep nostalgia the Greeks were experiencing. Moreover, it is at the coffee-house that their urge for some identification with Greece was satisfied—or was it perhaps only a natural functioning of remembrance? The walls of practically every coffee-house were filled with pictures of Pericles, of the Byzantine Emperors, or with scenes reminiscent of the victorious Balkan wars. The predominant picture, of course, was the one of the immortal Parthenon with which every Greek identified the magnificence of his country. There were also pictures of St. Sophia in Constantinople—the Greek Orthodox Church transformed by the Turks into a mosque—to remind the patriotic Greek immigrants that there were still parts of their country under brutal foreign yoke. What else was necessary to create a "small Greece"—the sacred picture of which they carried permanently in their hearts?

Moreover, many immigrants received their mail at the coffee-house —obviously some of them did not have a permanent address or even a dependable temporary address. One could see on one of the walls of any coffee-house letters pinned against it, waiting for the addressee to pick them up. The coffee-house was, therefore, a sort of post office as well. It was at the coffee-house that views were exchanged and news from the homeland discussed and given to those who had not received any letter from home for entire months.

Such was the importance of the coffee-house to the life of the new immigrants that one would frequently hear one say to the other: "I will see you at the coffee-house." Indeed what was heard or said at the coffee-house was sacred, because it was either news from Greece or something connected with the homeland.

The dark-skinned Greeks who came to the new world from almost every part of sunny, distant Greece, and whose existence very few Americans even suspected, did not have places prepared for them in the United States. They were employed in some factories because of their physical fitness and their willingness to accept any kind of menial work. However, this was a time when there was a dangerous scarcity of jobs and naturally native Americans and many other immigrants of various ethnic origins resented their arrival. There were also religious reasons for which the Greeks were disliked. Within a predominant Protestant population—including a certain percentage of Catholics—animated with deep bigotry, Orthodoxy was considered almost sacrilegious.

Strange as it may be the older immigrants who had fled from foreign lands because of religious persecutions had not learned their lesson and were, now, themselves, transformed into persecutors of a religious dogma which was not their own. Their newly acquired freedom had not helped them to recognize and to accept that others had the same rights to practice their own beliefs. Moreover, and curiously enough, according to Vlachos, "Resentment against the 'less developed' citizens of Europe arose among other foreign ethnic groups who were losing their jobs in the increasing competition, and also among Americans excited by a revived 'nativism,' which expounded theories of 'inherent inferiority' of the new immigrants. The alleged difference between Old and New Immigrants were also exaggerated by distrust of the predominant Catholicism of the New Immigrants as contrasted to the Protestant background of most of the earlier immigrants from Northern Europe. Thus great problems of assimilation were faced by the later immigrants, most of them came from comparatively poor and culturally and economically backward countries and were Catholic, Jewish, or Greek Orthodox in religion."

The development of the Greek-American community in the new world followed a given pattern in spite of the fact that because of the perennial microbe of dissidence and factionalism it was extremely difficult, if not impossible, for the Greeks to get together, remain together and live in peace in one and the same area. The first "concentrations" of Greeks in the United States, on a rather limited scale, were composed of close relatives who had decided to join their efforts in facing the unsurmountable problems. They were followed by the localities—villages or small towns, where people gathered as a result of the "chain" letters sent to one and the same region in Greece. The next development came in the form of what is called "society," that is to say the formation of social groupings of people who had come to the United States but from different areas of Greece.

The transformation of the original concentrations—which in the growing process had gradually become localities—into societies was inevitable as time went by and as some of the most enterprising immigrants, whether willingly or unwillingly, came into closer contact with the American environment and its principles.

Dissidence and factionalism existed, as they have always existed and still exist wherever there are Greeks—immigrants or natives living in their homeland—but there was a unifying factor: the parish built around the church. In accordance with the definition of the Greek Orthodox Church the parish is "... the body of communicants of the Greek Orthodox Faith in a given locality, organized for the support and maintenance of parish church and affiliated institutions." Yet, the definition might be somewhat dogmatic and perhaps too strict since some of the immigrants of Greek origin did reside in the area of one and the same parish without being necessarily members of the Church. In other words, a Greek-American community though theoretically united because of the existence of the church and the parish was not always composed of people discharging their financial obilgations to the church. Their failure to do so, however, did not change the structure of the community as a whole.

Tarpon Springs—
a North American "Greek Town"

I T WAS said that the development of the Greek-American community followed a given pattern—perhaps with one exception: Tarpon Springs, West Florida, on the Gulf northwest of Tampa, near the mouth of Anclote, which was founded in 1882. The encyclopaedias note that "it is one of the large sponge centers in the world. Greek fishermen take out the sponging fleet, and colorful Greek festivals draw many visitors."

> Tarpon Springs, the most Hellenic town of the United States. Most Hellenic in proportion to its population of Hellenic descent and in the maintenance of Greek traditions. Tarpon Springs, a piece of the Aegean in the Gulf of Mexico, only 29 miles north of Tampa, at the small harbor of which in 1528, a Greek set foot for the first time on American soil—the Greek Theodoros, who had come with the Spaniards of Narbaeth. (Babis Malafouris, *Ellines tis Amerikis*, New York, 1948.)

According to some other sources Tarpon Springs was founded in 1876 (and not 1882 as some sources indicate) by Anson P.K. Safford, Governor of Arizona. Originally, its inhabitants were simple fishermen from Georgia and other states. However, at the beginning of the 20th century some Greek experts in the sponge fishing arrived there and Tarpon Springs became a prosperous center of activities. The methods of sponge fishing, before the arrival of the Greeks, did not yield any satisfactory results. The first "expert" to be "summoned" to Tarpon Springs by John Cheney, an American businessman, was Ioannis Cocoris. He is rightly considered as the pioneer of the Greek industry of sponge fishing, which made Tarpon Springs famous. Within a few years thereafter, Cocoris and some of his compatriots had settled in the small town the situation had changed. Tarpon Springs became an important trading center—and at the same time a Greek town. Upon Cocoris' death a plaque was suspended on the wall of the Sponge Exchange building with the following inscription:

In memory of John M. Cocoris, from Leonidion,

the founder of Sponge diving Industry in 1905.

By the City of Tarpon Springs.

The definition of Tarpon Springs found in the dictionaries pertains to the past. Today, Tarpon Springs is no longer what it used to be. For one thing there are not enough sponges to fish in the surrounding waters. It seems that the industrious Greeks have exhausted the riches of the sea, and the little Greek town, always picturesque, nevertheless, seems to be gradually vanishing into oblivion. Religious festivals are still held there as they are held in every other Greek Orthodox community throughout the United States and all over North and South America, but the number of the curious visitors, who contributed to the income of the town, has decreased considerably.

This writer visited Tarpon Springs in 1949. It was then a booming town—a Greek town—very similar to any other Greek town built by the sea. Practically every inhabitant was Greek and Greek was the spoken language. The population came almost exclusively from the islands of the Dodecanese, where people were and still are experts in the fishing of sponges. Restaurants and tavernas were Greek; the names of the streets were Greek and the hospitality was, naturally, typically Greek. The Athenian visitor who had planned to stay in Tarpon Springs only one day found himself drawn into an unforgettable week in the town.

Tarpon Springs was not, in the past, a typical Greek-American community but rather a classical Greek town. Time and the scarcity of sponges in the region have, however, delivered a heavy blow to its "Greekness." Since sponge fishing is no longer the main occupation of its population some of its inhabitants have moved to other locations and "foreigners" have come there to undertake new enterprises.

It should be remembered here that the population of Tarpon Springs, made up exclusively from people from the islands of the Dodecanese, played an important role in securing the restoration of the 12 islands of the Dodecanese to Greece. As a result of a petition of the Greek-American community of Tarpon Springs, Senator Claude Pepper (Florida) introduced the following resolution to the Congress:

> RESOLVED, that it is the sense of the Senate that Northern Epirus (including Corytsa) and the twelve islands of the Aegean Sea, known as the Dodecanese Islands, where a strong Greek population predominates, should be awarded by the peace conference

106

to Greece and become incorporated in the territory of Greece. The 1946 Paris Peace Conference "awarded" the 12 Islands of the Dodecanese to Greece (they were under Italian domination after having been under Turkish rule) but Northern Epirus remained— and still remains—in the hands of the Albanians.

The Closing Gates of the "Promised Land"

ONE MUST remember that the distrust of other immigrants and the difficulty of the Greeks adjusting to the requirements of the industrial life in America had a negative influence on the existence of the first Greek immigrants.

The Greek-American poet Theodore Giannakoulis has described the way the early Greek immigrants felt in poignant words:

> We are strangers and no one talks to us, only they push us to all directions... There are no jobs for us here, outside railroad constructions and similar things... Here in New York, we get our daily bread with sweat out in the streets, in the rain, in the hot or cold weather, with baskets and the people keep pushing us... they stare at us as if we were murderers. It is a real hell with the street urchins... real devils. (Excerpts from Giannakoulis' unpublished *Introduction to the History of the Greek-Americans*, translated from the Greek and published in the magazine *Argonaut*.)

What a contrast between the tragic description and the letters full of "wonderful" experiences that most of the immigrants were sending back to Greece—letters which induced thousands of other immigrants to leave Greece and come to America to share with their compatriots all this unbelievable wealth and happiness that the new country was offering with such a profusion.

Between the years 1914 and 1924, the immigration policy of the United States changed briskly. In the past a form of unrestricted immigration had prevailed. The new policy appeared with the beginning of World War I.

Evangelos C. Vlachos (*The Assimilation of Greeks in the United States*, Athens: National Centre of Research, 1968), writes:

> The changing of attitude towards the immigrants came about as a combination of many events. There were first of all fears and apprehensions aroused by the various ethnic groups, whose countries of origin stood against the United States in the in-

ternational clash. On the other hand, the great waves of immigrants after the turn of the century imperiled the standards set by labor organizations and created fears of lowering the standards of living, pauperism and crime. A new policy of restriction started developing with its underlying assumption being the basic distinction between Older and Newer Immigrants.

Actually the first restrictions on immigration were imposed in 1917. After a long fight, over thirty years, the trade Unions succeeded in having the famous "Literacy Law" passed in spite of President Woodrow Wilson's veto. The law was enacted in 1918. In 1921 the law of "percentages" was voted according to which immigrants were permitted to enter the United States in proportion to the three percent of the figure of each nation which, according to the 1910 Census, was already represented in America.

In 1924, new laws restricted further the number of immigrants allowed to come to the United States. These new laws aimed at preventing the entry to the United States from Asia and Southeastern Europe which included Greece. When these laws were passed only 307 Greeks were permitted to come to America every year.

It must be added here that the fears of American racial deterioration were supported by a number of Emigration Committees, which in reality wanted to "protect" the Anglo-Saxon element.

This racist movement influenced the Greek immigrants. They experienced the humiliation of feeling inferior to other ethnic groups and at the same time they also felt compelled to struggle for a better status within the American environment. It should be remembered here that at the time many Americans used to refer to the Greeks with what were in their minds the derogatory labels "Slavs" or "people from the Balkans." This influence had also in many cases another quite different result: It forced the Greek immigrants to seek a deeper identification with Hellenic culture. It was in a way their only weapon against discrimination, and, moreover, most of them were deeply convinced that their cultural background or rather their origin should have been sufficient to permit them to acquire the highest possible esteem in the United States. They were wrong.

The McGarran-Walter Act of 1952 set a rather ridiculous quota for the Greeks, of 308 annually, which with some provisions for refugees and displaced persons, permitted the entry of approximately between 2,000 to 3,000 Greeks every year into the United States.

Evangelos C. Vlachos *(The Assimilation of Greeks in the United States)* writes that "the closing of the gates and the restriction of immigration after 1924, had many consequences for the Greeks in the United States. First of all, it resulted in stabilization of the ethnic population and increased acceptance of the United States as the place of permanent residence. Second, it stopped large population replenishment from Greece and thus cut off one of the sources of perpetuation of Greek culture in the United States. Third, it influenced decisively the trend for a return to Greece, since the difficulties involved with the re-entry of non-citizens, made irrevocable the staying in the homeland. The result of these was an increasing tempo of assimilation after 1924."

I believe that a fourth factor in favor of assimilation should be added to the above arguments: the passage of time, which exercises a tremendous influence on the thinking of people in general and on any immigrants in particular.

However, in 1968, the national origin system—a very unjust system —was abolished and visas have been allotted on a first-come-first-served system. As a result more Greeks will be coming to the United States, and since these new immigrants have an entirely different educational background from their "old" predecessors one will have to wait for their first steps in America before trying to predict how, and if they will yield faster to the process of assimilation. One will also have to watch how these new "visitors" from the old country will blend with the brand of Hellenism that actually prevails in the United States. Here again, only time will tell what will happen—and when it will happen.

It should perhaps be mentioned here that the self-sufficiency of the Greek Community in the United States is the product of a many centuries old necessity for the Greeks to safeguard their culture against foreign pressure and conquests. During the four hundred years of Turkish domination the best weapon of defense of the enslaved Greeks was the "community": there the Greeks stayed apart from the conqueror and alien influence through a deeper attachment to their ethnic and religious principles.

In almost the same way the first Greek immigrant arriving in America was armed with principles, customs and values, which allowed him to establish his own isolated community. Isolation was also prompted by his erroneous belief that in an environment where only money mattered his illustrious origin was sufficient to secure for him an economically safe place and special privileges. He did not acquire either.

It is only fair to mention that in the then cold, unfriendly cities and villages of the United States, the first Greek immigrants did indeed receive some valuable assistance. It came in the form of the Hull House, which was founded in 1889, and the League of the Protection of the Immigrant. The Hull House had been founded for the main purpose of studying the working conditions in various factories. Its founder was Miss Jane Addams—a devoted social worker who helped many Greeks to face the hostile entourage in which they had to live and work. Speaking at a mass meeting in Chicago, in 1909, Miss Addams said, among other things, that the young Greeks in the United States at that time were the descendants of heroes and philosophers who have given so much to the world. She said that these Greeks were often misunderstood by the Americans but that the moment had come for them to be recognized for what they really were.

The other organization, The League for the Protection of Immigrants, also played an extremely important role in offering help to the Greek immigrants. Its director, Miss Grace Abbot, wrote a lengthy report on the living conditions of the Greek immigrants (mostly in Chicago) in the *American Journal of Sociology* (Vol. XV No. 3), which was to influence a great many of Americans in regard to the Greeks, whom they originally disliked and boycotted.

The findings of Miss Abbot's report gave a very grim picture of the kind of life the first Greek immigrants were compelled to lead —whether in Chicago or elsewhere.

The Social System
and the So-Called "Melting Pot"

T O SOME writers the old notion of America as a melting pot seems to have been only a romantic idea about something that never really existed. They believe that the American system should not be considered a crucible in which the various national elements are fused in order to create a new amalgamation of homogeneous entities almost as uniform as the system itself.

Yale's Professor Robert Dahl, in a study of New Haven politics writes that "a genuinely ethnic group remains seriously ethnic only as long as it remains proletarian. But the time comes when large segments of the group are assimilated into the 'middling and upper strata' ... and look to others in the middling strata for friends, associates and marriage partners. To these people, ethnic politics are often embarrassing or meaningless." (*Time Magazine*, December 2, 1966.) He believes that most ethnic groups have become so much integrated into the general political community that they are only remotely identifiable ethnically in political terms. It is implied that economic interests have displaced ethnic interests. For one thing, and according to the views of many sociologists, this "new melt in the melting pot" extends only to the political and economic fields and for another it most certainly excludes the Greek-Americans. During the 1968 Presidential elections the Greek-Americans, who by tradition and for many years had always voted Democratic voted Republican just because the candidate to the Vice-Presidency, Spyro Agnew, was of Greek ancestry.

In an essay, *Time* Magazine (December 2, 1966) writes that:

> Big city bosses operated on the assumption they could deliver the vote to whatever candidate they chose—all they needed was a Christmas turkey, a memory for the names of the children, and a fluency in the mother tongue. We still talk about the Irish vote, the Italian vote, the Polish, Jewish or Greek vote. Statistically this is understandable: some 34 million Americans, or 19 percent, are listed by the most recent Census as of

foreign stock, which the Census Bureau defines as either foreign-born or with at least one foreign-born parent.

Another conclusion reached in this rather elaborate study of the evolution of the immigrants in the United States is that from the viewpoint of the politicians and the sociologists, the various minorities continued to behave separately and distinctly "only in the last decade, nearly 200 years after its enunciation, has the melting pot finally begun to perform as longtime myth would have it."

However, it is still true that the minorities' sympathies are considered important if not essential in civil affairs. For example, the Democrats have long counted the ethnic groups in their column. However, in the 1966 elections, minorities showed an unprecedented individualism. In Baltimore, 83 percent of the Negro vote went to the Republican (and ethnic Greek) Spyro Agnew—though two years before it had gone along its traditional Democratic lines.

Today the United States receives approximately 300,000 immigrants a year, and they still tend to join members of their own nationality and their own religion. However, the "old Neighborhoods" are in the process of being dissolved; in the very distant past the "block" leader would meet the newcomers at the pier, and being their only protector in a foreign land he would not only "settle" them in one and the same neighborhood but would also gradually influence their political preferences as far as their adopted country was concerned. Again ignorance played an important role in preventing most immigrants from expressing a free choice. There is no implication here that had they been in a position to distinguish the thin line that separates one party from another they would have gone the other direction from the one they had finally chosen.

Historian Richard Wade, of the University of Chicago (*Time* Magazine, December 2, 1966), points out that "Apart from the non-white groups, more than half the members of each other ethnic group in America left the old neighborhood and scattered across the cities." He seems to believe that the reason is rather economic; in other words that this was the result of a definite improvement in the life of the immigrants. However, one still finds large gatherings of Greek-Americans in New York, Lowell, Detroit, Chicago, etc., in one and the same section of these cities.

"Within 20 years, there will be no new Italian organizations" says the national director of the Italian-American Society. In 1914 there were an estimated 1,300 foreign-language newspapers and periodicals; today (1968) there are fewer than 400.

Another conclusion reached in the study undertaken by *Time* Magazine (December 2, 1966) is that: "Fear is disappearing. The ethnic groups, therefore, do not feel, as much, the need to cling together. They find security by losing themselves in the mainstream of American life."

These observations might be valid insofar as the political and economic spheres are concerned. In other areas the "structural separation" still persists. For instance, in religion, and in most social relations, minorities still resist amalgamation "although even here the lines are not nearly as sharply drawn as they once were." *Time* Magazine (December 2, 1966) concludes that "A great ethnic feeling is still enshrined in political rituals. In New York City, for instance, there are the infuriating, hopelessly provincial national parades."

It must be added here that the Greek-American newspapers perpetuated a great many ethnic clichés but the overall question of the Greek-American press will be studied elsewhere in this book.

In regard to the opposition to the process of the assimilation of foreign immigrants George C. Vournas writes that: "Each war that has been fought over a century and a half, plus the public schools, plus the political parties, plus freedom, have acted as a catalytic agent for nationhood. Why should a person be an Irishman, German or Greek when his personal interest, the road to distinction, riches and the pursuit of happiness lies through his unqualified loyalty to the American Constitution, law, and tradition—what, at times, slightingly is referred to as "100 Americanism?" *(Greeks in America*, Congressional Record. Proceedings and Debates of the 86th Congress, Second Session).

A small parenthesis is perhaps necessary at this point: all those conclusions and observations made at certain dates and on the basis of certain data pertaining to particular periods of time of the life, endeavors, experiences, misfortunes and achievements of the Greek immigrants have one and the same weakness: they may tend to be product of a rather static situation, while as years go by the overall picture slowly develops and changes considerably. This is perhaps unavoidable, but very often what was true yesterday is today false, or at least different. No one can escape this hazard. On the other hand, the factors which affect change are dynamic. These factors—which are aspects of their private and professional life—involved in the assimilation of the Greeks in America are their economic status, the establishment and purpose of their official

114

organizations, their involvement in politics—both American and Greek, their education, their language and their religion: these three last factors come under the jurisdiction and the immediate influence and control of the Greek Orthodox Church in America, which in a sense replaces the "mother country" in the United States for the perpetuation of the language and the religion. However, it is a Greek Orthodox Church in America, whose Archbishop must be an American citizen the way the Patriarch in Constantinople must always be a Turkish subject. The role played by the Greek Orthodox Church in the assimilation—or non-assimilation—of the Greeks in America will be examined separately. It is a most important question since what the Church has undertaken to do will affect the future of Hellenism in America.

The usual criteria for the classification of a person within the American environment seems to be his economic potential and his degree or type of education. The first Greek immigrants generally lacked both. However, today a first Greek immigrant, now a United States citizen, who had been an ignorant shepherd in the Peloponnesos or elsewhere in Greece, is not considered inferior from a social point of view provided he can prove he has acquired money, or that he is in the process of making a fortune.

There is evidence that many among the first Greek immigrants are evaluating their potential in proportion to the degree of their "embodiment" in the American social system and this in spite of the fact that they are still under the influence of the social class-system prevailing in Greece. In other words, the Greeks—or at least many Greek immigrants—consider that the emphasis put by the Americans on the materialistic aspect of life is "equal" to the respect shown in Greece to the system of values as accepted by the Greeks. The idea is perhaps only a fallacy since the differences between the extent of wealth or general prosperity in the United States, and the economic potential in Greece are indeed striking. They were more particularly apparent and acute at the moment when the first Greek immigrants set foot on American soil.

It is generally accepted that the Greek immigrant believes sincerely in the absolute harmony of American and Greek views on equality. Moreover, the Greek immigrant still feels immeasurable pride about his ancestors—the heroes, the philosophers and the sculptors who are highly appreciated and admired in the United States. This too often exaggerated feeling comes as a sort of compensation for the absence of other areas of agreement between native Americans and Greek-Americans.

In his book *The Personality of the Greek-American (I Prosopikotis tou Ellinoamerikanou,* Athens, 1964), Aris T. Papas comes to some conclusions about the character and the habits of the Greek-Americans in general with which one can only disagree. He writes that:

> The Greeks are very sensitive in regard to politics and the political institutions, but there is a general tendency on their part to feel satisfied when they discuss and advance arguments among themselves; they prefer the discussion to the actual participation in the wider American community.They are also satisfied when they have a representative in their own political party and they do not compete to secure such a position. This is at least one of the reasons of the failure of the Greek to respond to his personal obligations to the party as a whole. Another reason is the centuries old Greek experience of compromises to the demands of a "nominally" enemy, superior or "conquering" civilization. For example the conquest of Greece by the Turks led to the laxness of discipline and to the development of ways in avoiding pressure through the corruption of the local Turkish civil servants." Mr. Aris T. Papas adds that "The consequences of such a mentality (prevailing) in America are obvious: acceptance of the crime of bribery, of corruption of consciences of the civil servants and official. For the Greeks the adoption of such practices for many centuries has given birth to the idea that they (the actions) do not represent for them any crimes but that they are simply things that one has to do in order to acquire what he needs from those who govern.

Reference has been made to Mr. Papas' conclusions—reached with so much haste—only to reject these views which actually do not correspond to reality. For one thing, there is undoubtedly active participation and even some definite Greek-American representation in the civic and political affairs of the United States. This representation is found at practically every level of public life in America, and any objective research in this connection would easily reach this conclusion.

One cannot deny the fact that the Greeks like to discuss—discussion being a tradition and a legacy for all Greeks wherever they are—political or other issues of interest. However, the conception of the acceptance of bribery and corruption as a means to achieve success is completely erroneous and definitely unfair. This is not stressed here with the purpose of protecting the Greek-American community

116

but rather in defense of the truth.

To return to other aspects of the development of Greek life in America, a very interesting observation, which is at the same time a remarkable achievement, is the manner in which the first Greek immigrants finally pierced through the "thick wall" of difficulties, discrimination and in some cases even persecution, to achieve success in the United States, in their competition with either native Americans or members of other ethnic groups. They came a long way before attaining what some of them consider—and perhaps rightly so—absolute equality with those who had established themselves much before them on American soil.

> The early Greek immigrant on his arrival in the United States was most often employed as an unskilled laborer in the textile industry of New England, a miner in Utah or Pennsylvania, a laborer on railroads, all over the country, a fisherman on one coast or another, or a farmhand in the fruit farms of California. (Maldwyn A. Jones, *American Immigration*, Chicago, 1960.)

Of course these are not the only occupations chosen by the first Greek Immigrants: they became florists, bootblacks, waiters, restaurant owners, peanut vendors, hot-dog vendors, peddlers, etc. Though inexorably attached to Greece, they made a tremendous effort to adapt themselves—insofar their work was concerned—to American requirements.

> ... Americanization is the star that will guide us to prosperity, success and progress. Let us adopt this great country as our own. Let us be part of this land of plenty and not remain predatory aliens. America opens her arms to us. Let us embrace her with love and a desire to understand her laws, political and social life. (This is an excerpt of an appeal launched by some Greek community leaders published in the *Hellenikos Astir*, April 15 and August 15, 1904.)

"Love and desire" were there, but ignorance of the English language and a fear they might not be able to respond to the requirements originally kept most of the first Greek immigrants in a state of undestandable frustration.

Most writers who dealt with the first steps of the Greek immigrants in the new world seem to agree that at the beginning it was extremely difficult, if not indeed impossible, for them to accept the rigid discipline of the industrial American entourage. Back in Greece the tempo of daily work was much slower—and sometimes there was no work at all. In the United States the demands of the employers upon the immigrants were intolerable; this is perhaps why very few Greek immigrants attempted to make a career of working for fixed wages. However, there seems to be another reason for which they climbed one echelon after the other in their ascent to a better life: the innate individualism of the Greek character; the bootblacks, the waiters, the florists gradually became managers of shoe-repair stores, restaurant owners or owners of flower shops. They also got involved in tobacco industry.

Still another reason has to be taken into account: with the new immigration laws the competition between the various ethnic groups diminished and as a result the Greeks were in a better position than before to make quick progress within the American pluralistic environment.

Evangelos C. Vlachos (*The Assimilation of Greeks in the United States*) writes that:

> An indication of the changes in vocations between two different generations of Americans of Greek extraction can be seen in indices of relative occupational concentration ... the decreasing occupational specialization of the members of the Greek ethnic groups is ... one important index of assimilation. It shows that in the institutional area of occupation and the related economic status the Greeks have shown a high degree of assimilation.

Though no figures or statistics exist regarding the third Greek-American generation, there is evidence that "there is a rapid economic and occupational advancement of the Greeks in the country". (Theodore Constant, *Employment and Business of the Greeks in the United States,* Magazine *Athene VI,* winter 1945.)

It must be said that although there seems to be a considerable variation between the generations, the two institutions that have preserved the Greek culture into this third generation is religion and family life. These forces, plus economic and professional ambition, have led the first Greek immigrants to succeed in overcoming both the difficulties and their own weaknesses and in creating for themselves and their offsprings new opportunities, as they approached every aspect of American life. Yet, at the same time, they never lost their characteristics or their personality. Today, the children of the florists, the candy-shop owners—themselves owners of similar business—but also lawyers, doctors or artists are hardly distinguishable from other Americans—except, of course, for their names and their religion. Moreover, some of them do speak Greek—though rather badly.

Advantages and
Disadvantages of Greek Immigration

REGARDLESS of the positive or negative effects of the mass immigration of the Greeks to the United States, its results should be examined in the light of the fact that the confinement of people under conditions of poverty and misery in a country where they struggle for survival is undoubtedly a powerful reason that makes emigration imperative. The fallacious expectation of a miraculous recovery of the country is certainly not the best way either to halt immigration or to solve altogether the problem of steady expatriation.

The opinions on the advantages and disadvantages of Greek immigration to the new world—insofar as Greece is concerned—differ. However, in the final analysis, and in spite of some strong adverse views on the subject, the advantages of the mass exodus of the Greeks to America were indeed considerable. Mass immigration to the United States meant two different things to Greece: an influx of money from America and the withdrawal of laboring force from the country. The first compensated for the second. The resulting benefits were for one thing economic and for another cultural.

Though the Greeks came late to the United States and therefore their share in the exploitation of the "Virgin" land was rather small by comparison, their stubborn efforts to adapt themselves to the American environment led to their fast evolution and success among the native Americans. This view is supported by Professor Vasilios G. Valaoras (*The Hellenism of the United States,* Athens, 1937). He writes that Greece found in the first Greek immigrants the secret source, which covered for many years the deficit in its economic balance. At one time remittances from the United States had reached approximately one quarter of what Greece received from its exports. Thus, the first Greek immigrants can be credited with practically solving the economic problem of Greece.

From 1814, to 1930, there was a steady "wave" of remittances from the United States. After 1930, these remittances had decreased on account of the depression in America, but also because the first immigrants had fewer obligations to their relatives in Greece and had contracted new ones towards their families in the United States.

Professor Valaoras says that besides the economic benefits resulting from the mass immigration of the Greeks to America, their contact with a "much more civilized" American entourage "transformed" them into better people.

As to the negative aspect of the mass immigration of the Greeks one must acknowledge that it did not affect adversely the country they had left—probably because there was no industry in Greece at the time of their mass exodus. Since originally the immigration to the United States was an exclusive exodus of men, women stayed behind and worked in the fields—an old Greek tradition which still prevails in the country. On the other hand, the arrival of almost exculsively men in America created a problem for the family life of the first immigrant—and to some extent also a problem for Greece itself.

Professor Valaoras refers to another "small" disadvantage resulting from the immigration of the Greeks to America. He says that the Greeks in America acquired some selfishness—a natural phenomenon prevailing all over the world, which was the product of their rather easy success and the "exaggerated freedom of the individual which is preconized in the United States." This last argument is debatable and comes into contradiction with the recognition that for so many years the remittances of the Greeks from America not only helped their poor relatives in Greece but also solved the economic problem of the country. Moreover, the Greek-Americans are known for their generosity in donating considerable amounts of money for the establishment of schools and the building of churches and other institutions all over the United States.

The idea that the immigration of a rather considerable part of the population of one country is damaging to the economy of that country is undoubtedly sound. It is true that expatriation on a high scale has adverse consequences—both social and economic.

As a rule it is the young people who emigrate and thus the country is deprived of people who could eventually be helpful in building a better future for their homeland. But every rule has its exceptions and this seems to have been the case of Greece at the moment of the mass emigration of the Greeks to the new world. The conditions prevailing at that time did not offer any immediate possibility for all those young men, who had decided to emigrate, to be of any assistance to the economic recovery of Greece.

The wave of immigration to America started after a real economic catastrophe. The agricultural populations of the Peloponnesos faced a real dilemma when the grapes they cultivated could not find a market. In 1880, the only salvation for them seemed to be the road to America. From 1880 to 1890, approximately 200,000 Greeks emigrated to the United States. Their departure was the immediate result of a great crisis but brought also a sort of relief for the agricultural population remaining at home. Moreover, after a few years those who had settled in America started sending back money —their absence was felt, but favorably.

From 1910 to 1930, another 250,000 Greeks immigrated according to statistics left for the United States. This was quite a crucial moment in the history of modern Greece: the country had been through the Balkan wars, the First World War, the abdication of kings, and finally the tragic defeat at the hands of the Turks in Asia-Minor. At the end of 1922, Greece was forced to provide shelter for almost one million and a half refugees who lived in Turkey. Immigration at that time brought some relief to a country, which was unable to sustain the new burden.

In an article published in the *Argonaftis* (1958) Nikos Louros writes that modern Greece "has a surplus of population of about 100,000; that is to say the births exceed the deaths . . . the country is in no position to absorb this surplus...." Again immigration, though on a rather lower scale when compared to the previous mass exodus, helped in keeping Greece in a position to cope with the problem.

In a United Nations Report (Department of Social Affairs: *The Determination and Consequences of Population Trends,* New York, 1953, p. 288) a conclusion is reached that almost all studies of the effects of international and local immigration have been mostly concentrated on the industrialized countries. "The existing bibliography on the effects of immigration for the... economically underdeveloped countries still remains at the stage of a vague hypothesis."

This conclusion seems to cover the case of Greece, when one tries to determine in a scientific, documented manner the effects of the mass exodus of the Greeks to America at the end of the 19th century and the beginnig of the 20th century.

Prof. B. S. Keirstead ("Emigration and Economic Growth," *Quarterly Review,* September, 1965) writes that the economic analysis as to whether the exodus of immigrants represents a benefit or a loss to the exporting country is indeed vague.

In his book *Metanastefsis Kai Ikonomiki Anaptyxis* (Immigration and Economic Development, Athens, 1966) Professor Xenophon Zolotas, an academician and presently Governor of the Bank of Greece, offers a different approach to the examination of the problem. He writes that "In our view more important is the overall estimation of the advantages and disadvantages of immigration through a comparison of the various effects within the framework of the continuously changing social and economic conditions in the country."

Here is how he classifies both the advantages and the disadvantages:

Benefits	*Losses*
Remittances	Non-realized production
Decrease in consumption	Decrease in investments
Training of the laboring potential	
Formation of prices of equilibrium	Loss of human capital
	Danger of mass repatriation of the immigrants
Equal (or even) development	Demographic consequences

In regard to the first Greek immigrants to the United States, one has to recognize that their steady remittances over a great number of years not only helped the Greek economy but without any doubt contributed to improving the standard of living of the "weaker section of the population" of Greece.

Unfortunately, there are no complete statistics as to the exact figures of these remittances. The Bank of Greece, in answer to the inquiry of this writer provided only the following figures: For 1960:$64,-264,000; 1961:$64,977,000; 1962:$72,932,000; 1963:$73,749,000; 1964:$61,916,000 and 1965:$61,677,000.

The mass exodus of the Greeks to the new world deprived the country of human "material," which left the homeland and settled in America. Had the mass immigration not taken place, and if one accepts that this "human element" would have been multiplied, the population of today's Greece would have been approximately 10 percent larger—or more. This definitely represents a loss, provided the "human surplus" could have been employed to help improve the economic situation in Greece. However, the argument is based only on a hypothesis and cannot be presented as a scientific conclusion.

Moreover, even on the basis of this hypothetical view one has to remember that the "human surplus" of the Greek population moved—at a very crucial moment in the life of the country—to another, wealthy land where the immigrant was living free and could return at any time with no difficulty whatsoever to the homeland.

Besides sending their remittances to Greece the first immigrants assisted their country in more ways than one. Most of them got finally established in America. Since, thousands of them go regularly to Greece, where they spend a lot of money. Almost all of them were highly ambitious and wanted to do something for the "old country." Their ambition and love for Greece transformed some primitive Greek villages, from which they originated, into modern communities. The immigrants helped in building churches, schools and other educational institutions.

Another point, which calls for attention is the fact that as a rule almost all of the first Greek immigrants married Greek women —from Greece. This meant that the women coming from Greece to America brought new blood to the first Greek-American communities—something, which perhaps permitted the Greeks to keep their ethnic identity. We are talking here, of course, about the first Greek immigrants; since things have considerably changed. The new generations face marriage with different ideas in mind in spite of the fact that their parents are still exercising pressure on them to marry Greek girls—either from Greece or from their own Greek-American community.

Thanks to the presence of an increased number of "Greek elements" —a number growing every day—Greece has created a new source of some political influence in the United States. However, at this point one has to notice with some deep regret that during a recent dictatorship in Greece, 85 percent of the Greek-Americans—first generation—sided with the military regime. It proved, I think, that the process of assimilation of the Greeks in the United States is not proceeding at the speed that some people claim it does. It also showed that 50 or 60 years of life within the American democratic environment did not change the first Greek immigrants. For them the Greek Army could do no harm. It always represented the symbol of glory—of the victories of the Balkan wars or the crushing of the Communist uprising of 1946-49.

Naturally, there has always been philhellenism in America, in some form or another, but the presence of a numerically powerful Greek minority led the Americans to see Greece through their fellow-citizens of Greek ancestry, and in a different light.

It is said that the Greek-American vote is indeed taken into serious consideration in the American elections—whether national or local, and that in return the demands of the Greek-Americans regarding the United States policy towards Greece are often heard. "The ties between Greece and the United States are, to a certain extent, due to the presence of the Greek-American community—and help Greece politically, militarily and economically" writes Nikos Louros (*Argonaut,* 1958).

Not everyone agrees, however, that the mass immigration of the Greeks to the United States was beneficial. In the magazine *Argonaut,* 1961, Arist. Andreades writes that:

> When the statue of the former President of the United States, Harry S. Truman, was erected in Greece—as a token of gratitude of the Greek people to American assistance in their struggle against Communism—someone said that the statue must be erected in Greece to remind the Greeks to remain there and to build their country.

A. Andreades adds that: "It is an axiom that immigration from Greece represents a gradual racial catastrophe. The countries that are receiving immigrants like Australia, Canada, etc. demand young men and women and therefore Greece is deprived of its youth and of the most dynamic elements of its population."

An American sociologist calculated the economic value of a man of 25 to half a million dollars. He said that if the standard of living in Greece is only one fourth of the American standard of living one has only to figure the economic loss (from mass immigration) suffered by Greece.

There is another aspect—although perhaps only psychological or theoretical—that one has to remember. No one in the area of the Balkans at the time of the mass immigration of the Greeks to the United States, felt such an economic pressure as to abandon his country in search of a better life elsewhere. "No Albanian, Yugoslav or Bulgarian left to the extent the Greek left" (Andreades, *Argonaut,* 1961).

Still another point should not escape our attention: after graduation, the Greek students in the United States very seldom leave America to return to Greece. They marry in the United States or do anything to stay in the country. They fear the conditions that await them back in Greece, should they decide to return.

124

In an editorial the Greek-American Magazine *Hellenic Review* (New York, April, 1960) said:

It is very unfortunate that the internal political and partisan disputes instead of discouraging are in effect accelerating emigration to the great damage of the economic national interests of Greece. Ironically, the emigrants themselves with their remittances to their families, which are about to come close to some 100 million dollars annually, are undoubtedly offering a substantial contribution to the amount of foreign exchange needed by Greece to purchase the urgently required machinery for the industrialization. Should this not become the best lesson for those who are supposed to care and make them try harder and more earnestly to overcome their petty partisan quarrels and to concentrate all their efforts towards the one and only worthwhile target, namely to meet the legitimate demands of the Greek people for a better economic and social future?

In his book *Metanastefsis Kai Ikonomiki Anaptyxis,* Athens, 1966, Professor Xenophon E. Zolotas writes that: "Immigration has always represented for Greece, and more particularly for some of its regions, a substantial factor of democratic changes which had serious effects on the economic field." He adds that in the past "the immigration wave was changing at various periods and presented a sudden increase under the influence of conditions prevailing (at certain times) both internally and in the foreign countries, which were supposed to receive the immigrants." In the past the greatest mass exodus of the Greeks occurred during the years 1895-1912, when out of the 2,700,000 inhabitants over 215,000 people were "lost" (i.e. one third of the male population of Greece) mainly to the United States (males between 12 and 30 years of age).

On the question of the political involvement of the first Greek immigrants in the United States, Evangelos C. Vlachos *(The Assimilation of Greeks in the United States)* writes that: "The Greek ethnic group did not develop in general any 'ethnic vote.' There has been a certain concerted action to promote the cause of Greece, but whatever lobbying took place it was chiefly instigated by demagogues trying to arouse nationalism and ethnic pride. In some cases, however, manifestations of 'Greek vote' were apparent on the local level, where candidates for smaller public offices made special appeals to Greek-American constituents in the name of common ethnic background."

This is only partly so. We have seen during the 1968 Presidential elections in the United States, that Greek-American not only showed considerable interest—and even passion—in regard to the election of Spyro Agnew as Vice-President, but also changed their traditional democratic vote to help elect a Republican candidate of Greek ancestry. Is this a proof of a fast or rather slow pace of assimilation?

Yet one has to take into consideration that over the passing years the rate of naturalization of the first Greek immigrants increased rather considerably—not only because technically, so to speak, the Greeks were eligible for American citizenship—but because they started to feel more and more part in the American environment.

According to the available statistics—though the information is not extensive—in 1910, 74,975 Greeks (mostly males) were eligible for citizenship. Only 4,946 became naturalized citizens. In 1920, 29,479, out of 175,972, became American citizens. In 1930, of the total foreign born (174,526) Greeks only 65,977 were aliens, 78,059 were naturalized and 25,112 had taken their first papers.

Whether the pace of naturalization was considered fast or slow, one has to remember that the extreme nationalism of the Greeks and the impatience of the Americans for a faster assimilation played an important role in increasing hostility towards the first Greek immigrants. They had been the constant targets of prejudices and discrimination. This is why one does not understand the strange attitude of the first generation of Greek-Americans towards the problem of the Negroes in the United States. Most of them seem to share the prejudices against the black people of a certain percentage of the country. They seem to have too easily forgotten that they themselves had been, many years ago, subject to a definite discrimination and—in many instances—to cruel mistreatment.

Adjustment Problems

OST writers have come to the conclusion that the first Greek immigrants in the United States faced a number of psychological problems provoked by the influence of two different—and often adverse—cultural goals. However the problems of this nature do not pertain exclusively to the Greek immigrants. Assimilation is a process of adjustment to the cultural influence of a surrounding, superior and above all larger group of people.

It is generally accepted that the result of two opposing influences creates what is scientifically called "the marginal man": that is to say a human being torn between two loyalties and under pressure from two different sources of influence. This seems to be the case of the second Greek-American generation. The first Greek immigrants were perhaps willing to take up American citizenship but one cannot say that they were drawn towards a complete identification with America.

David Riesman ("Some Observations Concerning Marginality," in *Phylon,* XII, 1951) writing about the form and progress of assimilation says that:

> In the process of transformation the first generation is made up of the immigrants who have grown in an alien culture, the characteristics of which become deeply rooted in their personalities. The second generation is composed of children of the migrants, who, since they grow up in two cultures are seldom completely accepted by either culture groups. The third generation, the children of the second generation, can rarely be distinguished as members of any particular ethnic group.

The third generation of any minority group is subject to what is called "the ethnic revival" (Vladimir C. Nahirny and J.A. Fishman, "American Immigrant Groups: Ethnic Identification and the Problems of Generations," *Sociological Review,* 1965). The theory undoubtedly finds its application in the case of the third Greek-American generation. Its cultural identification with Greece, and indeed with almost anything "Greek," becomes more and more apparent—

127

mostly in respect to social events during which they display their preference and even a passion for Greek folk dancing and Greek music. Their regular attendance at the Greek Orthodox Church is another indication that the "ethnic revival," which is never foreign to one's "ethnic religion," is manifest among the third generation of Greek-Americans.

It is rather dangerous and it really does not serve any useful purpose to draw generalizations on the pace and form of assimilation of the first Greek immigrants in the United States. A number of factors, some imponderable ones, influence the progress—or should we say delay?—of adjustment. It seems that even the climate in the areas in which they are gathered, in conjunction with other living conditions, dictate the process of their assimilation or the extent of their struggle against it.

Many of the generalizations reached by some writers, who studied the problem are not necessarily applicable to the entire Greek-American community.

A Greek-American newspaperman, Paul G. Manolis (*Orthodox Observer,* May 1966) writes that:

> In many respects the development of social and community life (of the Greek-Americans) in the Far West and the South is far different for the Greek-American who is in the large industrial centers of the East and Middle West. In the South the immigrant is faced with a violent anti-foreign attitude not existing elsewhere. In the Far West assimilation into American community is much more rapid due to the smallness of the Greek communities and the notable lack of other large groups of foreign nationals as existed in the East and Middle West. Another factor to consider is that in the East the immigrant was faced with established society and institutions, while in the growing West he became an actual part of that growth. The Greek communities of the Western States never went through a phase as they did in the large cities east of the Mississippi.

Yet, one is inclined to agree rather with Professor Theodore Saloutos, who in his extensive study of the social and community life of the Greek-Americans *(The Greek-Americans in the United States)* states that the Greek-American community life is characterized by a typical, uniform pattern of activities and personal behavior.

Whatever the degree and the form of assimilation—or non-assimilation—the fact remains that nothing has prevented the Greek-

Americans wherever they are (first, second and third generations) from maintaining their heritage of language, religion and customs —three important factors against a rapid assimilation.

Many writers have come to the conclusion that as long as non-English language persist in the United States full assimilation has not taken place and that the continuing existence of ethnic language is a powerful indicator of non-adjustment.

It is true that over the years a Greek-American language has emerged, which is fully used and which has the distinct characteristics of a particular, often unattractive, dialect. What is curious is that this dialect—a target of sarcasm for the Greeks of Greece—is not only used either by the second or third Greek-American generation but also by the first immigrants who are still alive and who, as a matter of fact, are directly responsible for it. However, the existence of a dialect is not an exclusive trait—or sin, of the Greek-Americans—but rather an unfortunate product used by almost all other ethnic groups residing in the United States.

Another reason, which undoubtedly played—and still plays—an important role in delaying the process of assimilation of the Greek-Americans is the undeniable fact that their religion—Orthodoxy—is identified with Greece and its glorious contemporary history. Thus, Orthodoxy, and therefore the Greek Orthodox Church, have become powerful stimulants for an identification with Hellenism as a religious and cultural force. No other religion, except perhaps Judaism, is so completely identified with a particular nation the way Orthodoxy is identified with Greece.

Lowry Nelson ("Speaking of Tongues," *American Journal of Sociology,* 1948) writes that: "Greek-Americans (native or native parentage) are the last of all ethnic groups in persisting of speaking the mother language in the third generation and after." If one is willing to accept this statement as an axiom, and on the basis of the general principle that as long as non-English languages persist full assimilation is impossible, then the Greek-Americans will continue to maintain intact their identification with Greece. However, the problem of securing the survival of the Greek language is real and one should rather conclude that the identification of the future Greek-American generations—were the Greek language to be entirely forgotten or abandoned—will be rather with Hellenism as a cultural, spiritual force than with Greece itself as a nation.

The public school in the United States has been a very strong factor in the advance of the process of assimilation. In the public schools, regardless of the origin of their parents or grandparents, the children born on American soil are subject to the teaching of American history, and their patriotism and their allegiance to America are steadily cultivated—and rightly so since, after all, they are Americans.

The second, third and successive Greek-American generations are no exception to the rule and they have felt the influence of this immediate identification with America. They believe that if their parents or grandparents have the right to admire and to identify themselves with their own country, Greece, they are entitled to the same feelings for America. A deterrent against this unavoidable influence has been the creation of Greek schools (the question of the education of the new Greek-American generations will be studied in a separate chapter).

Evangelos C. Vlachos *(The Assimilation of Greeks in the United States)* writes that:

> We can understand the importance in the life of Greek-Americans and the assimilation in this institutional area as having two aspects. On one hand, are the effects of public schools, and the schooling completed; this means that the educational attainments and the general dissemination of American educational philosophy can be used as an index of assimilation. On the other hand, are the effects of the Greek schools in the United States, which basically tend to restrict assimilation.

The new immigration law passed by Congress in 1965 has produced basic changes in the nature of immigration to the United States and is probably bound to influence, in one way or another, the process of assimilation of the Greeks, who will be coming to America from now on. These new immigrants are people with an entirely different education from the non-existent educational background of the first Greeks who had emigrated to the new world some fifty or sixty years ago. Whether the new arrivals will influence the process of adjustment of those already settled in America is very doubtful, since from a chronological point of view their influence comes rather too late. However, the new immigrants will offer to the third and successive Greek-American generations a very different image of the Greek today when compared to the image of the first Greek immigrant.

The main features of the new law of 1965 was the scrapping of the old method of basing immigration on place of birth and giving each country a quota. Most of the quota had been assigned to

Western Europe and was usually only about half-filled, while other nations with incredibly tiny quotas piled up backlogs of applications.

The new law keeps an annual ceiling—120,000 a year from the Western hemisphere and 170,000 from other parts of the world. However, close relatives of United States citizens—and from any country are getting approximately 74 percent of the openings. The result of this basic change in the immigration policy is seen in the figures for the fiscal year that ended June 30, 1966, compared with those for the previous year.

The number of visas issued rose as follows:

In Italy, from 9,987 to 24,967; in Greece from 1,926 to 8,917; in Portugal from 1,698 to 8,719; in Nationalist China from 242 to 6,825. All had been low-quota countries with endless lists of relatives waiting for an opportunity to come to the United States and rejoin their families.

In contrast the number of visas dropped as follows:

In Canada, from 40,013 to 25,563; in Great Britain, from 28,698 to 20,831; in Germany, from 25,171 to 18,595.

It should be added here that under the new law anyone without any close relatives in the United States or a job skill needed in America can be admitted only if the Secretary of Labor certifies that the immigrant will not replace an American or "lower his pay." Some observers have come to the conclusion that the requirements of the new law will create some problems in the near or distant future. It is believed that the new provisions will lead to a large decrease in immigration when the lists of waiting relatives in former low-quota countries will run out.

At the time of the passing of the new immigration law, the then Vice-President of the United States, Hubert Humphrey, had stated: "Until last year (1964) the Greek quota was disgracefully low—only 308 a year. According to the latest figures, 6,583 immigration visas have already been issued to Greek citizens since the new law went into effect on December 1st of last year. This is good news for all Americans, for men and women of Greek descent have contributed to excellence in this country in many fields ... I think of Dimitri Mitropoulos and Maria Callas in music ... Dr. George Papanicolaou in the fight against cancer ... the Skouras brothers in motion pictures, and many, many others—not least . . . John Brademas, one of the ablest and most dedicated members of Congress, and Constantinos Doxiadis whose higher vision of the city has helped lift our sights and spirits."

Speaking about the 1965 new law on immigration, Senator Edward Kennedy said in an address to the 1966 AHEPA Convention that: "The Immigration Act of 1965 is one of the landmarks. It stands with legislation in other fields—civil rights, poverty, education and health—to reaffirm in the 1960's our nation's continuing pursuit of justice, equality, and freedom."

AHEPA (American Hellenic Educational Progressive Association) played an important, if not exclusive, role in the final adoption of the 1965 Immigration law which permitted the entry of larger numbers of Greek immigrants to the United States, and in general the Greek-American Organizations as a whole have played a definite part in the shaping of Greek-American life in the United States.

The Greek-American Organizations

WHEN away from their homeland and curiously enough the Greeks, who carry in them the indestructible microbe of disunity, feel the urge to look for other Greeks and even settle among them. They do so perhaps only to be given another opportunity to ascertain that the incurable disease has not disappeared. Unity and harmony are not most characteristic of the Hellenes and they do not seem to acquire these traits even when they are far from Greece and in search of other Greeks.

The first Greek immigrants to the United States had no reason to be different from their brothers in Greece. As soon as they would set foot on American soil they would look for some of those who had preceded them, yet they never failed to quarrel among themselves.

It is true that during the first years of the mass immigration of the Greeks to the new world an immigrant had no other alternative than to seek for another Greek, in the hope he might get some advice on what to do—and above all on how to find a job, any kind of job, which would permit him to remain alive in this foreign, hostile land he had chosen in the hope of finding a solution to his plight in Greece. An anecdote circulated at that time, which illustrates the blind belief of the Greek immigrants in the indescribable prosperity of the United States, goes as follows.

A Greek immigrant who had been told that dollars can be collected even in the streets of America, happened to find, upon his arrival at the port of New York, a wallet; he opened it and saw that it contained a few bills. He smiled and kicked the wallet away as he murmured to himself: "Well, I am not going to bother picking up money from the first moment I set foot in America."

During those days it was too early yet to think about a church, a priest or a Greek school. Top priority had to be given to securing the daily bread. The Greek immigrant, isolated within the terrifying vastness of America, became immediately aware that the establishment of an "organized Greek life" was indispensable for him and for the others who would continue to cross the Atlantic in search for a better future.

The gatherings at the coffee-houses had served as a preliminary step towards achieving some kind of collective "representation" in the United States. With the passing of the coffee-house era the creation of the "organization" became mandatory.

In his study *Assimilation of Greeks in the United States,* Evangelos C. Vlachos writes:

> Greek-American Organizations play a decisive role in the assimilation process. They help maintain and promulgate Greek culture and interaction between Greek members, and on the other hand by their functioning they accustom their members to basic requirements and working procedures of the larger American society. There is quite a number of organizations which emphasize the desire for continuation of Greek culture through interaction. We can distinguish categories determined mainly by the area of activity of the particular Greek organization.

Reference seems to be made here to the rather larger and well-known Greek-American Organizations on a national level, and to their most recent structure and purposes. The original intentions of some of these organizations have been slightly altered under the influence of the passing of time and the unavoitable process of assimilation, which, by the way, is one of the goals they seek to attain. The first Greek-American organizations, fraternities and clubs had not set as a goal the assimilation of the immigrants; to the contrary, most of them fought desperately against it.

Professor Theodore Saloutos (*The Greeks in the United States*) writes:

> The formation of fraternal societies was as much part of community life as was the establishment of Greek-language schools ... The immigrants demonstrated a mania for forming local, or *topica,* societies that many Americans found difficult to understand. It appears that every village and minute parish in Greece was represented in the United States by a society with an impressive array of banners, lengthy constitutions, and high-sounding names. The majority of these organizations, at least in the beginning, were composed of fifteen to thirty people and governed by councils of twelve to fifteen. Gold tassels and buttons adorned the officer's uniforms, which were worn on every possible occasion. An essential part of their equipment was the organization seal, whose use was confined exclusively to the president and

the secretary. About one hundred such societies were in existence as early as 1907; in New York alone there were thirty.

Mr. Saloutos attributes this profusion of Greek-American fraternities and societies to "the localism and provincialism of a naturally provincial people," and he says that "these traits were transplanted to the United States." But is not this "mania" of establishing innumerable organizations and clubs with the most impossible and unbelievable names and denominations also characteristic of the American environment? Could it be that the first ignorant Greek immigrants got their "inclination" from elsewhere than from the so-called provincialism supposedly inherited from Greece? Is it not perhaps only natural that under the psychological effect of the originally foreign, hostile atmosphere, the first Greek immigrants sought some solace, or substitute, by offering to themselves a semblance of official authority in connection with the conduct of their own affairs and which was denied them by the natives in other fields of activity?

One must recognize that even today after fifty or sixty years in the United States, the Greek-Americans still suffer from this "mania" of self-projection and organize pompous, pretentious parades, imposing, costly wedding ceremonies and social affairs. However, is this not the result of the influence of an overall American provincialism, as opposed to the traditional European sophistication or the weakness of a particular ethnic group? Moreover, is it not true that all minority groups indulge in such ostentatious demonstrations? "The immigrants' organizations were also, of course, characterized by activities: mutual aid, charity, and humanitarianism. These bodies came into existence before many of the members knew how to speak English; they were . . . organized according to villages, towns, districts and islands." (News from the paper *California*, February 3, November 17 and December 1, 1917; May 3 and November 11, 1918.) Gradually these organizations started collecting money to build churches, schools and waterworks in the native villages of most of their members. They were also used as "centers" for entertainment and above all for political activities and discussions about the situation in Greece—and sometimes in the United States about which, however, they did not know very much.

This superabundance of small organizations and fraternal societies in many, if not all, instances helped to isolate their members from non-Greek elements and, moreover, increased the degree of division and dissent among Greeks.

Theodore Saloutos (*The Greeks in the United States*) writes:

> In due time the local societies were viewed as obstructions to community progress. At first, they had kept the immigrants from becoming estranged from their language and customs and had furnished aid for their villages. But they soon became mere vehicles for personal aggrandizement. Their mortality rate was high, but so was their fecundity; new ones emerged from the ashes of the old. During the early years, they kept communities divided, fostered antagonism and hatreds, and impeded unification and cooperation.

The number of Greek-American Organizations and societies has, of course, decreased since these remote days, but divisions and quarrels among the members of those still in operation have not vanished. Babis Malafouris in his book *Ellines tis Amerikis: 1528-1948* (*Greeks of America: 1528-1948*), New York, 1948 writes that:

> Around 1890, all the Greeks of America were no more than 2,500, scattered in the big cities but also in remote parts of the country where they got jobs in mines and railroads. Therefore, the Greeks in New York were a few hundreds when they founded, in 1891, the first Greek society under the name of *Athena*. At that time *Athena* was a panhellenic society and had gathered almost all the Greeks of New York . . . with the same ideals and goals. The Greeks were politically divided and had different opinions on national issues but they set them aside in order to preserve their ethnical identity and their traditions and not to be carried away by the environment or change their religion.

Athena seems to have been the first Greek-American organization —at least in New York—which thought of the need of a "temporary" church and sent for a priest from Greece.

The number of organizations and fraternal societies augmented almost in proportion to the continuously increasing number of new arrivals from every part of Greece. Thus the Lacedemonians, the Macedonians, the Thessalians, or the Cretans and others had to have their own "localized" society. Professor Saloutos (*The Greeks in the United States*) writes: "The localism manifested in the societies also was reflected in the railroad, mines, and factories in which Greeks labored . . . The same divisions were observed among the coffee-houses and restaurants . . . The Greeks tended to work, sleep, eat and drink according to villages, districts, and provinces."

By 1906, the number of Greek immigrants to the United States was reaching the impressive figure of approximately 100,000. The necessity for the merger of all small societies and fraternities into something larger and more representative of the Greek as such became apparent. The immigrants thought they would be acquiring more power and perhaps a higher degree of recognition in America if they could present a cohesive organization, but also powerful from a numerical point of view.

The first organization of such "stature," the Pan-Hellenic Union, was established in 1907. The goals of the organization were stipulated in its by-laws:

1) The development among its members and through them among all the Greeks (in America) of the idea of solidarity and love for their own nationality;

2) The stimulation of respect and devotion to the principles of their adopted country and the cultivation of kind relations between the Greeks and their American co-citizens (or compatriots);

3) The teaching of the English and Greek languages, the maintenance of the Greek-Orthodox religion and the development and dissemination of principles of morality among the Greeks in the United States;

4) The offer of assistance to its members and protection—to the extent of its possibilities—to the Greek immigrants and laborers; and

5) The offer of moral and material assistance to the great needs of the *genos* (race, or in that instance the Greek nation).

However, in reality the purpose of the creation of the Pan-Hellenic Union was to bring together the "Greeks" in the United States in a common effort of establishing national identity and also promoting the Greek ethnic cause. The idea of full participation of the Greek immigrants in the American life was purely theoretical. As a matter of fact, the Pan-Hellenic Union had been established by the Greek Embassy in order to "instill a greater sense of patriotism and emotional ties with the homeland."

The character of the Greek immigration to the United States was considered only temporary both by the immigrants and by Greece itself. Thus at that time the Greek Government cared about securing the preservation of the nationnal identity of the Greeks rather than their eventual adjustment to the requirements of the new environment. On the one hand, the Greek Government had encouraged mass immigration to the new world and on the other, through its representatives in America, sought to stimulate the

137

immigrants in remaining Hellenes to the roots of their souls by avoiding assimilation. This policy of contradictions, which was also totally unrealistic, continued for many decades and has not entirely been abandoned even today.

The exclusive national character of the Pan-Hellenic Union was further established when the Balkan Wars broke out. The Organization assumed the duties of a semi-military order and it attempted to discharge the duties of a recruiting office.

Theodore Saloutos *(The Greeks in the United States)* writes that: "The Pan-Hellenic Union's recruiting was denounced as illegal. Critics charged that it was wrong for an organization known as a philanthropic agency to be used for recruiting purposes and to take advice from the leaders of a foreign government (the Greek Government). As soon as the Union committed itself to mobilizing reserves and raising funds for war, it ceased to respect the laws of the United States."

Babis Malafouris *(Ellines tis Amerikis)* writes that the Pan-Hellenic Union "had organized a special recruiting office and sent to Greece 15,000 reserves and volunteers 'from the Greeks of America.' At that time the Organization had collected 375,000 dollars from donations, which were used for national purposes."

When the Balkan Wars ended, the Pan-Hellenic Union was animated by confusion and indecision that "had characterized its earlier years" and was finally reduced to a "cipher."

Recruiting offices for the purpose of sending volunteers to Greece to fight the Turks and the Bulgarians were set up in many cities of the United States. Legions of Greek volunteers were founded all over America and the Greek Consuls in the United States were continuously receiving letters from various organizations asking how they could find arms and uniforms.

On August 10, 1910 (Babis Malafouris, *Ellines tis Amerikis*) "the secretary of the Greek Community of Ely, Nevada, ... sent to the Greek Consul General in Chicago, N. Salopoulos, the following letter: 'Because of the continuous slaps that mother Greece is receiving every day, the Greek Community (here) has decided to form a company of volunteers—the decision was accepted with deep satisfaction by our youth. This is why we appeal to your Excellency in order to be informed if we can find a capable instructor (a military instructor) and, moreover, where we can find arms and uniforms.' "

The Balkan Wars (1912-1913) were two short wars for the possession of the European territories of the Ottoman Empire. The outbreak of the Italo-Turkish war for the possession of Tripoli (1911) opened an opportunity for the Balkan states to increase their territories at Turkish expense. Serbia and Bulgaria accordingly concluded (1912) an alliance. In a secret annex, the treaty of alliance provided for joint military action and the division of prospective conquests. The outbreak of the war, in which Greece and Montenegro joined the original allies, was followed by the expulsion of the Turks from all Europe save Constantinople. After the conclusion of hostilities Serbia evidenced an intention to annex a large part of Albania, so as to gain an outlet on the Adriatic but this was opposed by Austro-Hungary and Italy and by the Albanians, who had proclaimed their independence. The Great Powers in London (1913) created an indepedent Albania of "fair size," thus cutting Serbia off from the sea. Dissatisfied with these terms, Serbia demanded of Bulgaria a greater share of Macedonia. Bulgaria thereupon attacked Serbia only to be attacked by Rumania, Greece and Turkey. As a result of the Second Balkan War, Bulgaria lost territory to all her enemies by the Treaty of Bucharest (1913).

> The Balkan Wars prepared the way for the First World War by satisfying some of the aspirations of Serbia and thereby giving great impetus to the Serbian desire to annex parts of Austro-Hungary, by alarming Austria and stiffening her resolution to crush Serbia, and by giving causes of dissatisfaction to Bulgaria and Turkey. (George Young, *Nationalism and War in the Near East*, 1915.)

Between 1914 and 1915, which coincided with the victorious (for Greece) end of the Balkan wars, approximately 50,000 Greek immigrants came to America. This figure included a few thousand Greek-Americans who had gone to Greece to fight, first the Turks and then the Bulgarians, and who were now returning to the United States. These new arrivals offered another opportunity for the establishment of numerous Greek-American organizations and societies. However, what is much more important is the fact that after 1915, the Greek immigrants were coming to the new world with the firm intention of settling for good. This was undoubtedly a turning point in the Greek immigration to the United States and indeed it changed its original "temporary" character into a permanent one. Once again, the Greek Government failed to realize the change and continued to believe and consider Greek immigration to the United States only a "provisional" enterprise, which was bound to come to an end, one day, as soon as the new immigrants would make enough money to return to Greece. Had they not really left for the new world because they wanted to help their poor relatives in Greece and build churches, schools and hospitals in their native villages and towns? Indeed, to many people in Greece, immigration of their fellow countrymen to America was nothing else but a temporary absence from the homeland, its main purpose being the earning of a small or large fortune. What else could force them to stay indefinitely in America? They did not seem to know that as the French say, "Il n'y a que le provisoire qui dure," and, dangerously confident in the Greek culture and pride, they never thought that the immigrants would ever be absorbed by the American environment; some went as far as to nurse the fallacy that even the second and third generations of Greek-Americans will be in reality "Greeks" like themselves. Greek views on many problems and situations, are a curious melange of myth and reality, in uneven proportions.

The First World War had already brought about a distinct change of attitude in connection with the future of all immigrants in America; this change was reflected in their organizations and institutions.

In 1922, and after the disastrous (for Greece) Greco-Turkish war in the depths of Asia-Minor, more and more Greeks arrived in the United States; they too were decided to settle in America for the rest of their lives.

The decision of the new immigrants to adopt America as their second fatherland was not the result of any emotional feelings or sentimentality but rather a fuller realization of what their destiny was to be from then on. Americanization as opposed to Hellenization seemed to have scored a first important point.

The Greek immigrants were willing, though perhaps only theoretically, to become part of this "restless and opulent America." Paul Javaras ("New Tendencies in the Thinking of the Greeeks in America," *American-Greek* Review, December 1926) wrote:

> Yesterday we thought ourselves as . . . foreigners. Today we view with the most ardent exponents of Americanism in excelling them. Along with the rest of the inhabitants of this fair land we proclaim it to be God's country; and since the barring of immigrants increases our well-being we too are in favor of the

enforcement of the immigration law. The constitution we revere and uphold, and in order not to be out of line from the rest of free Americans we too disobey the eighteenth amendment. An American air prevails over most of our social activities; our festivals have lost their purity and origin; the jazz has replaced our folksongs and the radio is sweeping away the last vestige of the connecting link—the phonograph record ... English is replacing the Greek in nearly all of our assemblies and has become the official language of numerous organizations ... As for the new generation, the American school will see to it that no hyphenated Americans emanate from it.

Though one cannot entirely agree with all these remarks since "the connecting link" with Greek traditions and customs has not been broken even today, but has rather been revived—there is no doubt that Hellenic traditionalism has come to some terms with Americanism.

It is perhaps through the establishment of two of the largest and most powerful Greek-American Organizations, AHEPA (American Hellenic Educational Progressive Association) and GAPA (Greek American Progressive Association) that the necessity of accepting these terms was seen and achieved in spite of the resistance of smaller organizations, groups and even individuals. These two Organizations, though with striking differences both in structure and purpose, were distinct from the other societies and fraternities in that they actually led "into participation and assimilation of the larger American culture," whereas all previous, to various degrees, were opposed and struggled against assimilation.

The idea to found AHEPA was conceived in July 26, 1922 by two Greek immigrants, George Nikolopoulos and Ioannis Angelopoulos, who met accidentally in Atlanta, Georgia—at that time a hotbed of the Ku Klux Klan activities and wider anti-foreignism. The absolute necessity to get seriously organized against such activities and feelings was one of the principal reasons for which AHEPA was founded. It was officially recognized by the State of Georgia on September 25, 1922.

The objects and purposes of the Order of AHEPA were:

a) To promote and encourage loyalty of its members to the country of which they were citizens;
b) To instruct its members in the tenets and fundamental principles of government;
c) To instill a due appreciation of the privileges of citizenship;

d) To encourage interest and active participation in the political, civic, social and commercial fields of human endeavor;

e) To pledge its members to oppose political corruption and tyranny

f) To promote a better and more comprehensive understanding of the attributes and ideals of Hellenism and Hellenic culture;

g) To promote good fellowship, and endow its members with a spirit of altruism, common understanding, mutual benevolence and helpfulness to their fellow men;

h) To endow its members with the perfection of the moral sense;

i) To promote education and maintain new channels for facilitating the dissemination and culture.

The foudation of AHEPA met great success, and the services it rendered to the Greek-Americans are indeed invaluable, though one might be inclined to say that AHEPA's attitude towards a military regime in Greece was, at that time, in flagrant contradiction with some of the stipulations of its by-laws.

Theodore Saloutos (*The Greeks in the United States*) who made an extensive study of the origin and the activities of AHEPA since the first days of its establishment writes:

> From the outset AHEPA was middle-class in orientation. It appealed to those who were climbing the social and economic ladder of success. It extended recognition to those who craved it but who found it difficult to obtain in non-Greek spheres. Its banquets, dances, and meetings furnished an outlet for many harassed businessmen who preferred the company of compatriots facing identical problems. The element of secrecy (AHEPA was influenced by the ritual of the Masonic and other fraternal orders) and exclusiveness also had its charm, for men regardless of race and nationality like to believe themselves among the select. The times were relatively prosperous and the dues were no obstacle to the well-off businessman. AHEPA, after all, represented Americanism, in a decade of conformity reacting sharply against the politics of the world, was desirous of shaking off all traces of foreignism by joining the greater American community. In short, the climate was favorable to the growth of the order.

AHEPA drew the attention of the American Government and of many prominent Americans who offered their support by accepting to speak during official banquets, gatherings and regular conventions. The speakers paid, and still pay, whenever they spoke before AHEPA's audiences, tribute to ancient Greece and to the "astounding" achievements of the Greek-Americans in the United

States. Nothing could please more the members of the Organization than these "two" recognitions. However, there were also some exaggerated statements in regard to the importance of the Organization. Thus George Demeter (AHEPA Manual, Boston 1926) wrote that: "The founding of the AHEPA fraternity marks a new era for the Hellenes of the United States—the Hellenic Renaissance . . . In a sense, the founding of this Order is a sequel to the Glorious Age of Pericles—the same Hellenic civic and artistic supremacy."

On the other hand, AHEPA was pressed to join forces with the Greek Orthodox Church to protect the Greek language and the culture of the mother country by abandoning its policy of non-sectarianism. *The Voice of Greek Orthodoxy* (Chicago, October 15, 1926) as a matter of fact asked AHEPA's members to become "the militant servants of the Greek Orthodox Church."

The attacks against AHEPA's intentions increased. The *American Hellenic World* (April 2, 1927) denounced its leaders as opportunists and pseudo-patriots. Saloutos (*The Greeks in the United States*) writes that: "Critics charged that AHEPA was downgrading the Greek school, disassociating itself from the Greek Church, and misrepresenting everything worthy among the Greeks in the United States. It was accused of offering a distorted picture of American Hellenism to the outside world."

Though usually AHEPA refused to react to criticism some of its members could not resist the temptation to stress their views. One of its members writing in *Archon Magazine* (August 1927) said:

The use of the Greek language in our meetings will turn our meetings to coffeehouse pandemoniums . . . you (its adversaries) were going to maneuver tactfully and slit open the red veins of the AHEPA and run its pure blood into the veins of the old defunct Pan-Hellenic Union, and declare Greek as the official language of the Brotherhood to please these old fogies . . . sinister propaganda has been started a year and a half ago for the purpose of injecting the old rules and policies of the Pan-Hellenic Union into the virgin, pure, sacred body of our AHEPA.

The fanatical cry of the old Pan-Hellenists "Pas Hellen Prepei na Einai Orthodoxos" (Every Greek must be an Orthodox) is outdated. We are Greeks, but we did not inherit our present religion from our ancestors—the ancient Greeks—as we did our blood and traits. Is Brother more a Greek because he is a convert to the Episcopalian denomination?

There are thousands of true-blooded Greeks who are members of

143

other churches. Must we deny their race owing to that? Finally the AHEPA is not a doctrinaire cult.

The problem of the exact relation between a Greek-American—second, third and successive generations, to the Greek language and to his religion—Orthodoxy, had already been felt at that time. It has become since those days more acute and much more difficult to cope with.

To many Greek-Americans, AHEPA, through its policy had committed itself to a philosophy of de-Hellenization—a "crime" of which the Greek Orthodox Church is accused today by some hasty critics.

It was indeed to counter AHEPA's alleged philosophy of de-Hellenization that GAPA was founded December 17, 1923. It decided to employ Greek as its official language and offer its full support to the Greek Orthodox Church, which AHEPA had seemingly ignored. GAPA's members had conceived the idea that Americanization meant the abolition of Greek traditions and thereby the elimination of the Greek language and to a certain extent of Orthodoxy as a "must" religion for the Greek-Americans.

Theodore Saloutos (*The Greeks in the United States*) writes that: "The philosophy of GAPA was idealistic, romantic, and somewhat impractical. It was embraced by people who lacked the resources and leadership to implement it with positive course of action. It made little appeal to the more affluent elements and its unwillingness to make too radical a break with the past left many potential members cold. It attracted the rank and file, some who felt insecure in an American environment, and others who sincerely believed that an unintelligent brand of Americanism was robbing the Greek-Americans of a heritage worth preserving."

AHEPA and GAPA seemed to agree on one thing: they both accepted the principle that the Greek-Americans—their members, were in the United States to stay. On the basis of this assumption the philosophy of AHEPA seemed to be much more realistic. AHEPA was looking rather into the future while GAPA wrestled with the perpetuation of a past which could hardly be preserved in its entirety within the American environment—at least not in the form dreamed by the organization and some, many, Greek-Americans of the first generation.

Where to draw the demarcation line between what has to be preserved and what has to be forgotten is the struggle undertaken by the Greek Orthodox Church of North and South America. The role and the problems of the church will be examined in a separate chapter.

Both Organizations have come to the assistance of Greeks when necessary and donated money for the relief of Greek refugees as a result of earthquakes and other disasters. Both Organizations have undertaken, mostly in recent years, regular excursions to the motherland, which most certainly helped in establishing closer and better relations between the Greek-Americans and the Greeks in Greece —the gap between these two different "categories" of Hellenes has been narrowed.

Another Greek-American Organization, though with different purposes than those of the previous ones, played an extremely important role in helping Greece at a very crucial moment of her national life. During World War II and within the two weeks after Greece was invaded the establishment of the "Greek War Relief Association" was announced; it immediately launched a drive for ten million dollars.

Saloutos *(The Greeks in the United States)* writes that:

> The first news release of the Greek War Relief Association on November 20, 1940 (Greece was invaded by the Italians on October 28, 1940) announced that more than three hundred local committees had been organized to coordinate the activities of the approximately two thousand Greek clubs and organisations in the United States. The local church communities, the hierarchy of the Greek church in the United States, and chapters of AHEPA, GAPA, the Pan-Arcadians, the Messinians, the Cretans, and other groups lent their support. But the greatest assistance came from AHEPA, which provided much, if not most, of the regional and local leadership.

In late April 1941, after Greece had been attacked and conquered by the Germans, and as a result of a visit of the officers of the supreme lodge of AHEPA to the White House, President Franklin Roosevelt issued the following statement, which is indeed an historical document and shows the influence that Greek-Americans exercised on the American Government in regard to its attitude towards Greece:

> During the Hellenic war of indepedence more than a century ago, our young nation, prizing its own lately-won independence, expressed its ardent sympathy for the Greeks and hoped for Hellenic victory. The victory was achieved.
> Today, at a far more perilous period in the history of Hellas,

we intend to give full effect to our settled policy of extending all available material aid to a free people defending themselves against aggression. Such aid has been and will continue to be extended to Greece.

Whatever may be the temporary outcome of the present phase of the war ... the people of Greece can count on the help and support of the government and the people of the United States.

Most of the "Greek War Relief Association" staff was provided by Americans who had lived in Greece for many years and by Americans of Greek origin; but very soon they were joined in their efforts by Americans of any origin and of all steps of life.

The "Greek War Relief Association" cannot be compared to any of the old or "new" Greek-American Organizations. It belonged to a special category—and served a particular cause.

Babis Malafouris *(Ellines Tis Amerikis)* writes that the "Greek War Relief Association" sent to Greece "foodstuff, medical supplies, clothing etc. amounting to 4,000,000 dollars" and that during the "three years from March 1942, until March 1945, the Organization of the 'Greek War Relief Association' contributed in money and goods nine million dollars." Malafouris adds that "In its report (The Greek War Relief Association Report) and in regard to its activities from the date of its establishment until the summer of 1946, the organization, without underestimating the generosity and willingness of the American public, stresses that the success of the programme of relief of the Greek people during the tragic days they were facing, was due mainly to the enthusiasm and the eagerness with which the Greeks in America had decided to support this programme."

Naturally, the "Greek War Relief Association" did not escape the criticism of some Greeks (in Greece) who objected to its "liberal" views. It was unavoidable and well within the lines of the perennial disunity and dissent of the eternally divided Greeks.

Speaking about the Greek-American organizations as a whole Professor Theodore Saloutos *(The Greeks in the United States)* comes to the following conclusion:

> The weaknesses of most Greek-American organizations were pretty much the same. They failed to attract or retain the active support of the better-educated and more socially active people, who tended to disassociate themselves from organizations that were even remotely Greek. The reasons for this disassociation varied from person to person ... but the estrangement was per-

sistent. A common heritage was not enough to bind persons to ethnic or quasi-ethnic organizations—interests and associations changed. If recognition was needed, it could be had more meaningfully elsewhere. As a result, many organizations had to content themselves with inadequate leaders or "left-overs."

It seems that on the contrary it is rather the "ethnic" or "quasi-ethnic" nature of these organiaztions that attracted its members, and that disunity among them, on the other hand, would sooner or later lead to their dissolution or to a diminution both of their numbers and of the influence they exercised at one particular moment in the life of the Greek-Americans—and, in some instances, in the life of Greece itself.

What is true is that the gradual removal of these organizations from the problems of education and preservation of the Greek language created a vacuum which was to be filled by the Greek Orthodox Church of North and South America. The creation of this vacuum was also prompted to some extent by a steady indifference of the Greek nation to the Greek-American community.

The Greek-American
"Social Class" and Social Classifications

E VEN in a country which enjoys the best possible democratic system the existence of social classifications—or social classes— is unavoidable. There are "social classes" in America, with different characteristics both in the mentality and behavior of its citizens, which in so far as the immigrants are concerned influence— in a positive or negative manner—the process of their assimilation.

The existence of social classes is indeed an important element in the life of the immigrant. In the United States many years ago and in some instances still today, the immigrant was considered an inferior human being—a needed laborer who was not entitled to the privileges of the native Americans. This attitude did not escape the attention of the Greek immigrants and most of them suffered the consequences of its unjust and cruel presence.

The intricate, modern societies have established a system by which people are placed on various levels according to their activities and their financial status.

W. Lloyd Warner (*The Social System of American Ethnic Groups*, New Haven: Yale University Press, 1945) speaks about the following "social classes" in America: the upper-upper and lower-upper; the upper-middle and lower middle; the upper-lower and lower-lower. The first category comprises the "old families," the "old aristocracy"—descendants of truly well known and successful people. The lower-upper is composed of the "nouveaux riches" whose ambition is to accomplish extraordinary deeds. They struggle in order to be accepted by the first classification. They usually belong to exclusive clubs, and politically they lean towards the extreme right. So the analysis goes, through the middle and lower classes.

To which of the above "social classes" does the Greek-American belong—or wants to belong? Usually, the Greeks are more interested in appearing to be prominent people in the eyes of other Greeks, and therefore it is rather difficult to determine very accurately to which of all these classifications they really belong. The "Olkott's

Handbook of Chicago Real Estate" places the Greeks before the Negroes, the Mexicans and the Jews of Russian origin but after any other minority group.

Aris T. Papas (*The Personality of the Greek-American—I prosopikotis tou Ellinoamerikanou*) writes that: "... the Greeks are not allowed to become members of certain clubs like the Negroes and the Jews are prevented to do so . . . ." He adds that "This 'lowest' classification stems from the habit of the Greeks to self-isolate themselves from the American cultural life because of their original allegiance to the principles and values of Greece . . . in brief it seems that the Greek system of evaluation has retained something from the attitude of the Greeks, during ancient times, towards the Barbarians."

Finally Mr. Aris T. Papas comes to the conclusion that:

> If the Greek has chosen not to circulate among the Americans it is because he does not wish to do so and that he prefers his close relatives and the close relationship and mutual influence of the members of the community who are oriented towards the church of the Greeks. Not because there are any obstacles. This is probably the most obvious reason . . . though one hears, on the other hand, that the Greek does not succeed to achieve any contact or reach the level of higher classes of the American social life."

These observations, however, seem to fall within the dangerous domain of generalization. Quite a great number of Greek-Americans are part of the highest so-called "superior" American social class. They did not seem to hesitate or have any difficulty in approaching the so-called superior American social class and, on the other hand, there was no reluctance on the part of that particular social class to accept them in its midst as long as they could keep up with a certain "prosperous" way of life. Ecoonmic equality was able to set aside all other—if any—considerations or differences.

W. Lloyd Warner writes that the factors that influence the process of assimilation are:

1) The power of the church which is exercised on its members and the degree of declination from the American prototype.

2) The existence of separate schools and the amount of control they exercise.

3) The political and economic unity of the ethnic group.

The Greeks are classified as more darkly complected people of the

Caucasian race (type 2 and cultural type 4) and it is believed that the time necessary for their assimilation could be described as "moderate" (not excessive).

According to the Warner theory it would take about six generations before Americans of Greek ancestry are completely assimilated. It must be repeated here that whether the arrival of new immigrants from Greece—people with a different educational background than their "old" predecessors—might influence the process of assimilation by presenting quite a different picture of what a Greek is today to the new Greek-American generations, is not known.

What is American culture and how do the Greek-Americans fit into it? American culture has been called "the civilization of paradoxes" (Clude Klukhohn, *American Culture: Generalized Orientation and Class Patterns*). Some writers have come to the conclusion that American civilization—or culture—is in reality a culture of a middle class in which the lower classes are less adjustable to the traditional American ideological system than the so-called superior class because they include—to a great extent—elements of immigrants.

Julius Dreschler *(Democracy and Assimilation,* New York: Macmillan Co., 1920) writes that when the "parent-immigrants" will die the children born in America will not need to be americanized. America was not always that patient in regard to the evolution of its immigrants. In 1918, President Theodore Roosevelt declared that "we must insist that every immigrant learns English. If after five years he has not learned English then he should return to the country from which he came from." *(Report of Americanization—* Conference called by the Secretary of the Interior—1918).

Insofar as the Greek-Americans are concerned one has to acknowledge that they have already achieved a certain degree of assimilation though they have been affected by a process of dual cultural adjustment rather than by total assimilation.

Aris T. Papas says that:

> It appears that those of the Greeks who settled in the United States many years ago have created a standard mentality of their own to which the new immigrants (Greeks) should adjust if they wish to be considered Greeks. On the other hand, there is no way of knowing how many of the new immigrants have removed themselves from the pattern of the Greek community because they refused to abide by the local idea prevailing in America in regard to what a Greek must be.

Once again the danger of generalization becomes apparent. A great many factors seem to dictate the attitude of certain groups of Greek-Americans, according to the regions in which they live or because of their economic status—regardless of whether all of them continue to be inexorably attached to Hellenic traditionalism. Thus what is true for some particular groups is not for others.

The Greek Orthodox Church of North and South America is trying to establish some basic religious and educational principles, and rules, which might help preserve some sort of Hellenic consciousness in the Greek-American generations of the future. It is indeed these future generations that will represent Hellenism—in whatever form—in the United States, and it is on them that attention should be concentrated.

In his book *Apodimos Ellinismos (Greek Immigration* or *Greeks Abroad*, Athens, 1961) Panos Ch. Pamboukis takes a rather dim view of the future of the Greek-Americans. He thinks that immigrants have always lived with the dream of repatriation; he believes, however, that during the years after the World War II the living conditions of the Greek immigrant have changed in such a way that not only is his return to Greece prevented but also he is forced to become a citizen, lest he find himself completely isolated from the economic life of the country in which he lives. Thus, Panos Pamboukis concludes, the danger of assimilation becomes more serious. ". . . The problem therefore" he says "is how, in the middle of a politically, economically and culturally foreign environment will the immigrants maintain their national identity, their language, their religion and their love for the Greek fatherland?" He goes on to say that this problem was never faced by the Greek State; Greece saw it as an immigration problem and not as a national issue.

Most of the Greek writers who dealt with the problem of Hellenism in America seem to believe that whatever was preserved or "saved" from Hellenism abroad is, without any doubt, due to the initiative and the organization of the immigrants themselves. Some of them insist that since Greece has entered a new phase of her contemporary life there should be a steady, basic immigration policy and that Greece should try to solve some of the many problems of the immigrants by maintaining them within the framework of the Hellenic National Community. The idea seems to be more of a dream than an actual plan. Planning has never been one of the best qualities of any Greek administration. Something else which seems to escape the attention of those who study the problem of

Hellenism in America, is the attitude of the United States towards a second, third or successive generation of any ethnic ancestry, who, by the way, are genuinely American. Nobody wants to take into consideration that if the future generations, which are the product of various ethnic provenances, were to maintain all the particular characteristics emanating from the origin of their ancestors (parents, grandparents or great grandparents) then an American could be simply identified as a man or woman carrying a United States passport—and, irony of fate, there are thousands of United States citizens who do not speak a single word of English.

When speaking or writing about Greek immigration to the United States, in reality one refers to two different aspects or products of one and the same immigration: the past and the present, the first immigrants and the successive generations. Too often the first and successive generations are not clearly identified and cannot be distinguished as two separate entities. Thus, one might get the illusion that some of these first Greek immigrants, for example, have lived over one hundred years in America. The term "Greek-American" is often used in such a manner as to embrace a variety of generations of men and women of different background except for their ethnic origin; some are faithful to the Greek Orthodox Church; others stay away from it; still others are always fascinated by Greece while some others do not even talk about Greece if it means they might be identified with the country of their ancestors. Which is really the representative type of a Greek-American?

Theodore Saloutos (*The Greeks in the United States*) comes to this conclusion:

> ... (this) study of the Greek people in the United States suggests some striking parallels between their problems of adjustment and those of the older and even pioneer groups. One is that they never lost interest in the country they left behind, any more than did the English, the French, or the Germans. They became embroiled in the political and religious upheavals of the mother country and on various occasions fought them out with a passion that equaled and even exceeded that of their compatriots abroad ... If the Greeks seemed less adaptable it was because too much was expected of them. Their detractors never realized that these same criticisms had been hurled at earlier immigrants who were now accepted as respectable members of American society. The Greek's late immigration was a temporary handicap, but it was no deterrent to a people who took pride in their individualism and national background.

It is true that the Greeks, whether immigrants or not, never realized that what happened to those among them who emigrated to America, in reality happened also, to a lesser or greater degree, to the immigrants of other ethnic origins. They sincerely believe that the contempt shown to them by native Americans, especially during the days of acute anti-foreignism in the United States, was exclusively directed against them and thus made them the constant target of American puritanism and snobism. Of course this is not so; during the first days of the formation of the United States almost all immigrants had to face the same ugly visage of rudeness and disdain. The Greeks were not the only ones to attract criticism; scorn was there as an inherent part of the American attitude that was displayed then towards the "foreigners."

Greece likes to talk about the "danger" the future Greek-American generations face of being completely assimilated—of completely identifying themselves with the United States. One has the right to wonder if "danger" is the proper word to use in order to express an historical—and not ethnic—interest in the evolution of Hellenism in America. One feels that the whole issue is seen through an illusory prism, which leads to a misinterpretation of the problem. It should perhaps have been the other way around— the United States expressing concern over the possibility of its citizens one hundred years from now still being conspicuously Greeks, Italians, Poles, Germans or anything else.

New Orleans—
Birthplace of a New Organized Orthodoxy

THE Centennial of the Greek Orthodoxy in America was celebrated in 1964-65. The closing ceremonies of the commemoration took place in the Holy Trinity Cathedral in New Orleans, Louisiana, where a century ago the first Greek Orthodox Church in the Western Hemipshere was founded by a small group of Greek merchants. The Greek Orthodox of America were entering the second century of their religious life in the New World. When the Battle of New Orleans in the War between the States was decided and the Union troops under Admiral David Farragut took New Orleans on the 25th of April, 1862, the Greeks in the city had already become a permanent settlement, which was the product of a continuous flow of Greek immigrants arriving from Greece in search of better opportunities but also of a place for worship.

At a time when the Sixteenth President of the United States, Abraham Lincoln, was delivering his famous Gettysburg Address on November 19, 1863, and was reminding his audience that "Fourscore and seven years ago our fathers brought forth on this continent a new nation, conceived in liberty and dedicated to the proportion that all men are created equal," some devout Greeks had already founded the First Greek Orthodox House of Worship in the war torn city of New Orleans.

The glamorous, picturesque largest city of the South enjoyed a lasting reputation of gay living, elegance but also of wickedness. It was also a major port where international trade was booming, and the city soon became a center of business, of commerce and finally an impressive metropolis of many cultures. In 1852, New Orleans was the third largest city in the United States and a few Greek merchants and dealers in cotton were contributing their own particular flavor to the prevailing atmosphere but also their innate genius in the field of commerce. As one commentary notes:

> As they were making adjustments to their new economic, social and cultural environment they failed not to turn their attention

to the more profound values in their life. Conscious of their ethnic, religious and cultural heritage they sought to so preserve, foster and nurture these values, as in a measure commensurate with their capabilities and numerical strength, they may enrich the unrivaled, in its harmonious diversity, American civilzation and its newborn heritage ... And in the exercise of this freedom (reference is made to Lincoln's address) they have given birth to the first Greek Orthodox Church Community and House of Worship of the Holy Trinity, one hundred years ago, in the historic city of New Orleans. They strongly believed that Orthodoxy in America had a mission to accomplish, not only in the religious life of its people, but also in their ethnic and cultural heritage to which they are the historical heirs and privileged advocates, defenders and preservers. (From the *Centennial Album of the Greek Orthodox Cathedral of Holy Trinity in New Orleans, Louisiana*, New Orleans, 1965.)

One cannot help thinking that there is perhaps a curious coincidence, which permits an historical observation of the fact that the First Greek Orthodox Church in America was founded in New Orleans. The city was built within a great bend of the Mississippi river and was, because of that, called the "Crescent City." The crescent is an emblem representing the half-moon with the horns turned upwards. The crescent and star were of course ancient Byzantine symbols, which became the emblems of Constantinople. However, the crescent was assumed as the standard of the Ottoman Turks after their capture of the city. Since then, the Cross for Greeks and the Crescent for the Turks—Orthodoxy as opposed to Islamism—have been the very symbols of an historical, racial and religious struggle between the Greeks and the Turks, which has been going on for centuries. The observation does not claim the discovery of a fact of any historical value; there is simply another kind of symbolic "encounter" between the Cross and the Crescent within the American environment.

Writing about the establishment of the Greek Orthodox Church in New Orleans, Professor Theodore Saloutos *(The Greeks in the United States)* says that:

Even though the immigrants became the bulkwark of support for the faith, the first Greek church in the United States—the Holy Trinity of New Orleans—was founded in 1864 by non-immigrating merchants and factors representing commercial firms owned by Greeks. The principal benefactors of the New Orleans church were agents of the Ralli brothers and of Benaki; they also happened to be the consular representatives of the Greek Government. One was the well-known Demetrios Botassi, the Greek Consul general in New York City, who reached the age of one hundred and four; the other, Nicholas Benaki, was the Greek Consul in New Orleans. In this church worshipped the merchants of New Orleans and their families, Greek sailors who happened to be in port, and a few Syrians and Slavs...When Greek merchants liquidated their commercial interests in the southern states and their agents departed for other assignments, the New Orleans church passed into the hands of the remaining Greeks, Syrians and Slavs... As might be expected the first priest was a member of the Russian Orthodox church. The minutes of the parish were kept in English until 1906, since some of the officers and members knew little, if any, Greek.

Though it is generally accepted that the first priest of the Greek Orthodox Church in New Orleans was a member of the Russian Orthodox Church, nobody seems to be able to trace his name— at least not in any responsible manner. Those who did not hesitate to identify him gave his name as Rev. Agapius Honcarenko. In his book, *O En Ameriki Ellinismos Kai I Drasis Tou: I Istoria Tis Ellinikis Archiepiskopis Amerikis Voriou kai Notiou (Hellenism in America and its Activities: The History of the Greek Archdiocese of North and South America,* New York, 1954) Vasilios Th. Zoustis writes that: "The first priest of this church (Holy Trinity in New Orleans) was supposed to be someone who belonged to the Russian Missionaries in America. But his name is not remembered by anyone and cannot be found in the minutes of the Board of the Church."

From 1880 to 1901 the priest officiating in the New Orleans Greek Orthodox church was a certain Mihail Karydis, from Philippoupolis (Bulgaria) who committed suicide in a New York hotel, in June 1901. The reasons for which the priest took his life are not known, but it has been said that he had become insane as a result of a nervous breakdown—he had been busy designing an engine for a bicycle which, he said before his death, would have been capable of speeding at 100 miles per hour.

In his book *Ellines Tis Amerikis, 1528-1948, (The Greeks in Amerrica)* Babis Malafouris writes that:

Until it is definitely established, as a result of an historical research, that the few Greeks who settled in St. Augustine, Florida, after the dissolution of the New Smyrna settlement in 1777, were worshipping in their own church . . . the most ancient Greek Orthodox Church in America is the church of the Holy Trinity in New Orleans, of Louisiana. The church was founded in 1867(?) by Greek merchants . . . ."

Though some writers have contested the accuracy of the exact date the First Greek Orthodox Church was built in the United States, there seems to be no doubt whatsoever that it was indeed built in June 12, 1864 and demolished in December 4, 1950. Actually, there is probably some discrepancy arising from the fact that both the words "foundation" and "construction" of the church have been invariably used in connection with the establishment of the First Greek Orthodox Church in New Orleans.

A letter found in the archives of the City of New Orleans shed some light into the story regarding the establishment of the First Greek Orthodox Church in America. It is signed by a certain A.J. "Bob" Bordes and was written on the stationery of "Vilacs Service Station—1113 N. Broad Street, New Orleans, La." Unfortunately the letter is not dated. The writer, who says he lived at 2534 St. Philip near Dorgenois (Dorgenois is the name of the street on which the church of the Holy Trinity was built), had this to say:

> It was in the early 1875 that a family moved in the neighborhood of Dorgenois and Barrachs Hospital, by the name of Theodore. They were Greeks; at that period they were but a few handful of Greeks in the city of New Orleans. The family I am about to refresh your memory (at this point it must be said that the name of the addressee is not mentioned in the letter, which could mean that Bob Bordes wrote perhaps a sort of "story" regarding the Greek church and the activities of the Greeks in New Orleans) were known by the name of Costa Nich Theodore, a river captain who had a fleet of Tug Boats and who was a very charitable man and who in time bought nearly the whole front of Dorgenois St. Hospital and Barrachs, and between the years of 1875-1878 donated a plot of that ground to build a Greek church. In that neighborhood resided a few Greeks who had accumulated a few dollars; these men known as John Stratis, George Theodore, his brothers Christo and Peter, Peter Baker, John . . . (the name is illegible) started by filling that plot of ground and built the church; a small frame structure and that was the work of those men up to 1878 to 1888. For the years of 1878-1888, a priest was brought from Greece but he was not versed in the American way and he

157

did not stay here long—about six months and then the church was closed and in the period of 1881 a father by the name of Gregory was brought from Greece and he only remained a few years and then a father Michael was brought here and to him deserves a great deal of credit. He remodeled the church; had a house built on the grounds and lived there, taught school at certain periods of the year, but the attendance was very small; but he remained many years and was somewhat of an inventor, and I believe he wanted to make a flying bicycle and the worry of so many things he had to overcome and . . . he died. In the years that followed other priests took charge until the present time; it is today a beautiful edifice and an honor to the Greek colony of New Orleans. Between the years of 1880 to 1890 there were a few American friends of the Theodores by the name of Alexander Bordes, Jos. Dancas, Adam Dorn, James Degelos, Billi Zambelli, John Bordes and a few others . . . they came and played cards and they made jack-pots to help the Church. Mr. Alex. Bordes was one of the first to contribute five dollars to the church and so was J. Dancas and James Degelos . . . so you see we were the three great friends of captain Nich Theodore. George Theodore reared a family, but captain Nich Theodore had no children but had nephews and nieces and one of them in the family of Tomarovitch and they had a large family . . . and the children of Peter Christo are still living and have a family; this is the best I can give you about the church . . . I am still living, I am 76 years old and have a family and never resided no further than three blocks from the church all my life.

The letter is reproduced in its original form. It seems that Mr. Bordes had confused his dates.

There were some Greeks in New Orleans long before the First Greek Orthodox Church was built there. One of them, Alexander Dimitry, played an important role in the cultural life of Louisiana.

"Teacher, editor, diplomat, first state superintendant of education, he made an intellectual investment on the culture of Louisiana that paid rich dividends." He was born in New Orleans, February 7, 1805. His father, a Greek, came from the island of Hydra. His maternal grandfather, also Greek, emigrated to New Orleans in 1760. His mother's mother was of a family long resident in the state and one of her ancestors was an Indian. Alexander Dimitry became the first English editor of the *New Orleans Bee*, a newspaper published in French. He married Mary Powell Mills. The President of the United States, James Buchanan, appointed him United States Minister to the republic of Costa Rica, in 1859. When the war of the States broke out and Louisiana seceded, Dimitry promptly resigned and returned to New Orleans. President Jefferson Davis, of the Confederacy, appointed him chief of the Post Office Department. He died in New Orleans in January 30, 1883. He was familiar with eleven languages and there is a school in New Orleans which bears his name." (Archives of the City of New Orleans).

The Greek Community of New Orleans, which should have been extremely proud because it was in their city that the First Greek Orthodox Church was built, suffered from what all Greek communities—indeed all Greeks—suffer from: the disease of disunity. Neither religious faith nor patriotism, which are the characteristics of the Greek soul, mind and heart, have eliminated the perennial microbe. The objective observer comes to the unhappy conclusion that such is the extent of disunity among the members of practically every community that the urge to build large and expensive churches, schools and other institutions is prompted by the desire of the members to project themselves; to have a rostrum where they can display their sharp differences—most of them the product of personal dislikes or quarrels.

Research in the archives of the Greek Orthodox Church of New Orleans brings to light that the community there was torn by internal disputes, year after year. Resignations and accusations followed one another.

In May 5, 1909, one of the members of the Board of Trustees of the Church, N. Bellamore, resigned and stated, in his letter to the officers and members of the Board of the Church of the Holy Trinity, "Try as you will and do what you can for the interest of the congregation; there is absolutely no gratitude and no thanks. No matter what the result of elections might be or what the Board might do, there is trouble and lots of it."

Another member of the Board of Trustees by the name of M. Popovitch, in his letter of resignation states that: "Continuous discussions and wrangling among the members of the congregation, which will not redound to the benefit of the church and in time will disrupt the whole congregation."

Unity has been urged upon the members of every community and the priest of every parish—almost every priest, because some of them have themselves indulged in "improper" contacts with their parishioners—has played the role of "rehabilitator." The sermons

159

have been directed to induce the members of every community to help in creating a spirit of unity so much needed for greater progress—not only of the Greek Orthodox Church but of the community itself.

The Greek Orthodox Church in America has been often accused of having failed to establish a harmonious rapport with the communities. This is perhaps true. However, it should not escape one's attention that the lack of unity in practically every Greek-American community has not been conducive to the establishment of such a relationship. This is not stated in defense of the Church but rather as an undeniable fact.

An opinion on the efforts of the Greeks of New Orleans to build a church was offered by Judge Walter Hawlin of Louisiana, in his address during the ceremonies for the celebration of the Centennial of the Greek Orthodoxy in America:

> Within the half century 1850-1900 changes of profound significance occurred in the life of the few immigrants Orthodox in New Orleans affecting every phase of Christian life. Greek immigration on an unprecedented scale phenomenally increased the population of New Orleans notably modifying its ethnic composition. A greater city arose to become a principal factor in social, political and commercial life. A great challenge was imposed by the immigration. Since a large number of Greek immigrants were arriving at this port of entry virtually penniless, it was inevitable as religious people that they should establish an Orthodox house of worship. Insistent calls came from the immigrants anxious for a church and school. As the years went by these appeals continued to be heard. The missionary Orthodox minded Christians were becoming more and more aware of the great need of the church. Early attempts had failed to establish a church. Financial support was at its lowest. Immigration brought only poverty. Although bitter defeat commonly appeared, it did not weaken the spirit of the early immigrant settlers.

Judge Hawlin went on to say that: "The reality of a church was finally to take shape and materialize. Contributions were solicited for renovations; the church took shape and form. A request was made to the Greek Consul Dimitri Botassis of New York City to secure a priest. Patiently the settlers waited to hear the hymnology of the Orthodox worship. It wasn't until the early month of April in 1865 that Reverend Agapius Honcarenko (1832-1916) from Greece arrived in New Orleans. Through his ministry Orthodoxy was to begin extending its rays throughout our great land teach-

160

ing the true principles of Christian worship. Here was to begin the first established congregation to have a continuous existence." The construction of the First Greek Orthodox Church in the New World—a small, inconspicuous wooden church, located at 1222, Dorgenois Street, in New Orleans—begun late in 1866, and the inaugural services were held there only in July 1867. The church remained in use for approximately 83 years; then in April 12, 1950, it was demolished and a new church was erected adjacent to the original site.

One wonders if the first "wooden" church should not have been kept intact as a monument, which would have not only reminded the Greek Orthodox of their first House of Worship in the United States but would also have been part of America's historic wealth. For the Greeks it would have been a constant reminder of their humble first steps in the western hemisphere, and for the Americans an evidence of the religious and ethnic diversity of its population. Curiously enough the Greeks, who at home are struggling to preserve the past and its ruins, were, in the case of the New Orleans church, eager to erase the past by building a new, spacious church, obviously in the belief that such an imposing edifice would automatically improve their position within the American environment. The urge for larger, richer churches all over the United States has never abandoned the Greek-Americans. "Until the turn of the century this little New Orleans church remained as the lone beacon and solitary outpost of Greek Orthodoxy in the Americas. With great effort and even perhaps with divine intervention it somehow miraculously managed to survive until the commencement of Greek immigration in the late 1890's salvaged it from certain extinction." (Peter T. Kourides, in his address delivered at the closing Centennial Observance in New Orleans, on October 15, 1965).

In considering the necessary efforts to build the First Greek Orthodox Church in America, it is to be noted that those who built it were men without education and with very little money; yet they were fanatically resolute that their church, and through it their heritage, might be somewhat maintained in the New World. They also became an example for those who came later, found a place to worship, and gradually were animated by the same feelings of respect and devotion to their tradition and their religion, as they spread throughout the immense vastness of the United States, building their churches and their schools.

161

Greek Numerical Strength in America

THE United States Constitution went into effect in 1788. When the Bill of Rights was made part of the Constitution in the year 1791, the first article thereof, known as the First Amendment, provided for the freedom of religion. The founders of the young and vigorous country were determined that those who were fleeing religious persecutions in their own countries, would have freedom to pray in the United States, along with freedom to speak or print—rights which they had been denied in their native lands.

In his address, during the Greek Orthodox Centennial in New Orleans in 1965, Judge Walter Hawlin of Louisiana said:

> Only seventy-three years after the adoption of the first amendment to our Constitution, and I refer to the year 1864, Orthodoxy, which now totals to over four million souls in America, started from this parish. The Greek Orthodox Cathedral of the Holy Trinity in New Orleans is the first established Church of Eastern Orthodox Faith in the Western Hemisphere. And when we take time to think of it, this total of four million is a tremendous phenomenon. It is a substantial part of the heterogeneous nature of our population and religions. Our nation is unique and different because of our mixed population and religions.

It is not possible either to deny or to confirm the accuracy of the figure of four million "souls" attributed by Judge Walter Hawlin to Orthodoxy in the New World. However, whether contested or accepted, the figure does not refer, in its totality, to the Greek Orthodox in the United States, but rather to all Orthodox in America regardless of their ethnic provenance.

It has been already said that the exact numbers of the Greek-Americans will never be known and the reasons were more or less explained. Nobody can say precisely how many are the Greek immigrants in the United States who actually were born in Greece, or whose maternal tongue is Greek, and how many are their children who were born in America. Neither the figures of the Census nor those of the Greek Orthodox parishes or, for that matter, of any organizations can be considered as absolutely accurate. On the other hand, the Greek-Americans like to speak about one or two million of them being in the United States but the gap between one and two million in their rather frequent references serves only to illustrate the absence of official, precise figures. The Greek Orthodox Church of North and South America also speaks about one million and a half of Greek Orthodox or Greek-Americans but there is no way of knowing how close the figure is to reality.

It is important to bear in mind that the Census of 1940 included among the so-called "foreign stock" only the first immigrants (born in their own country) and their children born in the United States. Since 1940, the third and successive generations of any ethnic group have not been comprised in any official Census because these generations were regarded as 100 percent assimilated.

In his book *Ellines Tis Amerikis, 1528-1949* (New York, 1949) Babis Malafouris writes that: "People of Greek origin in the United States are on the increase while the number of the immigrants born in Greece is continuously decreasing . . . According to the 1940 Census the total number of people (foreign stock) of Greek ancestry in the United States was 362,672, out of which 163,252 were born in Greece, and 163,420 in the United States—this figure, however, did not include the third generation."

It is obvious that after the year 1940, it becomes impossible to evaluate the exact numbers of the Greek-Americans, since officially they have been incorporated in the total figure of the overall population of the United States. However, the population of America has steadily increased since 1940 and it is fair to assume that the percentage of Americans of Greek descent—third and successive generations—has also increased proportionally.

Though the assessment of the exact numerical strength of the Greek-Americans might be of considerable interest from an historical point of view, what is extremely important is to follow their course within the main stream of American life, since it is this course that will determine what will become of Hellenism, in one form or another, in the United States.

It is interesting to notice, for instance, that the percentage of illiterate Greek-Americans is smaller than the percentage of illiterates in Greece itself. Inasmuch as the first Greek immigrants in the United States came from the usually ignorant agricultural classes one has to come to the conclusion that the educational improvement of the Greek-Americans is without any doubt due to the influence of the higher cultural level of the American environment.

In regard to the capability of the Greek to learn English—the official language of his adopted country—the figures show unfortunately that he is not—contrary to what is believed the first among other immigrants to have captured the language. According to official statistics the Greeks come after the Danes, Swedes, Germans, French, Roumanians, Russians and Czechoslovaks and ahead of the Turks, Armenians, Yugoslavs, Poles, Italians and Portuguese.

Another interesting aspect of Greek immigration to the United States is the fact that although the first Greek immigrants were in their great majority farmers, laborers and shepherds they chose to live in American cities and were employed in a variety of professions or jobs. Only a very small percentage of them were employed on farms.

The following figures are characteristic of this contrast between the original occupations of the Greek immigrants in their homeland and the type of work they did once in the United States.

Nationality	Farmers	
Germans	30	percent
Scandinavians	19	,,
British-Irish	12	,,
Russians	5	,,
Poles	4,8	,,
Czechoslovaks	5	,,
Italians	3	,,
Dutch	2.5	,,
Swiss	2	,,
French	1.1	,,
Yugoslavs	0.8	,,
Roumanians	0.4	,,
Greeks	0.1	,,

It appears as though the first Greek immigrants had come to the United States in the hope of doing something different from what they were doing in their country among unsurmountable problems and difficulties. They also came with the ardent desire to become affluent as far as possible—and farming did not seem to offer such an opportunity.

This explains perhaps why people who had lived and worked in the fields or the rugged mountains of Greece, chose to be florists, waiters, shoeblacks, etc. Naturally, a number of first immigrants were extremely successful—and rather rapidly, in various larger and different enterprises—but they were the exception and not the rule.

A rather peculiar aspect of the first Greek immigration to the United States is that the Greeks, at least during the first twenty or thirty years, remained convinced bachelors, and according to statistics showed the highest percentage of unmarried men among all other ethnic groups. This, of course, did not help either in the formation of Greek families or in the increase of the Greek race as a whole. The Greek men among the first immigrants did not want to marry because they wanted to wed only Greek girls, who were not available in the United States since the original exodus of the Greeks to the New World was an immigration of men. Moreover, the Greek immigrants considered their presence in America only temporary and therefore carefully avoided contracting any ties or obligations in that country, which at that time they had not yet finally adopted as their second fatherland.

Finally, the geographical distribution of the Greek immigrants all over the United States is typical of the wandering mood of the Greek. According to Professor Vassilios G. Valaoras *(The Hellenism of the United States*, Athens, 1937) this geographical distribution of the Greeks is "the result of the lack of a spirit of collaboration with other compatriots and an exaggerated belief in the individual —characteristics which have been (responsible for) diffusing modern as well as ancient Greeks, to all the countries of the world. Anyway ... this diffusion (of the Greeks) contributed to a faster adjustment to the heterogeneous environment of the United States and, at the same time, gave birth to many Greek nucleuses throughout the immense land in the best interest of the individual but also of the national goals towards which Greek immigration was aiming at from the very beginning."

One is forced to accept only part of Professor Valaoras' conclusions. If the goal towards which Greek immigration was aiming was the return to Greece at the earliest possible date, then the "faster adjustment" did not serve the best interest of the "national goals." On the other hand, the "diffusion" of the first Greek immigrants throughout the United States does not seem to have been a factor, which might have activated the tempo of their assimilation. To the contrary it seems that wherever they were, either as isolated individuals or as very small groups, the Greek immigrants remained as far as possible from actual participation in the American way of life and even avoided contacts with Americans, probably out of fear or perhaps some sort of inferiority complex. Wherever there was no "isolation" assimilation was easier or faster—but then again we have to bear in mind that when we talk about assimilation of the first generation of Greeks in America, we are speaking about something that in reality has never happened.

The Political Problems
of Greece "Transplanted"

T HERE was something genuinely Hellenic—less valuable but more powerful than a handful of Greek earth—that the first immigrants had not forgotten to bring along with them to America. The perennial disunity of the Greeks had automatically crossed the Atlantic together with the early expatriate.

Regardless of their social origin or their intellectual background all Greeks have an innate passion for politics; an instinctive interest and devotion either for the government in power in the mother country or for the opposition, which bides time until things change in its favor. The shepherds, farmers, or laborers from Epirus, Thessaly, and elsewhere, were no exception to the rule. Thus from the very beginning the adopted country was no obstacle to the promotion of a small Greek civil war within a foreign land, whenever the occasion would arise. And there were many unfortunate opportunities for the Greeks to quarrel and to fight among themselves for political reasons.

Thus Professor Theodore Saloutos (*The Greeks in the United States*) writes:

> The Greek-Americans found it quite impossible to divorce themselves from the internal politics of the mother country. This was inevitable, since they had been in the United States for only a few years and many had planned to return as soon as circumstances warranted. Being people with strong political inclinations, they organized themselves into rival factions; both sides issued propaganda, held public rallies, and denounced each other with passion. Both sides attempted to influence American foreign policy towards Greece ...

It is the fact that the Greeks are people with strong political inclinations that should rather be considered exclusively responsible for the divisions among the Greek-Americans—an inescapable result of the dissensions existing in Greece itself. The contention that the Greeks could not divorce themselves from the politics of the mother country because they had been in the United States only for a very short time does not seem valid. Today, almost a century after the first arrivals of the Greeks in America, they are still deeply divided over politics in Greece. On April 21, 1967, when a military regime was established in Greece, once again, the Greek-Americans found themselves tragically divided—with a clear majority, however, siding with the regime.

Every political crisis, every revolution or military coup in Greece has split the Greek-Americans into two hostile camps. The deep hatred prevailing among the feuding factions in Greece was felt by the Greek-Americans—sometimes with more violence and more absurdity than in Greece itself. There could be no better evidence that these first immigrants were the direct descendants of the Hellenes and the genuine brothers of those fighting against one another in the old country. No wonder over the years all Greek Governments, as well as all their opponents, never ceased to regard the Greek-Americans as native Greeks temporarily residing abroad. "Some people considered the Greek population of the United States a psychological and cultural, if not an organic, part of the Greek nation," states Saloutos in *The Greeks in the United States*. Nobody could believe, and still does not believe, in Greece that there could ever be a conflict between race and nationality among the Greek-Americans—and, as a matter of fact, there has never been one.

It is during the First World War that Greece lived through a most tragic division of her modern history. King Constantine favored neutrality but—the pro-allied Eleftherios Venizelos—one of the greatest statesmen that Greece has ever had, negotiated an agreement with the allies, to land troops in Salonica, where, in 1916, he formed his own revolutionary government. Greece entered the war in 1917, but the country was tragically divided and royalists and liberals (Venizelos' followers and supporters) were at each other's throats. The repercussions of this division (which in reality amounted to a civil war) among the Greeks in the United States were perhaps without any precedent in the annals of the history of any ethnic group living in a foreign land.

The communities, the individuals, but also the churches, were divided. To some people Christ was either royalist or liberal, according to their own preferences and convictions. Fanaticism led to ugly scenes within the American environment, which did not help enhance the image of the Greek-American.

Fuel was added to the existing fire by the two opposing newspapers. Theodore Saloutos writes that "The royalist and Venizelist factions in the United States were quick to assert themselves. *Atlantis* lost little time in making known its royalist preferences... The first major Venizelist broadside in the United States was fired by the *National Herald,* which started to appear as a daily on April 2, 1915. Its publisher and editor-in-chief, as noted, were Petros Tatanis, a merchant of moderate wealth, and Demetrios Callimachos. Both came from the "unredeemed" portions of Greece. Earlier challengers of the *Atlantis* had been motivated more by personal ambitions to obtain a foothold in the Greek journalistic world of the United States. But this latest challenger of *Atlantis* was inspired by its own set of principles and, as a result, succeeded where the others had failed."

It is extremely difficult to state precisely how many Greek-Americans were with King Constantine and how many with Venizelos. Both sides claimed to hold a majority. However, it is true that the sequence of events in Greece itself, with Venizelos forming his own government at the side of the allies, impressed many Greek immigrants. Finally, when the United States entered the war against the Germans and their allies the percentage of the Venizelists must have been substantially augmented.

On October, 21, Venizelos, fully aware of the role that the Greek-Americans could play in influencing American public opinion and therefore the United States Government, sent the following message to supporters in New York:

> We wish to express our warmest thanks and appreciation to all organizers and collaborators who took part in the great national rally... and for the courageous expression of an undying patriotism. We congratulate the worthy Greeks of America and their heroic representatives who toil with honor and dignity. You are living in a great land where you enjoy individual and social freedom, feeling, however, as Greeks and as residents of the United States cognizant of your objections to a nation proud of its past and concerned over its future... Pursue your efforts with care... support our military organization... establish a treasury... for the support of the families of our soldiers.

An event which deeply impressed the Greek-Americans in favor of the liberals in Greece was the excommunication of Eleftherios Venizelos. In 1916, the then Archbishop of Athens, Theoclitus, decided to inflict punishment on Venizelos by performing the "medieval rite." Although it sounds unbelievable, it did happen and the hierarch helped by some bishops representing the royalists chanted: "Cursed be Eleftherios Venizelos who imprisoned priests, who plotted against the King and his country"—and each participant did not fail to shout "Cursed he be, and cast a stone upon the cairn." (The newspaper *California,* January 6, 1917.) All over the United States the divided Greek-Americans quarrelled and even struggled in hand-to-hand fightings whenever they met in force, either during parades or in rallies.

In the Orthodox Churches—royalist as well as Venizelist—the priests preached political sermons according to their own political inclinations and those of their parishes. Each faction accused the other of "disloyalty to the Greek cause, stupidity, and base motives." (*Ibid.,* February 1917.)

Curiously enough when the United States entered First World War in 1917, the Greek-Americans unanimously supported the American war effort but never forgot their own differences and in the basement of some churches fist fights were reported. The American Press was unanimous in criticising their behavior. The prestige of the first Greek immigrants had never sunk so low. Moreover, Greek Orthodoxy, and as a result the Greek Orthodox Church in America, received irreparable blows from which it took years of patient efforts to recover.

The Second
Greek-American Generation

THE second Greek-American generation seems to have had, at least from a psychological point of view, a harder time than the first immigrants, though for different reasons. It occupies a very special place in the development of Hellenism in America, because in a way it has been a sort of intermediary, evolutionary element between the original, rather primitive source and the generation following it. It is animated by more sophisticated motives and has already scored more impressive achievements.

While the adaptation of the parents of children born in the United States was conditioned upon their capability or their willingness to accept assimilation, their children were automatically a genuine, inherent part of the American environment, both physically and intellectually. However, how American could these children be or feel with their parents still deeply attached to Greek traditions and customs, which in many instances—if not in all instances—were strikingly different from American habits? These children were brought up between two different worlds and they did not always know to which one they belonged.

In 1930, of the 303,751 residents who were of Greek ancestry, 129,225 were born in the United States. This generation born of Greek parents in America, has grown rapidly. It was 9 percent of the total Greek population in 1910, 23 percent in 1920, and 43 percent in 1930. Today, it has reached, without any doubt, 75 percent—if not more—of the total Greek population. Moreover, this second generation is already producing its offspring—another type of Greek-American.

The second generation of Greek-Americans was subjected to unbelievable pressures which very often were tantamount to psychological torture and presented tremendous problems of loyalty. Theodore Saloutos (*The Greeks in the United States*) writes:

> The early years in the lives of children born of immigrant parents were hardly joyous ones, for they were exposed to the realities of life at a tender age. They heard parents and their

friends tell of their hardships in Greece and the early years in the United States, the unemployment, discrimination, and difficulties with the language. They were told in clear and often blunt language that their principal purpose in life was not to have fun, but to work, take advantage of the opportunities denied their parents, assume responsibilities, make a success of themselves, see their sisters happily married, and provide for their parents in old age. All children did not abide by this regimen, but it was the kind of rhetoric to which almost all were exposed.

On the other hand, these children who were going to American schools and who had American friends, were gradually becoming aware that none of these strict requirements were imposed upon their friends. They wanted to be accepted by a society to which they belonged by the right of birth and also because they were convinced it was a better world in which to live. They resented the severe, at times incomprehensible, admonitions of their parents, of the Orthodox priests and of their teachers—if they happened to attend Greek schools. It was impossible for them to understand that while they were born in the "land of the free" they were supposed to lose their freedom by abiding by the traditions of the parents. What they also failed to comprehend was why their parents who had lived in a state of half slavery and total ignorance wanted their children to follow their path. The fact that their parents insisted they should have an education never calmed their fears and never eliminated their suspicions that something was wrong with their parents, with the Orthodox Church and even with Greece.

In his book *Ellines Tis Amerikis, 1528–1948* (New York 1948), Babis Malafouris writing about the problems of the second Greek-American generation says that if the adaptation to the American environment of foreign-born Greeks and of immigrants of other nationalities presented difficulties and contradictions, the problem of adaptation of the second generation was even more difficult and more complex. He says that born in America, the children of the immigrants were Americans but very often their contact with the Greek environment inflicted deep psychological, emotional wounds because they were often the object of discrimination and scorn on the part of other ethnic groups with deeper roots in America. This, Malafouris contends, was a problem faced not only by the children of the second Greek-American generation. It was a problem with which all the children of all immigrants who had come to

America during the first decades of the 20th century were confronted with. These children attributed the discriminations against them to the fact that they still kept many of the habits of their parents or of the ethnic group to which they belonged.

It was unavoidable that these children—including the second Greek-American generation—would develop a profound dislike for whatever was related to the customs of their parents. They were in a hurry to eradicate any influence of their origin and many of them did not like Greece either. Their main goal, as they came into closer contact with American reality, was to enjoy to the fullest the American way of life. Naturally, they did not show any eagerness to attend Greek schools or to listen to their parents' annoying scolding. It is indeed surprising that the second Greek-American generation did not drift totally away from all things "hellenic" but gradually managed to keep a happy equilibrium between myth and reality without losing its own particular characteristics. Still the second Greek-American generation can be described as a "moment" in the evolution of Hellenism in America, which had been deeply wounded because of the problems arising from uncertainties and pressures from two different directions.

It must be added that the attitude of the second Greek-American generation towards Greece changed considerably when the Greeks scored an unexpected victory over the Italians at the beginning of the Second World War. The change of their attitude coincided with different views adopted by the American public opinion as a whole towards Greece. Moreover, after the war frequent visits to Greece helped the Greek-Americans of the second generation realize that the country no longer fitted the picture made of her by their parents. They found a modern country with an emancipated youth very similar to American youth.

Taking into consideration the problems that the second Greek-American generation had to face (especially teen-agers) one must come to the conclusion that its participation in the professional and intellectual life of the United States is most certainly impressive. Today there are innumerable doctors, lawyers, engineers, artists, whose parents came from the rugged mountains and the sterile plains of Greece, and who never stopped telling them that only the Hellenic world was worthy of their attention and their devotion. The second Greek-American generation succeeded also in keeping away from political issues regarding Greece, except perhaps in moments of serious crisis—and this is another achievement.

The Greek Language Press

T
HE Greek language press in America together with the
Greek Orthodox Church were natural influences, which could
and should have directed and shaped the thinking and the
attitude of the Greek immigrants within the American environment. A close collaboration between the Church and the press
was, therefore, indispensable but the nature of such collaboration
has always presented a number of problems mainly because the
church often wished to assume a privileged, leading role in a task
which pertained to a great extent to the Greek-American press.
On the other hand, the press as a whole, and in many instances,
expected more substantial help from the church.

It seems that from the very beginning the objectives of the Greek
language press were dual: the Greek immigrants had to be influenced in preserving the Greek language, the Greek traditions and
the closest possible contacts with the mother country. They also
had to be acquainted with the ways and habits and the requirements
of their adopted fatherland. Whether this second objective was ever
attained is debatable. The Greek language press faced from the
very first moments of its appearance enormous economic and tech-
nical problems, and it really never enjoyed the full support of the
Greek-American community though the immigrants were eager
to be informed about what was going on in Greece and in their
communities. Such support was necessary, but one is forced to
doubt whether the immigrants understood the magnitude of the
task undertaken by the Greek-American press on their behalf;
and some of its failures must most certainly be attributed to the
indifference shown by the Greek-American community as a whole.
The immigrants seemed to demand everything in return for nothing
—or indeed very little. Ignorance had never helped to fully realize
the role of the media of communication, and the improvement of
their quality depends on the economic assistance they are entitled
to in order to fulfil their mission. A newspaper is a financial enterprise but it is also a voice on behalf of the people and a

forum which they can use to express their own opinions. In other works, it is a two-way project.

In his book *The Greeks in the United States* Professor Theodore Saloutos has hard words in connection with the first Greek language press. He writes:

> It (the Greek language press) kept the immigrant with little or no knowledge of English in contact with happenings in the homeland, perpetuated Old World feuds and gave rise to new ones...This kind of personal journalism got off to a quick start in the United States, even though newspapers with broader issues were also published. Newspapers, however, did appear for the sole purpose of attacking or praising certain individuals, of exploiting the weaknesses, prejudices, or petty vanities of the naive. Men presuming to be editors wrote vituperative articles against a particular individual, showed these handwritten pieces to rivals of the attacked man, received from them the cost of the newsprint or the salary of the typesetter, and then printed the articles as "newspapers."

Elsewhere Professor Theodore Saloutos states that: "There were newspapers engaged in personal journalism of another variety, less venal but equally pointless. Usually having a handful of subscribers, they wrote two and three-column articles about the wedding of some person, with laudatory accounts of the bride and groom and numerous other details; or they ascended to unbelievable heights in praising the deeds of some local society or organization. And there were newspapers which on one day would heap praises on Mr. X, calling him a merchant, a man of eminence, a friend of the people, and a patriot and on the next would denounce him as a nonentity, a traitor, an illiterate, and a bootblack."

Unfortunately, though the quality of the Greek-American press has improved since the first days of its original appearance, the silly habit of unbelievable laudatory accounts of weddings, christenings during which "the best priest in the country" baptizes "the most extraordinary and the most beautiful baby'" of the Greek race or descriptions of the qualities and the achievements of any old immigrant who has passed away, continue to fill the columns of some newspapers. These "tales" occupy valuable space, which could have been used for better purposes.

Whether the newspapers are solely responsible for these accounts is doubtful since most of their subscribers insist on being ridiculously described to other readers. Some of these descriptions are indeed pathetic. However, were these utterly distasteful accounts of social events, of tremendous deeds of certain individuals or successful performances of some organizations to disappear, those interested in reading these absurdities would probably discontinue their subscriptions.

This unfortunate situation shows the degree of indifference and ignorance, and also a degree of human vanity, that exist over the real purpose of the news media and explains why in the case of the Greek language, its quality is in no proportion to the years of its publication. The newspapers had to compromise and they still do, between quality, taste and their own survival.

The Greek language press still represents the sentiments of the older generation, which wanted and still wants to read in print real or imaginary accounts about its achievements and never a single word about an eventual failure. Thus it seems that the Greek-Americans have imposed a sort of censorship on their own newspapers, which has been detrimental both to them and to the real purpose and progress of the Greek language press. Glancing through these special columns one gets the impression that the Greek-American community is a paradise where only angels with supernatural qualities and powers live—the phoniness of such a paradise escapes only the self-appointed "angels."

The birth, the existence, and some sort of continuation of the Greek language press, was not only a normal, natural phenomenon but a necessity for the Greek-American community. It is indeed too bad that the members of this community did not always realize the proper role that such a press could have played in improving their knowledge and in facilitating their gradual adjustment to the requirements of American life without departing from its primary objectives: the perpetuation of the Greek language, religion and tradition. They saw the Greek language press through a very narrow prism and as an instrument they thought they should use only for their own personal interests and petty quarrels.

Before 1900, the few thousands of Greek immigrants who had already settled in the United States had gathered in certain cities and lived in their own, separate sections of every town they had chosen to make their home. Whether consciously or unconsciously they had created Greek ghettos. Theirs was a life of isolation from American influence. As a matter of fact, such an influence was considered by most immigrants a mortal enemy against which they wanted to put up a fierce fight. They thought that by erecting their own ghettos and by presenting a strong numerical appearance they had found the best deterrent against the process of assimilation.

In these efforts on the part of the first Greek immigrants to stay away as much as possible from whatever was American, except the dollar, lies one of the paradoxes of evolution—but obviously not of immigration. The first immigrants had left Greece, where the prevailing, precarious conditions did not permit them to live a decent life. They had crossed the Atlantic to come to America— penniless, some hungry and barefoot and after a number of years of hardships a new, different, better life was smiling at them. Yet, there was even hostility towards the United States among some of these expatriates. It took years before the original hostility due to psychological reasons, changed into a gratitude much deserved by their adopted country.

The Greeks who had gathered in the same cities and towns all over America did not know English. Gradually they became more and more interested in what the future would be for them and in what other Greek immigrants elsewhere were doing. Moreover, as time went by they were becoming more nostalgic about Greece— and nostalgia can be treated only through a contact with the source that provokes it. This was an opportune moment for the publication of a Greek newspaper.

It seems that the first newspaper printed in the Greek language in the United States was *The New World*, which appeared in Boston in 1892. It did not last very long. Its editor was Constantine Fasoularides, who had studied in Constantinople and had worked with the Greek newspaper *Neologos*. In the United States, Fasoularides attended the Massachussetts Institute of Technology. Fasoularides' short lived experiment was to be followed by many other ventures in the field of publication. The mortality rate of the Greek language newspapers, was high, but so was the rate of their fecundity. Frequent "births" but also frequent "deaths" proved only that no one had as yet tried to print a serious newspaper capable of attracting the interest of the Greek-American community.

George C. Vournas (*Greeks in America,* Congressional Record Proceedings and Debates of the 86th Congress, Second Edition) writes that: "It appears that the first newspaper printed in the Greek language in the United States was the *New World,* first appearing in Boston, Mass. It was short lived. After that, many have been the newspapers that have been published in many sections of the United States—some living weeks; others, months, and others

for years. The major portion of them were weekly newspapers ...
many weekly, bi-weekly, or monthly magazines have appeared here
and there from time to time in Chicago, New York, Detroit, Boston
and San Francisco ...."

There are no complete statistics regarding the activities of all Greek
language newspapers and magazines, which were ever printed in
the United States from the early days of the mass immigration of
the Greeks to America. Even Seraphim Canoutas limited himself
to enumerating most of them. Dr. Demetrios Callimachos, a priest-
journalist, is perhaps the only one who in a series of articles
published in the *National Herald,* in 1955, tried to analyse the
role, the objectives and the achievements of the Greek language
press in the United States.

The only available statistics regarding the foreign language newspapers printed in the United States including the Greek language
press are those which were gathered by the Common Council for
American Unity. These statistics, which were published in 1943,
are far from accurate, moreover, since that date there have been
numerous Greek language publications, most short lived, which
were never comprised in any official statistics.

In his book *Ellines Tis Amerikis, 1528-1948,* Babis Malafouris writes
that "all the Greek newspapers of the United States—those which
do no longer appear and those which are still published—are the
following (by order of the date of appearance):

1892 *Neos Kosmos* (Boston).
1894 *Atlantis* (New York).
1900 *Thermopylae* (New York).
1902 *Hellas* (New York).
1903 *Greek Star* (Chicago).
1905 *Simaia* (New York), *Sanita* (Chicago).
1906 *Paraxenos* (New York), *Athena* (Chicago).
1907 *Ethniki* (Boston).
1908 *California* (San Francisco).
1909 *Frouros* (New York).
1911 *Satyros* (New York).
1912 *Diaplasis Efivon* (Chicago).
1913 *Thessalonike* (Chicago).
1915 *National Herald* (New York).
1916 *Chronos* and *Hellas* (San Francisco).
1917 *Dimokratia* (Boston).
1918 *Anorthosis* (Boston).

1920 *Ethniki Anagennisis* (New York), *Nea Zoi* (Chicago).

1921 *Ekklisiastikos Kirix* (New York).

1922 *Kosmos* (Washington), *Kathimerini* (Chicago).

1923 *Embros* (New York).

1924 *Tahydromos, Proodos, Estia* (Chicago).

1927 *Vima* (Detroit).

1928 *To Vima* (Atlanta, Georgia).

1931 *Kosmos* (Los Angeles), *Athenae* (Detroit).

1932 *Stentor* (Pittsburgh).

1933 *Neon Vima* (New York).

1934 *Orthodox Observer* (New York), the official organ of the Greek Archdiocese.

1938 *O Estiator* (New York), *Hellenic World* (Boston.

1939 *Athenae* (Boston).

1940 *The Hellenic Spectator* (Washington).

1941 *Greek-American Volume* (New York).

1942 *Ergatis Thalassis* (New York).

1943 *Eleftheros Typos* (New York).

1944 *Anexartitos Epitheorisis* (New York).

1945 *Ethnikos Frouros* (Chicago), and *Life of Greece* (Boston).

This list is far from being complete. Since 1945, however, there were few additions to the existing Greek language newspapers or magazines—and some of those who came to life for a very short period are perhaps not worth mentioning. Moreover, in recent years there has been a tendency to publish newspapers in English, in order to reach the second and third Greek-American generation. Some of them were extremely successful—like the *Hellenic Chronicle* and the *Greek Sunday News,* Boston—both weekly. One should perhaps draw a valuable lesson from the success of these newspapers printed only in the English language but full of news regarding the activities of the Greek-American community and also some aspects of life in Greece itself.

All writers who have studied the evolution and the activities of the Greek language press in the United States will agree that the history of this press is indeed the story of the two Greek dailies of New York—the *Atlantis* and the *National Herald.* The first has been appearing for seventy-seven years and the other for sixty-one. This is quite a record if one takes into consideration the economic difficulties faced by the press, the lack of trained, competent, professional journalists and the indifference coupled with a complete misinterpretation of the real role that such a press could have played in the life and progress of the Greek-Americans.

Christian Xanthopoulos Palamas—former Greek Ambassador to the United Nations (and later to Washington)—in an address delivered at the Auditorium of the Fashion Institute of Technology in New York (January 30, 1960), speaking about the Greek-American press had this to say:

> We speak very often about the Greek press in America. The periodical, but above all the daily press. And we all agree that Greek press is the daily Greek breath of the *omogenia* (the Greek-Americans), however, what is of a substantial interest is the account of the facts. How many Greek papers did we buy during the year that went by? How many did we read, what place did we give in our home to the *National Herald* and to the *Atlantis*, and to the other known Greek newspapers? This is the responsible account we owe to ourselves and to Greece.

Atlantis was first published in March 3, 1894, by Solon J. Vlastos, who was born on the island of Syros in August 1852. He arrived in New York in 1873. In 1904, the *Atlantis* became a daily. As Saloutos states, "The paper attributed much of its early success to the interest of Americans in the Greek language and the affairs of Greece. It made periodic references to John Stuart Mill, Lord Dufferin, John Stuart Blackie, and teachers of modern languages who believed that to teach Greek in the schools was to begin at the wrong end: 'It is only through the living and spoken Greek that the ancient can be mastered.' Some American colleges used the paper for reading exercises; special subscription rates were given clergymen, professors and students. But in the long run the success of the *Atlantis* may be attributed to the patronage of the immigrants."

Early in 1915, the *Atlantis* got its first real competition, the *National Herald (Ethnikos Kiryx)*, which immediately opposed royalism and neutralism and showed liberal ideas as opposed to the conservative views preconized by the *Atlantis.*

Professor Saloutos writes that: "The paper (*National Herald*) quickly acquired the distinction of being more than a foe of the *Atlantis*. It came into existence at a crucial time in Greek-American history ... perhaps the most dedicated advocate of Greek liberalism in the United States was Demetrios Callimachos, who served as the editor of the *National Herald* for twenty-seven years. Few editors could claim the wealth of experience and education that Callimachos brought with him to the United States (the *National Herald* was founded in 1915 by Petros Tatanis, born in Amalias, Greece). Born in "unredeemed" Thrace in 1879, he was educated in the three cultural centers of Hellenism, Constantinople, Smyrna and Athens. Trained as a clergyman he nevertheless spent most of his life in journalism, where he expounded his profound feelings with "apostolic fervor."

The role played by Demetrios Callimachos as a journalist and as a prominent figure in the affairs of Hellenism in America, is probably unique in the annals of the history of the Hellenes in the United States. His contribution to Greek-American journalism and to the promotion of liberalism among the first immigrants in America, has been invaluable and he most certainly stands out as an extraordinary personality, which has left its imprint on the vast field of his activities.

In his book *Demetrios Callimachos—Mia Artia Agonistiki Syneidisi* (*D. Callimachos-A Genuine Fighting Conscience*, Athens, 1963), Sifis G. Kollias writes that "D. Callimachos has been without any interruption a volcanic human being. The ardent fighter was also an ardent orator. He always spoke from the surplus of his heart and this is why he captivated and moved his audiences."

D. Ch. Christoforidis in his book *I Elliniki Dimosiografia os Istorikon Didagma kai os Synhronos Koinoniki Anangi* (*Greek Journalism as an Historical Institution and as a Modern Social Necessity*) writes: "Callimachos' religious sermon—whether written or spoken—interests religion as much as it interests literature ... it is life with the modern religious color, and it is religion with the modern color of life."

Writing about the two New York dailies, the *Atlantis* and the *National Herald*, Babis Malafouris (*Ellines Tis Amerikis, 1528-1948*) says that the *Atlantis*, through the exercise of a journalistic monopoly, which lasted for twenty years, imposed its views upon a great percentage of the Greeks in America; however, as it was to be expected its enemies tried repeatedly to express their own views through other publications, which they founded or financed ... however, they failed in their efforts and the life of these publications was of short duration. From 1915, the appearance of the *National Herald* led to a stubborn fight of extermination between the two dailies. The fight, which lasted almost continuously, resulted in dividing the Greeks in America into two fanatic camps and halted their progress. This conflict illustrated by passionate editorials, which often came down to personal quarrels, kept the

Greeks in a constant turmoil and without any doubt harmed the moral and material interests of the Hellenes in America. The result was that the two newspapers, as well as the Greek-language press in general, in America lost the esteem of a great percentage of the readership. It is true, Malafouris says, that Greek journalism in the first years of Greek immigration dealt more with the political problems of Greece and much less with the vital issues of the Greek immigrant.

This situation was perhaps unavoidable since the immigrants had brought with them to America their own fanaticism and division stemming from the political problems of the mother country.

The rivalry between the *Atlantis* and the *National Herald* (the first was published by Solon G. Vlastos, a nephew of the original founder, before it ceased publication in 1972, and the second by Babis Marketos) has taken a different form today but has not vanished altogether. The *Atlantis* stuck always to conservative views that brought the paper close even to the most "abnormal" political situations in Greece, while the *National Herald* follows a traditional liberal policy and has been presenting developments in Greece with commendable objectivity. It is fair to say that both papers had realized that a diminution of their own antagonism might be helpful in protecting, if not preserving, the unity of the Greek-American community. Whether this was achieved or not is another question.

The Greek-language press and the two New York dailies have been the target of violent criticism expressed even by their own readers; though some of this criticism might have been justified, the Greek-language press has rendered, and is still rendering, invaluable services to the Greek-American community. Without any doubt it helped maintaining the Greek language—though the quality of the language used, especially in the accounts of social events, has been far from satisfactory. Moreover, the two dailies, in spite of their constant antagonism served also as a sort of intermediary between the first Greek immigrants and their new environment. This role, however, was not always successfully fulfilled and the Greek-language press in America has probably neglected this particular aspect of its mission by assuming (together with the Greek Orthodox Church) the almost exclusive task of perpetuating Hellenism in the United States. I believe that one of its main concerns should have been to take into consideration what was also required of the immigrant as an American citizen.

The following figures show the growth and the fluctuation of the publications in Greek in America from 1900 to 1964:

Year	No. of publications	Dailies
1900	1	—
1909	—	1
1910	9	—
1914	—	2
1920	15	3
1923	—	—
1930	20	2
1934	15	—
1943	30	2
1958	—	2
1964	30	2

The Greek-language radio programs have also played a role mostly in entertaining the Greek-American audiences. The owners of the various radio programs have faced and are still facing the same economic difficulties encountered by the Greek-language press. This is one of the reasons the quality of the programs with some commendable exceptions has been of a very poor standard. However, here again, the responsibility seems to rest more with the peculiar exigencies of the audiences and the lack of sufficient sponsors, than with the owners of the programs who fought and still fight for survival.

It is extremely difficult to foresee the future of the Greek-language press in the United States. A lot depends on the attitude that the new immigrants from Greece will show to the Greek newspapers. On the other hand, this attitude will also depend on what the newspapers will have to offer the new immigrants—people of a much higher education than their predecessors in America. Moreover, the Greek newspapers published in Greece are reaching the United States within a few hours after publication—they represent a formidable competition for the Greek-language press in America, which has already been felt.

Finally, if the second, third and successive Greek-American generations have to be reached and initiated to Hellenism, ancient and modern, the Greek-language press—whether we like it or not—is not the best way for doing so.

The success scored by some weeklies published exclusively in English proves that the new Greek-American generations are interested in Greece and in Hellenism in general but would like to learn about it through their own language, which is English.

Again time can only tell what will happen with the Greek-language press in the United States—the press which is fighting a delaying action battle.

The Relationship
Between the Greek-Americans and Greece

G REECE has always looked upon its immigrants in the United States the way she had always looked upon Greek immigrants anywhere in the world: Greek citizens temporarily absent from the motherland. They were, therefore, considered capable of defending themselves against assimilation because they themselves believed they would return one day to Greece where they belonged. It was an enormous mistake that often led to serious misunderstandings and moreover never helped Greece to face the Greek-American reality; for the Greek State the Greek-Americans were just Greek citizens living abroad.

Every Greek official coming to the States would address a Greek-American audience and praise its achievements but also lament because of the continuing expatriation—as though the Greek immigrants had been "loaned" to America for a certain period of time. It has never been sufficiently understood in Greece that the power of absorption of the American environment could not be compared to any other similar influence anywhere else. It was also thought that because of the materialistic form of American civilization the Greek-Americans would be immune to such an influence. This fallacious belief was extended to the second and even to the third Greek-American generation. The extent of the absurdity often annoyed the native Americans and in some instances even the United States Government.

During the first years of the mass immigration of the Greeks to America the immigrant was indeed a temporary visitor who worked hard to save some money and go back to his village in Greece as soon as possible. Many of these first immigrants had not taken up American citizenship as a sort of guarantee of their eventual return to Greece. However, gradually the first immigrants decided to settle for good in the United States and their decision was accompanied by the necessity to become American citizens. Still in Greece the newly acquired American nationality was not considered valid and many Greek-Americans returning for a while to the old country were forced to join the Greek army although some of them had already served in the American Armed Forces. The second generation of Greek-Americans was not exempt from this rather strange requirement either.

Greece continued to believe that she had not only rights to influence the Greek-Americans but legal rights as well. In 1936, the then Prime Minister, John Metaxas, had decided to set up a Commission, which would have been entrusted to study all the issues related to the Greek living in North America and prepare a program of legal and other measures to "protect" the Greek-American community. The decision was indeed unbelievable. Here the Government of a foreign country—regardless of how friendly America might have been to Greece—was about to adopt legal measures in order to organize communities, churches and schools for Greeks who, however, had become United States citizens. Fortunately, the idea was abandoned due to some sound, last minute, reconsideration of the matter.

Many of the Greek officials either visiting or working in the United States have often misunderstood the purpose of their mission in America. There is a distinct difference between conveying a message from Greece to the Greek-Americans and telling them whom to accept or reject in Greece itself. Recently after a military regime was established in Greece (on April 21, 1967) some visiting officials have indulged in open propaganda in favor of the regime while proclaiming, on the other hand, that the Greek-American community should remain united and never get involved in Greek politics. Moreover, some of the Greek officials of the diplomatic corps have also misunderstood their task and have confused their duties.

The relationship between the diplomatic representation of Greece and the Greek-American community has always been of a very delicate nature—especially when political divisions in Greece were felt among the Greek-Americans the way they have always been felt, with deep emotion and even uncontrolled passion.

It is about time that the Greek State, regardless who might be in power, realizes that the Americans of Greek descent are American citizens. No other Government or any other foreign diplomatic representation in America has considered it its duty to influence politically those Americans whose parents or grandparents happened to have been born on the other side of the Atlantic.

The Urge for Repatriation

I T WAS already said that the dramatic story of the first Greek immigrants in America, which naturally begins in Greece itself, unfolds in the United States and in many instances—if not in all instances—ends in Greece. Only then is the historical cycle completed.

There has always been something passionate, at times incomprehensible, about this obsession for speedy return to the motherland, which has haunted the early Greek immigrant since his first steps on the American soil through the many years of his struggle to establish an identity. Inexorably attached to the idea of repatriation as though attracted by a formitable pulling force, immigration was a temporary "state of mind," a necessity, for the first Greek immigrant. It was a provisional condition, which, however, lasted an entire life.

It was among those immigrants who had been successful in America that the urge for repatriation seemed to be imperative—an incurable disease; they were perhaps in a hurry to go back to the motherland in order to show to their relatives how they had conquered the land on the other side of the Atlantic; some wished to return only to be able to use the money they had earned to improve the primitive villages where they were born. Those who had been less successful or who had entirely failed, those who did not meet the requirements for a triumphant return could not think of going back; theirs was a tragic destiny: the unbearable nostalgia was aggravated by the realization that the "return trip," like the original crossing of the Ocean, was only an illusory goal.

Repatriation, which is a sequence to immigration is, of course, a social phenomenon of a general nature. The Greeks were not the only ones among the other immigrant groups to repatriate themselves.

From 1908 to 1931, for example, a total of 4,077,262, immigrants of all nationalities returned to their native countries. Of the half million Greeks who had emigrated to the United States by 1931, only forty percent—or 197,000—returned to Greece. Since the process of repatriation has slowed down or has perhaps changed in form; because of the means of communication the Greek immigrants have an opportunity to visit Greece more often—once, and sometimes twice a year. Thus there is not enough room for exaggerated nostalgia.

A statistical breakdown of repatriation of first immigrants of all nationalities (Annual Report of the Commissioner General of Immigration, Fiscal Year ended June 30, 1931) reveals that the Greeks ranked fourth among the returning expatriates:

Immigrants Who Had Left the United States—1908-1931

Nationality	Number
Italians	1,240,884
Poles	339,428
English	201,081
Greeks	197,088
Germans	161,324
Magyars	156,019
Slovaks	132,763
Scandinavians	125,308
Croatians and Slovenians	118,129
Russians	115,188

As to the reasons why the first Greek immigrants wanted to return to Greece, Professor Theodore Saloutos (*They Remember America*) writes:

Among the repatriates were many who were simply fulfilling their original intention of returning home as soon as their economic status permitted. But these, as well as immigrants who had never contemplated a return journey, were impelled by differing reasons to leave the United States. Motives varied from person to person, from period to period. Often not a single motive, but a combination of circumstances, contributed to an immigrant's decision to go home.

Though there is no doubt that in many instances there was a more tangible prosaic motive behind the sentimental urge to return to Greece, one has to accept that the principal reason for repatriation was the motherland itself. Very few Greeks had forgotten the picturesque village, the parents left behind—a primitive life to which they had been accustomed and which they considered an inherent part of what Greece had always been for them: the land of gay poverty.

It is almost impossible to know the exact number of Greeks who repatriated to Greece—returned to the United States or settled again in the motherland. What is known is that many of them after having spent a few years or even only months in Greece, crossed again the Atlantic in the opposite sense to settle for good in an environment, which had helped them to progress. The extent of their progress had appeared greater when they visited Greece, to find out that the people they had left behind twenty, thirty, forty years ago had not improved. Their gratitude for America reached its peak.

Some of them had enormous difficulties in adjusting themselves to the Greek environment—especially if they had to live in Athens, where sophistication and even scorn reminded them of their first years of calvary in America, which they had, however, overcome. Very few had the courage to start a fight all over again. Moreover, it was one thing to fight the hostility of the native Americans and another to face the disdain of their own compatriots.

If we were to compare immigration and repatriation of the first Greeks in order to find out which of the two social phenomena attracted the immigrants more—though the first was a natural sequence of the second—we must conclude that it is immigration that proved—in many instances—less painful, than a repatriation attempt after many years in the United States of America. Sentimentality was not always strong enough to ignore reality. Moreover, it is always more difficult for one human being to immigrate twice in a lifetime than once. And the return trip to the motherland had often the characteristics of a new immigration.

In several instances the reasons that led to the repatriation of many of the first Greek immigrants were almost similar to those which had provoked the original wave of mass immigration of the Greeks to the United States. Only the numbers of the first immigrants and those of the repatriates differed substantially.

In 1907, the United States went through an economical crisis. The Greeks working in steel mines, tanneries or railroad constructions felt automatically the impact of the unexpected recession. A great number of them were discharged so that jobs could be secured for either naturalized or native-born American citizens. Prejudices and racial discrimination are familiar products of our society.

Thus several thousands Greek immigrants started leaving for the motherland. The accounts of these new misfortunes appeared both in the Greek-American press and the Greek press at home with the usual, unavoidable exaggerated tone. Moreover, those among the first Greek immigrants who managed to return home "often dramatically corroborated these tales of hardship with firsthand accounts, sometimes highly colored to attract sympathy and thus compensate for their misfortunes." (Saloutos, *They Remember America.*)

Greek chauvinism was mostly responsible for the dramatization of the situation.

A striking example is offered in the following description of some of the returning immigrants to their fatherland in the newspaper *Panhellenios,* August 6, 1908:

> Yesterday morning the Austro-American Liner, *Laura,* arriving from New York docked in Patras where 150 Greek immigrants disembarked from the land of gold. We met many of the returned ones who gave us a melancholy picture of conditions among the Greeks there. Some who have been established in America for some time have the necessary means to support themselves, but those among the later arrivals have been faring rather poorly. The others returned with money sent by relatives, or by barely scraping together the necessary funds. They assured us that there are many thousands of Greeks who wish to return to their homes, but do not have the means. And not only because of this, because if they returned they would have greater difficulties since they sold what they had to go to America. Therefore they are compelled to remain there enduring hunger with the hope that conditions might improve. They are capable of returning but fear that if they did they would face economic disaster, especially if they learned that the economic crisis in America had ended. Others, including those who had returned, were overcome by panic and decided to return even though they would barely eat here (in Greece) and in America gold predominates. Employment opportunities are limited. Many are working on railroads in America, but because they continue to be railroaders in America, these people do not have steady work. They work there days and are laid off ten. Most of the employees have been exploited by various middle-men. The unbearable heat also affects them. Many have died from sunstroke. In general the returned portray the conditions among the immigrants in the United States as frightful.

These and other gloomy accounts of the life of the Greeks in the United States brought about a change in the immigration policy of the Greek Government. In 1907, the Minister of Foreign Affairs advised all nomarchs (prefects) of the "miserable" conditions that most of the first Greek immigrants in the United States had endured and asked them to discourage immigration.

There is very little doubt that most of these reports were highly exaggerated. Some of the accounts were dictated by psychological reasons; by some sort of complex, felt by these immigrants who had failed to establish themselves in America the way they had dreamed of and spoke about in the letters to their relatives left behind. Curiously enough not too much attention and even less publicity was given to the thousands of Greek immigrants who had been successful and who were continuing to send money back—an evidence of some prosperity.

There were as much doubts and uncertainties about repatriation as there had been about the original immigration to the United States. In reality a repatriated immigrant or a man about to return to his motherland after many years of absence, entered a new unknown adventure and some of the Greeks who returned to Greece faced the same problems and the same difficulties they had met when they had crossed the Atlantic in the opposite direction.

Who were these repatriates? They were mostly small businessmen, owners of second rate restaurants and luncheonettes but as a rule very few professional men (exept perhaps dentists); the latter had already settled rather comfortably in the United States. Sentimental reasons were not always strong enough to make repatriation a necessity.

Nostalgia had affected all the first Greek immigrants with, however, different degrees of pressure. Age probably also played a role in some of the decisions about repatriation. Those who many years ago had decided to come to America in search of a better future were at the time of their departure young men full of dreams, ambitions and of physical strength. Now, at the moment of indecision in regard to the eventual return to the motherland they had become adults with more experience—therefore with fewer dreams, and perhaps less physical endurance to go through new trials.

Greece as a whole, and more particularly the Greek provinces, owes a lot to these repatriates—these "Americans" as they will always be called even by their relatives when they return to the villages where they were born. Whether successful or failures they bring with them something from America, something which will help improve the environment in which they want to live from now on—unless they once again decide to cross the Ocean.

In many instances the repatriate will demolish the old house of his parents or grandparents not because he does not respect it—the Greeks always respect ruins, but because he wants to build it all over again. He wants it bigger. He has, now, after a prolonged stay in the United States, acquired a different conception about dimensions. His perspective of things has considerably changed; his horizon has larger frontiers—or no frontiers at all. From the house he will go to the field or the small factory in the area. There again he will bring some of the more advanced methods he learned in America. He knows how to exploit the earth through scientific means.

One will meet the former immigrant in the Peloponnesos—or for that matter anywhere else in the country. One will immediately recognize him. He is dressed differently and his conversation is a strange mixture of English and Greek—very often, if not always, quite inadequate. Indeed he needs time to forget what he has not learned in the United States: the language.

The repatriate is regarded as a wizard, a sort of financial demigod by some and by others a ridiculous "copy" of a man who is half of something and half of something else; for the latter these two halves never form an acceptable entity. The former immigrant brings to the village along with his nostalgia, which by now has changed into reality, his desire for work, the discipline he has respected in America. All he wanted was to be able to relive the dream—the myth he had kept intact in his mind. However, America has taught practicality and practicality is an enemy of the dream; he has to find a way to keep a happy equilibrium between myth and reality—between Greece and the United States. The task is not always easy but he is willing to try. He does not always succeed in going through his new experience. When he fails—which is quite often, then a new, different nostalgia burdens his thoughts. A new decision becomes indispensable. Once again he reaches a difficult moment in his life.

It was said that "once an immigrant always an immigrant"; for some of the first Greek immigrants who returned to Greece the dilemma was of enormous proportions. Not all of them were capable of taking the right decision, whether they stayed on or went back to America. At this rather late date in their lives any decision, whether positive or negative, could never be satisfactory.

Theodore Saloutos (*They Remember America*) writes:

> Possibly to enjoy a respite from tedious working conditions, or to regain their health in a salubrious climate, or to see again parents, many Greek-Americans went home for a brief visit, intending to return after a short time to the United States. A surprisingly large number of these visitors, however, became permanent residents of Greece.

Things have considerably changed. For one thing the parents of the first Greek immigrants are dead and for another the new means of transportation have abolished the distance between America and Greece; a nostalgia which can be satisfied within a few hours is no longer as imperative as it was in the days when the crossing of the Atlantic would take many days of an often painful voyage.

There are no statistics as to the exact numbers of the Greeks who returned to the motherland. Again Professor Saloutos offers in his book *They Remember America* some interesting data:

> Beginning July 1, 1907, the United States kept a record of all immigrant aliens departing for foreign lands. Although official records for earlier years are unavailable, it is believed that for some time the immigrant outflow had been about one-third of the inflow. According to the Trans-Atlantic Passenger Association, from 1899 to 1910 about thirty-seven steerage passengers left the United States for Europe for every hundred such passengers brought into the United States from Europe.
>
> During the early years, the number of Greek immigrant aliens leaving the United States fell considerably below the general average for all nationalities. Of the 88,205 Greeks admitted from 1908 to 1910, some 21,852, or about 25 percent, departed. . . . The number of Greek immigrants who reached the United States between 1908 and 1923 has been placed officially at 366,454. Of this total, 168,847 made the return trip to Greece with the intention of repatriating themselves. In other words, over the sixteen-year period about 46 percent declared their intention of returning to live in Greece, whereas 197,607, or 54 percent, indicated that they planned to remain in the United States.

It is necessary to point out that of all eastern Mediterranean people the Greeks were the least inclined to leave in spite of their evident nostalgia and the fact that most of them—if not all of them—had always dreamed and worked towards a "final" return to Greece.

Some of the repatriated played an important role in the opposition of Greece to the Italians and Germans during the occupation of Greece by the Fascists and Nazis. In his book *The Greek Trilogy* (London, 1945) British author W. Byford-Jones, had this to say about the role of the Greek-Americans (some 250) in the operations against occupants:

> Their task had been to stiffen the *Andartes* (the guerrillas) working in detachments of 24 men, with two officers, against exit railways such as those from Jannina-Agrinion, Lamia-Salonica, Lamia-Larisa and the main Athens-Salonica railway. So successful did they operate that the Germans dared not move their trains faster than ten or twelve miles an hour, despite the fact that they had created pillboxes every three kilometers and guarded the line with wire and mines and troops armed with mortars and twenty millimeter cannons. The practice of the Greek-Americans was to fire bazooka shells into the locomotives, tearing the tubes, and a second shell into armoured cars, before spraying the carriages with machine-gun fire. The Germans were terrified by these attacks.

In Salonica during the occupation, according to Saloutos, *They Remember America*, the Greek-Americans helped the British escape, "found them jobs and fed them." "On the island of Rhodes, in the attractive village of Kremasti, an athletic association initiated by Greek-Americans symbolized resistance."

A question should perhaps be asked in connection with the former immigrants who turned repatriates at some stage of their lives: where did they deserve, geographically speaking, the characterization of "repatriates" when they remained in Greece after their return from a long absence in the United States or when, after a new disappointing experience, they came back to America?

A human being who does not fit entirely in either of the two environments in which he lived for a time and who does not speak correctly either of the two languages of these environments could be an unhappy person regardless of his materialistic achievements.

The Contribution
of the Greek-Americans to the Arts

A S FOR almost everything else related to the first Greek immigrants in America detailed, responsible information about their artistic activities and achievements is rather difficult to be obtained. This does not mean that there have not been many extremely successful Greek-American artists. To the contrary, there have been quite a number who are a credit both to the United States and to their profession. However, all their names are not available; neither do we know the degree of success achieved by everyone of them. This is why when speaking about them one is compelled to avoid mentioning names. The best he can do in fairness to all of them is refer only to the most prominent and then again with the reservation that he might have left out some of the best of the entire lot.

There is another thing: when a Greek praises or criticizes another Greek there is always a measure of exaggeration in the formulation of his opinion. There is almost always something personal, which obscures the objective judgment of any achievement. Moreover, there is another deplorable habit and we must be frank about it: when a Greek speaks about one of his compatriots he is always more enclined to criticize than to praise him. Thus it is quite impossible to evaluate the artistic achievements of the Greek-Americans solely on the basis of what some Greek writers have said about them. It is equally difficult to form an opinion on what the artists themselves have been saying about their performances; some of them have stayed away on purpose from every publicity; others have used publicity to increase a popularity which they did not always deserve.

Some of the writers who have dealt in length with the activities of the Greek-Americans in the arts seemed rather surprised to find out that whatever achievements were attained they were scored almost exclusively in the fields of painting and sculpture, with very few, if any indeed, in the domain of literature.

In his analysis of the Greek-American artists (*Argonaftis*, Athens,

1958) Elias Ziogas writes that "The Greek-Americans scored their first serious successes in the arts (painting and sculpture) in a way that attracted attention to the small ethnic group, which had come rather late (to America). The phenomenon," Ziogas thinks, "which can be explained is not a natural one. What is natural is exactly the opposite—literature (in the case of the artistic activities of any immigrants) is bound to appear first, then come the arts."

One cannot agree with this conclusion. It seems that the reason why the Greek-Americans were prevented from writing poetry, fiction or for that matter anything, was because of the language. They did not know English and therefore could not write in a language they did not even speak. It is said that the prehistoric man knew how to draw before he learned how to converse.

In his book *Ellines Tis Amerikis, 1528-1948*, Babis Malafouris has this to say about the Greek-American artists and their successful activities:

> Only through a deep analysis of the Greek soul, only through the spiritual—regardless of how poorly it was cultivated—strength, which is hidden in the race (the Greek race) one can explain, at least to a certain extent, the fact that the Greek immigrants in the middle of their struggle to settle financially and socially in this country (the United States) found the desire and the time to create artistic activities. Time was of great value during the first years of their efforts since neither the theater nor music or any other arts were financial enterprises for them, but to the contrary they meant expenses and luxury. However, it was a necessity as this can be proved by all the activities of their artistic life—a necessity which at the beginning they wanted to fulfil through their own meagre means and later through their support to the artists who came from Greece, or to those who were their offspring—the new Greek generation of America.

What is implied here is the fact that an artist is born an artist and that regardless of the environment in which he lives—and sometimes even regardless of the circumstances under which he struggles—he will create if the power of creation is in him. One can offer thousands of examples of great artists who practically starved when they produced their best work.

Who were—indeed who are—the Greek-American artists? How can one identify them? They came to America from the mainland and the isles of Greece, but also from Constantinople, Smyrna and

196

the depths of Asia-Minor—the unredeemed parts of Greece; they also came from foreign lands. Some were children when they first set foot on the American soil; some were slightly older; others were adults; still others were born in America—the sons of the first Greek immigrants.

Dimitry Mitropoulos, the great conductor came to the United States in 1936. Does this make him a Greek-American artist? He loved America but he really never left Greece spiritually in spite of all sorts of accusations made against him by most Athenians, jealous of his great talent. Elias Kazan, born in Constantinople, came to America when he was a very young boy. He is one of the most successful movie directors and a writer whose book *The Arrangement* became a best seller. Is Elias Kazan the typical Greek-American? Nikos Moshonas, the well-known baritone, came to America in 1938, and was hired by the Metropolitan Opera of New York. In 1939, the daughter of the famous Greek actress Kyveli, Aliki, came to the States where she has been performing at various intervals. Is she indeed the representative type of a Greek-American actress?

There is an endless list of names of men and women who distinguished themselves in the field of the arts in the United States and—let's repeat it all over again— it is quite impossible to mention all of them or even to know all of them. Besides, this is not the purpose of this book. The names already mentioned were offered as an example of the difficulty one is encountering when trying to describe or to identify a Greek-American artist.

Some of the Greeks who settled in the United States became famous painters and sculptors. The painter John Xceron won worldwide recognition; Polygnotis Vagis was a great sculptor; John Vassos is another great painter, and George Constant's paintings were bought by the State Department to be included in the works of great American native artists. Here again these are but a few names of an entire pleiade of talented artists who contributed a lot to the artistic life of the United States.

There were also a number of writers who most definitely left their mark: Dr. Demetrios Callimachos, editor of the *National Herald;* Adamantios Polyzoides, editor of the *Atlantis* for a number of years—and others.

Writing in the Congressional Record (Proceedings and Debates of the 86th Congress, Second Session—*Greeks in America*) George C. Vournas whose judgment on people and situations is always accurate has this to say about one particular writer:

> The one writer, however, who best reflected and interpreted the Greek immigrant was the editor and publisher of the satirical weekly, *Satyros,* 1911-1954—the late Constantine Zambounis; he was a gifted writer of both verse and prose; a moralist and a philosopher, to boot. His newspaper was written in verse, prose and in a wholly new dialect under the caption "Letters of Marigoula Farfalia." His lines reflected the American environment as truly as those of *Romios* of George Souris reflected Athens. In addition, Mr. Zambounis authored more serious works ("Moments of Melancholy" and "When I Died") both written in verse, and are classics in their field. He also wrote short stories and four volumes of essays, entitled "On the Wings of Thoughts." His devastating satire—in verse, prose and through cartoons was directed mercilessly against all pretense and exploitation. No one was feared or favored and no one was exempt—be it a church dignitary, Government official, or private individual. The Greek of America and his welfare claimed his undivided loyalty, and woe to the person who would do him harm or seek to exploit him.

The second Greek-American generation produced many excellent writers but we consider them as Americans and this is why they are not mentioned here. If every minority group in the United States would claim a second generation writer as its own then there would not be any American writers as such.

There were other fields of activities in which the Greek-Americans excelled. There were also failures. Within a number of years after they came to America the first immigrants launched themselves in various—small and large—enterprises. They opened restaurants —for which they are still known, candy stores and factories, bakeries, night clubs, etc. They also went into the tobacco and fur business with great success. They were also successful in the chain movie business and food markets.

Theodore Saloutos (*The Greeks in the United States*) writes that "The problems of the Greek merchant were essentially those of the small businessman, though multiplied by the waves of anti-foreignism. During the earlier years, the individual merchant predominated in the confectionary, restaurant, shoe-repair, and other retail businesses. He continued to flourish until he felt the menacing hand of the chain store ... He recognized the peril, yet his ego caused him stubbornly to pursue an individual course of action and refuse to unite with others ... The better informed also realized that poor management, rather than persecution and intolerance, was the cause of many business failures. Many small businessmen simply were incapable of keeping books; they probably knew how to add up profits, but they were unable to calculate their opening expenses and losses."

In the final analysis it must be recognized that the first Greek immigrants demonstrated that it was not impossible for ignorant people of very simple origin to compete within a very ruthless environment and achieve a positive success.

Gradually those among the most successful went into larger enterprises and their activities came closer to American reality and its difficult requirements; they were more easily absorbed by the process of Americanization.

The Greek Orthodox
Church of North and South America

THE GREEK Orthodox Church of North and South America is not only an inherent part of the very life, evolution and progress of the Greeks in America; it is above all the guardian and the protector of their religious and spiritual ideals in the Western hemisphere. It could not have been otherwise. There was no other organization which could assume such a mission. As it could have been expected some strong objections have been raised against this historical role of the Greek Archdiocese of North and South America and some people challenged the competence of the Church. However, whether we like it or not it is the Greek Orthodox Church in America, which will be responsible for whatever form Greek Orthodoxy and Hellenism will retain in the future in this part of the world. Moreover, the Greek Church of America developed gradually and in conjunction with the growth of the first Greek immigrants; in many aspects the Church faced the same difficulties they encountered until they succeeded in overcoming most of the numerous and varied problems.

The first Greek immigrants started from scratch within a hostile environment; the Church also was established in the United States in the middle of a chaotic situation. Today it stands well organized and in rather good financial condition. It is impossible to agree with the contention advanced by some quarters that it is becoming more and more merely a church and nothing else. As a mattter of fact, the exact opposite view could easily be sustained. This, of course, does not mean that the Church did not have, or does not have, its shortcomings. Moreover, the extent and the burden of its multiple responsibilities were bound to produce some decisions which were far from being popular.

Orthodoxy was brought to North America by way of Alaska by Russian missionaries. Following the destruction of the Russian Orthodox State as a result of the Bolshevik Revolution in 1917, the Greeks in foreign lands assumed officially the leading role as representatives of Orthodoxy.

In spite of its rather rapid growth during the early years of the 20th century Greek Orthodoxy remained a very small and a minor religion in the United States, hardly known and very seldom recognized. This was to be expected since the first Greek immigrants in America, though large in proportion to the total population of their motherland were indeed a small group when compared to the numbers of other nationalities that had come before or at the same time with them to America.

Today, thanks to the efforts and the activities of the Greek Orthodox Church, Orthodoxy has taken its place among the major faiths in the United States; it is recognized as such over the inexplicable hesitations of some Orthodox, who would have liked the Church to keep following the road of isolation.

The position of Orthodoxy within the American environment and towards the other three major faiths is today similar to the position of a man to whom attention is paid for the first time by other men and whom they expect to offer evidence and justification for his presence. It is really up to Orthodoxy to make its presence necessary and to attract due attention of the other religious creeds to its goals and to its activities.

The first organized community that established a Greek Orthodox Church in the United States was that of the Holy Trinity in the city of New York—in the year 1892. It was chartered by a special act of the New York Legislature in 1896 and it is the only Greek Orthodox Church in the United States, which was legally created prior to the incorporation of the Greek Orthodox Archdiocese of North and South America.

It must be said that regardless of the gradual development of the Greek communities in the United States the situation, from an administrative point of view, was chaotic. Under the Patriarchal Decree of 1908, the Greek Orthodox Church of America was under the jurisdiction of the Holy Synod of Greece. It is only in 1918, when Metropolitan Meletios came to America to organize the Church that things started to change. On September 19, 1921, Meletios, who was to become Patriarch later, incorporated legally the Greek Archdiocese of North and South America under the Religious Corporation Law of the State of New York. When he assumed his post as Ecumenical Patriarch the year after, he revoked the 1908 Decree and terminated the dependence of the Greek Orthodox Church of America on the Holy Synod and placed it under the supervision and control of the Ecumenical Patriarchate of Constantinople.

On May 11, 1922, the Greek Archdiocese of North and South America was canonically created and its legal establishment formally ratified by the Ecumenical Patriarchate. Alexander Rodostolou became the first Archbishop.

The certificate of Incorpation of the Greek Archdiocese of North and South America stipulates that the objects for which such Corporation is to be formed are:

> To edify the religious and moral life of the Greek Orthodox Christians in North and South America on the basis of the Holy Scriptures, the rules and canons of the Holy Apostles and the seven Ecumenical Councils of the ancient undivided church as they are or shall be actually interpreted by the Great Church of Christ in Constantinople and to exercise governing authority over and to maintain advisory relations with Greek Orthodox Churches throughout North and South America and to maintain spiritual and advisory relations with synods and other governing authorities of the said Church located elsewhere.

According to Peter Kourides, *The Evolution of the Greek Orthodox Church in America and its Present Problems* (New York, 1949):

> Unfortunately the eight years reign of Archbishop Alexander Rodostolou were literally a nightmare. During this interval our churches and communities had become divided battlegrounds in which Venizelists and Royalists used physical violence even within the sanctuary of the Holy Altar. Police were stationed at strategic positions within some of our churches to actually prevent bloodshed. And, of course, those shameful and disgusting incidents were reported on the front page of the American press to the awful humiliation and irreparable damage of our people throughout the country. With the ascendance of Photius II to the Ecumenical Throne, the Metropolitan of Corinth, Damaskinos, was dispatched to this country in May 1930 as a Patriarchal Exarch in an effort to bring peace amongst the two warring factions that had devastatingly divided and destroyed our church in America. Fortunately, on August 13, 1930, Athenagoras, the then Metropolitan of Kerkyra, was elected as our Archbishop.

A new era of reconciliation was about to begin. However, the civil war within the Greek Orthodox Church in America was one of the darkest moments of Hellenism in the United States, which affected the status both of the Church and of the first Greek immigrants in America. As years go by the first immigrants—the actual participants in the civil war—tend to disappear and today whatever divides the church and the communities has no political motivation.

> The civil war of the twenties had come to an end; a new leadership, energetic and determined to place great authority in the archdiocese and the parish priests, had emerged. But the leadership was hampered by the toll that had been taken by more than a decade of strife, the worst economic depression in history, and a church orientation that was more Greek than American. The early thirties also witnessed the beginning of a new chapter in church history—that of the steady decrease in the influence of the layman in community affairs and an increase in that of the clergy. The church, in addition, was girding itself for a more aggressive role and making efforts to appeal to the disaffected second generation. (Professor Th. Saloutos, *The Greeks in the United States*.)

What were the achievements of the Greek Orthodox Church of North and South America, from the days of the internal crisis until the present days?

Its principal achievement was perhaps its ability to survive when its parishioners were so few and its financial resources so negligible. Another major achievement was the devotion and the determination of its immigrant communicants, which permitted to build 482 churches, community and educational centers, parochial and afternoon schools. In the meantime, under the primacy of the then Archbishop Athenagoras, the church organized itself into one solidified, disciplined church and succeeded in eliminating all dissidence.

Another extremely important—and of historical significance—achievement was the realization of the church that it could not survive in America as a church unless it was able to adapt Greek Orthodoxy to the requirements imposed by the American environment.

This realization, which called for some drastic decisions made the Church the target of violent criticism emanating mostly from the first Greek immigrants. This criticism was echoed and promoted by the Greek-American press in a way which was not always in harmony with the facts.

The Church created educational facilities within the United States for the training of the American oriented clergy and teachers needed for the staffing of its churches and its parochial schools.

Moreover, Greek Orthodoxy has achieved a de facto major faith recognition with the participation of its Archbishop in presidential inaugurations, with the designation of Greek Orthodox chaplains and the introduction of Greek Orthodox identification tags in the United States armed forces.

Finally, the Greek Orthodox Church in America has played an important role in the accelerated trend toward Christian ecumenicity. It is significant to recall that Archbishop Iakovos accompanied Partriarch Athenagoras to the historic meeting in January, 1964, with Pope Paul VI in the Holy Land.

It is recognized that the modern organized period of the Greek Orthodox Church in America dates from the beginning of Athenagoras' administration. He succeeded through unrelenting efforts and because of his dynamic personality to unite the Greek Orthodox communities under a centralized Archdiocese "thus coordinating and ensuring the future of Greek Orthodoxy in America."

Archbishop Michael, succeeded Athenagoras and was Archbishop until his death in July 1958. He was a scholar who further "enhanced the prestige of the Church." He promoted the campaign for recognition of Orthodoxy as a major faith in the United States. He was the first Greek Orthodox Archbishop in America to be invited by the President of the United States to deliver an invocation as the official representative of the Greek Orthodox Church at the Presidential Inauguration in January 1957.

The present Archbishop Iakovos assumed his position on April 1, 1959. There is no doubt that in the last 15 years he has strengthened and reshaped Orthodoxy so that it could make concrete contributions to the American environment. His aim was to present a Greek Orthodox Church to the new Greek-American generations—to the perpetuators of Hellenism in America—which would not be in striking contrast to the churches of different creeds in the United States. These churches, because of a more realistic, practical approach to the demands of our time, might have a stronger appeal to the Orthodox youth of America. The Archbishop must also be credited for improving the excellent relations that Orthodoxy enjoys with other faiths. He is also a determined proponent and a frequent spokesman of ecumenical unity and has served as one of the Presidents of the World Council of Churches.

Archbishop Iakovos has been often criticized, still is, for some of his decisions—but who can be exempt from criticism when he tries to introduce reforms in a church in the hope it will better serve its mission and answer the pressing demands of a new era? Whether some of his decisions were considered too hasty will not be known before some years to come.

Is the Greek Orthodox Church of North and South America attracting more people today than it did in the past?

According to data compiled by the National Council of Churches, church membership in general is lagging behind population growth in the United States.

The Council's report is based on official figures from 251 religious bodies of all faiths in the 50 states and the district of Columbia. It includes the major faiths—Jews, Roman Catholics and Protestants —as well as the Eastern Churches, the Buddhists and a number of smaller Catholic denominations not affiliated with the larger bodies.

Total church membership in the United States was put at 124,682,422. Protestants, including Eastern Orthodox communicants, accounted for 69,088,182 church members in the latest total. Roman Catholics numbered 46,246,175 and Jews 5,600,000. The Eastern Churches were listed as having 3,172,163 members, while Old Catholics, Polish National Catholics and the Armenian Church's Diocese of America had 483,901. Buddhists numbered 92,000. The figure of membership to the Greek Orthodox Church of North and South America was given as 1,770,000.

There is no way of establishing in a responsible manner whether the Greek Orthodox Church in America has lost or gained followers within the last ten years. While it is true that some American born Orthodox have joined other denominations mostly through marriage to persons of other creeds, it is equally true that many people of various faiths have come to the Greek Orthodox Church.

The Greek Orthodox Church has often been accused for showing interest and taking a position in political matters. However, there are also those who criticize the Greek Archdiocese of North and South America for not having taken a more positive stand against the regime that was established in Greece in April 1967. The Church refused to take an open stand in fear that it might lead to deeper division of the Greek-Americans in connection with the situation which prevailed in Greece since 1967.

Archbishop Iakovos has often commented on political issues and has even sent encyclicals to all parishes of the Archdiocese in which he requested that Doxologies and special prayers be offered to commemorate a political event or decision of the past.

In May 1967, he asked the parishes to offer prayers to commemorate the twentieth anniversary of the Truman doctrine. (President Harry S. Truman addressed a joint session of Congress on March 12, 1947, asking for the appropriation of 400 million dolllars in economic and military aid to Greece and Turkey, in an attempt to prevent Communist domination of those two countries).

The Greek Orthodox Church of America often takes a position on world peace or on the issue of Human Rights. During the 18th Biennial Clergy-Laity Congress held in Montreal, Canada, in 1966, the Committee on the Church and the Moral and Social Issues of our Times, expressed "the profound concern of the Church that discrimination in all forms be eradicated, and we appeal to our parishes and people to stand steadfast in the protection of individual human rights, particularly in such areas as employment, housing, education and hospitalization."

On the issue of Vietnam, which the Archbishop visited a few years back, the Clergy-Laity Congress of 1966, adopted a resolution to the effect that "The Greek Orthodox Church recognizes the God-given right of all men to live a life of dignity in peace. However, the sad lessons of history reveal that the peace of Christ has always demanded a long and relentless struggle, and the forces of evil in our own day, as in the past, are adamant in destroying that peace. The eternal commitment of the Greek Orthodox Church to the cause of world peace will not permit it to ignore the suffering and oppression of our fellow-men and therefore wholly supports America's commitment to the pursuit of peace in Vietnam. We deplore, however, such hypocritical acts of pacifism as draft-card burning and the evasion of military service, for we affirm that freedom is not and has never been totally free. The preservation of our cherished rights and liberties requires the solemn obligation and duties of citizenship among which the Church recognizes as most important the service to and defense of country in time of need."

The Greek Orthodox Church of North and South America is democratically organized although the Archbishop is vested with tremendous power, and as a matter of fact, there are few things that are not either controlled or decided by him. Spiritual matters are determined by the Archbishop and his auxiliary bishops. All other matters are theoretically decided by the legislative body of the Archdiocese, which is the biennial congress at which each community sends both clergy and laity representatives. However, in reality no issue can be decided without the Archbishop's consent.

"The actual administration of our church is wholly in the hands of the Archbishop. The auxiliary bishops merely carry out the dictates and directions of the Archbishop. The entire executive authority is vested in the Archbishop." (Peter Kourides, *The Evolution of the Greek Orthodox Church in America and its Present Problems.*)

The Greek Orthodox Church in America and the Ecumenical Movement

T HE importance of the commitment of Greek Orthodoxy to the Ecumenical Movement was emphasized by Archbishop Iakovos, in his report to the 17th Biennial Clergy-Laity Congress of the Archdiocese in July 1965. He said:

Our interchurch relations give a new substance to our Church. One can see this in the parish, in his city and in his state. As the youngest church in America, we lived in relative isolation, yesterday. Today, we enjoy a happy and fraternal relationship with other Churches. Today, we are looked upon as a noteworthy Church with ethnic values. Yesterday, we were a Church of ceremony and pomp. Today, we are a vital Church, living not in the past, but in the present. Our position in interchurch relations is that position which has been set forth by the Holy Synod of the Ecumenical Throne: that of direct dialogue. We have much to learn and much to teach. Constantinople, Rome, Geneva, London and New York, together represent the music staff of our ecumenical symphony. Our primary concern is our inter-Orthodox relations, and then our dialogue with the World Council of Churches, with the Church of Rome, with the Anglican Church, and with the National Council of Churches of Christ. That goal which we have sought in our contacts with our Roman Catholic Brothers is a closer relationship in a communion of love. For we believe that love alone can abolish such terms as "schismatic" and "separated brethren," and enable us to tear down the barriers, penitently repair the robe of Christ and resolve that we shall never permit anyone to rend it again.

The initiative undertaken by the Greek Orthodox Church of America in regard to the Ecumenical Movement is, without any doubt, one of its most commendable undertakings. The task has not been, and is not, an easy one. The Greek Orthodox Church of America had to face bitter criticism from the Church of Greece and unfortunately also the opposition of some Orthodox faithful in the United States. Most—if not all—first Greek immigrants are opposed to the movement and are determined enemies of any rapprochement between the Church of Rome and the Eastern Church. Orthodox participation in the Ecumenical Movement has augmented as years have gone by. At the First Assembly of the World Council of Churches in Amsterdam in September 1948, there were 15 delegates and 3 alternates; at the Fourth Conference on Faith and Order held in Montreal, in 1963, there were 50 Orthodox theologians participating. Today, the Orthodox Church has two bishops as permanent representatives at the World Council of Churches in Geneva, and Archbishop Iakovos, a dedicated leader of ecumenism, has been one of the presidents of the WCC and was the first permanent representative of the Ecumenical Patriarchate to its Geneva headquarters.

The Problem of Greek Education
in the Hands of the Greek Orthodox Church

THERE is no doubt that the task of infusing Greek education into the future Greek-American generations rests exclusively with the Greek Orthodox Archdiocese of North and South America. The task is as enormous as the responsibility carried by the Church.

Many have been the attempts to establish and operate schools in the United States with the Greek language as the principal medium of learning. A Greek educational institute was organized in New York City about 40 years ago, supported by the local community at first, and then laying claim to support by all Greeks in the United States. Other Greek schools were organized privately with a decidedly limited capacity either for boarders or day students. All, for that matter, succumbed to the inexorable economic law. Very few families were financially able to send their children to be educated at the Greek schools, which were no wise equal academically to public schools, and the limitations in accommodations were such that even if more were financially able, no facilities were available. (George C. Vournas, Congressional Record Proceedings and Debates of the 86th Congress, Second Session.)

Mr. Vournas, speaking about the Church's schools and educational program comes to the grim conclusion that "Instead of instilling love and affection for the Greek language or the Greek Orthodox religion, it provokes antagonism. Such being the facts, it is sad but not unreasonable to expect that with the passing of time Greek Orthodox Churches and communities in the United States, with the exception of a few centers—New York, Chicago, Boston and San Francisco—will suffer and eclipse." (*Ibid.*)

It is against this "eclipse" that the Greek Orthodox Church in the United States is fighting an extremely difficult battle.

Refuting the contention that the fact the Church was becoming the most influential Greek institution in the United States was a "general cause of alarm," Paul G. Manolis, an executive editor of the Oakland *Tribune,* California, writes (*The Orthodox Observer,* May, 1966):

It must be understood that the reason the Church has become the most influential institution is because it is the only all embracing "organization" in the United States ... AHEPA, GAPA (and) various provincial federations such as Pan-Arcadian, Pan-messinian, etc. ... really have a membership which is a mere fraction of the Greek-American population of the United States. The centralization of authority in the Archdiocese ... was not first invoked by Archbishop Athenagoras. The Tome setting out the reorganization of the Archdiocese of North and South America was issued by the Patriarchate in 1931, abolishing the up to then existing synodical system."

In the yearbook issued by the Greek Orthodox Archdiocese of North and South America one can find data and figures concerning the efforts undertaken by the Church in the field of education. In 1969, parishes, large and small, in North and South America numbered four hundred and sixty. Twelve others were in the process of being organized in South America, four in Canada, four in the Far East and ten in the United States.

In addition to the churches, four hundred afternoon schools, seventeen parochial, fifty-five nursery and fifty evening schools function in the parishes having a total student body of 24,700 and a teaching staff of 640. Also 709 Sunday Schools with an enrolment of 64,471 and a total teaching staff of 5,764 function in the Parishes. In addition, 285 chapters of youth and scout troops with a total membership of 8,340 belong to the Parishes. Finally, 440 Philoptohos Society Chapters, having a total membership of more than 30,-000 belong to our Parishes. Members of the Parishes, that is, those who are active and regularly support the Parish work, number over 80,000.

During the period between June 1st, 1966, to May 31st, 1968, the following building activities and purchases of buildings and property were noted in the Parishes:

Sixteen Parishes built new churches having a total value of $3,430,-500.00. Five Parishes erected new school buildings having a total value of $1,598,900.00. Eight Parishes renovated or enlarged their building facilities at a cost of $817,100.00; and twenty-one Parishes purchased new properties with the view in mind of building either churches or community centers having a total value of $2,249,-000.00. Seven Parishes purchased or built rectories at a cost of

$145,000.00. Sixty-six Parishes, therefore, spent more that $10,000,-000.00 during this two year period, in order to more firmly secure the present and assure the future.

As a result of the initiative of the Parishes, a number of summer camps are in operation: one in New England, two in Canada, one in Michigan, one in Minnesota, one in California and one in Pennsylvania.

Fifty of the priests are celibate and for the most part graduates of theological schools. The rest are all married. Of the 470 priests, 262 are graduates of the Theological School of Halki (Turkey), Athens and Thessaloniki. Approximately 70 of the priests come from preparatory theological schools, normal schools, and *gymnasia* (high schools) of Greece.

All the Bishops are graduates of the Theological University of Athens, and nine of them have earned graduate degrees from American theological schools.

The responsibilities of the Greek Orthodox Church in America in the domain of education are discharged through various institutions it has founded.

St. Basil's Academy, situated in Garrison, New York, is one of them. The Teachers Training Department of the Academy functions as an educational institution for the purpose of preparing young women of the Greek Orthodox Faith to teach at the schools of the Greek Orthodox Archdiocese or to continue further studies in the Liberal Arts or the Teachers Training Colleges.

In pursuing this twofold purpose, the Academy offers studies aiming at bringing the student into cognizant contact with:

a) the Western civilization and its constituent elements as the latter are particularly expressed in the history and life of the United States by way of culture, literature, and arts,

b) the Greek Orthodox cultural and religious traditions, including the Greek language (classical and modern), history and civiligation of ancient and contemporary Greece, together with whatever is considered to be the student's parental heritage in culture and life,

c) contemporary American teaching methods and skills for the purpose of enabling the graduate to teach at the schools of the Greek Archdiocese of North and South America.

The Byzantine Fellowship, another educational organization, is functioning under the aegis of the Archdiocese. Its program is dedicated to the service of its members and the advancement of charitable and educational causes. The Byzantine Fellowship offers its members a program of services through travel opportunities to Greece, the Patriarchate of Constantinople, and the Holy Land.

The Philoptohos Society is the official organization for women of the Greek Orthodox Faith in America. The Society conducts benevolent programs and service projects and has chapters in nearly all parishes of the Archdiocese.

St. Michael's Home for the Aged of the Greek Orthodox Church, Inc., houses and cares for the senior citizens of Greek extraction. A total of 139 residents had been admitted "to date" (1969). Men are accepted at the age of 65 and over, while women must be at least 60 years old. Among other requirements for admission a priest's certificate is necessary to the effect that the candidate is of Greek Orthodox faith, of Greek origin and a member of the Greek community.

The Guadalupe Home for Boys of the Greek Orthodox Church admits "pre-delinquent and delinquent adolescents between the ages of 12 and 16." This Home for Boys, licensed by the State Department of Social Welfare of California, serves youngsters regardless of race, creed or color.

The most ambitious project of the Greek Orthodox Church in America is without any doubt the foundation of Hellenic College in Brookline, Massachussetts. Actually the Hellenic College is the outgrowth of the Greek Orthodox Theological School, established at Pomfret, Connecticut, in 1937.

According to the *1969 Yearbook of the Greek Archdiocese* (New York), the Hellenic College "realizes the aspiration of the Greek-American community to make its own contribution to higher education in America in the form of a distinctive college, expressing both the cultural tradition of Greece and the religious tradition of the Greek people, the Orthodox Christian faith. It also marks the first major step in attaining the objectives set nearly a decade ago with the establishment of the Hellenic University Foundation." The Hellenic College is as ambitious as it is an expensive project and only the future will tell if it will serve the purposes for which it was founded amidst tremendous difficulties and some strong objections.

The Greek Orthodox Church is facing the problem of educating the future Greek-American generations with more realism than mere sentimentality. The Church fully realizes that the language assimilation to the environment is leading to many other forms of assimilation. The Church has been studying the evolution of Hellenism in Austria, Italy, Rumania, Hungary and Russia—where there are Greek schools and newspapers.

In a conversation with this writer, Archbishop Iakovos said in this connection that: "In our own case there are similarities but also some differences. One of them is the lack of an homogeneous religion in America. Another is our numbers (the numbers of Greek-Americans) as individuals and as organized communities. Another is the 'inspection' of our communities by our bishops. A fourth one is the abolition of distance. A fifth one is the frequent contact with Greece. A sixth is continuing immigration. Finally, there is the dangerous decline of spiritual, moral and intellectual values."

The education of the future Greek-American generations should, therefore, be twofold and aim at: the cultivation of the racial origin and the religious or ecclesiastical identification with Greek Orthodoxy. The Greek language without being ostracized should be taught not simply as a maternal language but as a means and as an organ of intellectual and religious evolution.

In another conversation with this writer (1967) Archbishop Iakovos commenting on the question of the preservation of the Greek language among the future Greek-American generations said: "The Church knows that the day might come, when the Greek language will not be spoken among the Greek-American generations either because of ignorance or necessity—as in the case of mixed marriages. However, the Church rejects any internal or external pressure for the total replacement of the Greek language in the liturgy or in its life in general."

In the "Course of Study" prescribed for the Greek Elementary Schools (Greek Archdiocese of North and South America, New York Professor Philippos D. Emmanuel writes that "The broad interpretation that the Greek Archdiocese makes to its mission is inspired by: 1) The tradition and the character of the Greek Orthodox Church, 2) Complete faith in the cultural power of Greek Education, 3) The correct interpretation of the spiritual and cultural needs of the American citizens of Greek descent, as well as their obligations towards the American society and community, 4) The historical and emotional ties of the American citizens of Greek descent with Greece, and the common nature of the cultural trends and interests of the peoples of both America and Greece."

Professor Emmanuel comes to the conclusion that "the Greek education of the American citizens of Greek descent is not and should not be conceived as an independent and complete educational enterprise. This education is not and should not be conceived as a special and complementary side of the education that the American society provides by its comprehensive system of education to all the citizens of that country.

The future Greek-American generations face the problem of bilingualism. Some educators have supported the idea that bilingualism is advantageous for the mental development of the child; others argued that the pressure of a second language on the child at a time he is not ready to absorb it is definitely detrimental to the intellectual development of the child.

The Need for a New Orientation

THE passing of time, which in our days is carrying much faster and much stronger evolutionary pressures and changes is making necessary the revision of previous attitudes and concepts about life in general. It would be irrational to support the idea that whatever was established in the past is immune from the impact of evolution.

The changes brought about in the world as a result of an unprecedented technological progress and the fact that science has invaded the privacy of previously unexplored areas of the physical world but also of the human mind are as considerable as they are varied.

Very little, if anything, has remained what it used to be. Very few things, today, are accepted or believed the way they were adopted and trusted in the past. Our environment has been radically transformed. The air we breathe is no longer the same. Moral values are differently interpreted and some of them have been altogether shelved. Even man's faith has been deeply affected by the sharp changes. Today's Christian is not the devout he was some years ago. The basic reliance and belief in God have not vanished but new methods had to be devised to maintain or instill the acceptance of divine power. The immediate need for a different orientation of the dogmatic practices of the Church has become apparent and imperative. The Church—every church— had to meet the new situation with realism and even make some concessions in regard to the legacy of the past.

It is within the prism of the awareness of an overall change in the physical and spiritual world and the dictates of historical evolution that the Greek Orthodox Church of America had to approach the problem of the future Greek-American generations. Moreover, additional factors had to be taken into consideration in trying to foresee and evaluate this future, namely:

1) The needs and the demands of the new Greek-American generations for a more pragmatic Orthodoxy and a specific degree of

Hellenic indoctrination, which would not be contrasting with their natural allegiance to the United States.

2) The practicality of an eventual autonomy of the Greek Orthodox Church of America—a revision of its dependence on the Ecumenical Patriarchate of Constantinople. Such an autonomy might, on one hand enhance the position of the Greek Orthodox Church of America vis a vis the newly established Russian Orthodox Church of America and, on the other might be considered indispensable in view of the fact that the Ecumenical Patriarchate, because of the special conditions under which it functions within a hostile entourage, has remained in almost complete isolation from the reality of today's American environment.

3) The establishment of a new, independent, autocephalous Russian Orthodox Church in America. The effects of such an important decision, which was condemned by the Ecumenical Patriarchate and the Church of Greece, had to be very carefully examined by the Greek Orthodox Church of America.

There is no doubt that it is with these evolutions and factors in mind that the 20th Clergy-Laity Congress, held in New York between the 27th of June and the 4th of July, 1970, adopted some decisions. These decisions, which were in many aspects misinterpreted, created a deep confusion among those Greek Americans who feared that the Greek language was abolished by the Greek Orthodox Church of America and that, thus, their ethnic identification with Greece and their religious identification with their Church were coming to an end.

The above mentioned factors should be examined in some length and depth. An objective examination of their real meaning might help in placing the entire problem in its right perspective.

Whether we like it or not we have to bear in mind at all times that necessity imposed by historical evolutions becomes a powerful force much more decisive in reaching certain decisions than even the cherished tradition. We are often detached from symbols we love not on our free will but because of forces beyond our control. It should be added here that ironically enough when reforms are decided people are always thinking about what might have been lost that belonged to the past and never what might have been created for the future.

The task of the Greek Orthodox Church of North and South America is twofold: Continue and maintain Orthodoxy in the hearts of the Greek-American generations and educate them—find a modus operandi of Greek and American culture, which would be attractive to them.

In order to achieve such a difficult goal the various negative and positive influences on Orthodoxy in general, and on the new American generations could not have been overlooked.

Needs and Demands of the
New Greek-American Generations—
American Orthodoxy

THE necessity to meet the needs and demands of the new Greek-American generations for a more pragmatic Orthodoxy within the American environment—in other words, for a more religiously oriented and less influenced by ethnic considerations Orthodoxy—does not permit to ignore either the first Greek American generation or the new immigrants arriving from Greece. Nor can the existence of other Orthodox jurisdictions in America be overlooked.

In his book *The Individual and His Orthodox Church* (The Orthodox Observer Press, 1970) Rev. Dr. Nicon D. Patrinacos writes that:

> The American Orthodox of today, having come of age as regards his personal religious experience and that of a group within which he moves, seeks a more definite and more convincing articulation of his Faith and a way of practicing it to which he could fully subscribe without hesitation or reservations and without fear of being severed on account of it from his American environment.

Yet, the American Orthodox is not only a believer of the second or third Greek-American generation. He is also a first immigrant residing in this country and a new immigrant arriving from Greece.

It is a fact that with the passing of time the first Greek American immigrants are gradually disappearing. However, it would be a serious mistake to contend that because of this disappearance there will be no longer a first Greek-American generation and that, therefore, all efforts should be exclusively concentrated on how to deal with the new generation.

There will always be a first Greek-American generation as long as new Greek immigrants will be coming to America and to Canada. They will be replacing the first disappearing generation and they will become, in their turn, the first generation. They will not be the original source of Hellenism in America but they, too, will try to adapt themselves to the American environment and they, too, will be the starting point of future Greek-American generations.

The new immigrants, like the first ones, are more closely attached to Orthodoxy as viewed in Greece—a more dogmatic and less realistic Orthodoxy. They will be less enclined to adopt American Orthodoxy. They will be probably objecting to the label with the firm conviction that Orthodoxy is exclusively Greek. Yet, there is a Russian Orthodoxy, a Serbian and a Bulgarian Orthodoxy— and others. The various Orthodox ethnic groups have always be linking "their" Orthodoxy to their ethnic identification with their native country regardless of the dependence of their church from one or another Mother Church. Indeed, nationalities—at least as far as the common believer is concerned—are a dividing factor and not the fundamentals of Orthodoxy.

Can the differences be forgotten within an eventual merger of all Orthodox in America? Can we have an American Orthodoxy capable of surviving as a fourth major faith in this country, without the weakness of internal divisions and quarrels?

In regard to the traditional American pattern the Orthodox Churches in America have developed as colonies of their mother sees in Eastern Europe and the Middle East. Now, like the Protestants and the Catholics before them they seem to have matured to a point which—if they were to unite—would permit them to stand on their own among the autocephalous or independent churches of the Orthodox world. But it is only fair to state that behind the Orthodox in America stand today the Ecumenical Patriarchate of Constantinople and the Patriarchate of Moscow through the Russian Orthodox Church of America to which it granted autonomy. Their views differ on what Orthodoxy should be in this country.

Eastern Orthodoxy in the United States is America's fourth major faith but perhaps still the most fragmented. The Orthodox Christians in the United States are mostly second, or third generation immigrants with strikingly different cultural backgrounds and their churches have developed as daughter colonies of ancient sees. Theoretically nothing would be more logical than to link Greeks, Russians, Serbs, Syrians, Ukrainians and others into one American Orthodox Church. But is this possible from a realistic point of view?

The Greek Orthodox Church is the largest and the wealthiest among the United States Orthodox jurisdictions. However, is this undeniable fact to be accepted by all Orthodox jurisdictions as to the prevalence of the Greek-Orthodox Church?

In an interview in *Newsweek* Magazine, Archbishop Iakovos of North and South America said: "We have been struggling to establish a platform for cooperation (bringing the Greeks and Slavs together in the Standing Conference of Canonical Orthodox Bishops in America), but we have not matured enough yet for real unity...."

In his book *The Individual and His Orthodox Church,* Father Nicon Patrinacos writes that: "... most Orthodox want progress for their Orthodox Church. But what kind of progress and how? Most of them view progress from the institutional viewpoint. There seem to be two schools of thought. The one urges: Americanize the Church. The other demands: Unite all the Orthodox national jurisdictions into one. The motive, though, behind both of these requests seems to be the same: institutional strength and a vision of effecting an impact on the American scene."

It appears that the difficulty in achieving eventually an American Orthodoxy stems rather from cultural than essentially religious reasons.

The Ecumenical Patriarchate
and the Greek Orthodox Church of America

ALL Orthodox Churches, Patriarchates as well as autocephalous and autonomous Churches, recognize the Ecumenical Patriarchate of Constantinople as the main and essential body of the Faith of the Eastern Orthodox Church. The Ecumenical Patriarch is accepted as the first among equals with certain distinct privileges regarding the projection of the Eastern Orthodox Church as a whole.

The Eastern Orthodox Church is made of the following autocephalous and autonomous churches. First, the four ancient and original Patriarchates:

The Ecumenical Patriarchate of Constantinople.
The Patriarchate of Alexandria.
The Patriarchate of Antioch.
The Patriarchate of Jerusalem.

Then,

The Patriarchate of Russia.
The Patriarchate of Serbia.
The Patriarchate of Rumania.
The Patriarchate of Bulgaria.

Finally, the autocephalous Churches:

The Church of Cyprus.
The Church of Greece.
The Church of Iberia (Georgia).
The Church of Poland.
The Church of Albania,

and more recently the Russian Orthodox Church of America.

The Ecumenical Patriarchate of Constantinople has under its immediate supervision the Greek Orthodox Metropolis of Europe, the Greek Orthodox Church of North and South America (the Archbishop is the Patriarchal Exarch and was recently vested with additional powers), the Greek Orthodox Archdiocese of Australia and New Zealand, the Church of Korea and the Church of Africa.

The tremendous historical significance of the Ecumenical Patriarchate is an undisputed fact and the symbolic importance of its location cannot be denied. Yet, it is its geographical position and the continuous frictions between Greece and Turkey that have undermined, perhaps not its prestige, but most certainly its original power.

The Ecumenical Patriarchate of Constantinople is no longer what it used to be. This is said with deep sadness by someone who remembers with unbroken nostalgia the days when Fanar, surrounded and backed by hundreds of thousands of Greeks residing in Turkey, was projecting all the radiance and the splendor of its legendary mission. However, history has undertaken with unjustified malice to diminish both its splendor and its power.

In an article published in the *Orthodox Observer* of June 1970, Elliott Wright, who visited the Ecumenical Patriarchate following the decisions of the 20th Clergy-Laity Congress of the Greek Orthodox Church of North and South America writes that: "Most of the wordly splendor of the Church of Constantinople is gone . . . Today, of course, the Church of Constantinople is quite small in comparison to former times. There are 60 Parishes, nine of which are on the Asia-Minor side of the Bosporus in Chalcedon. All others are in Europe and on the islands in the Sea of Marmara. . . ." And Mr. Wright adds: "The physical size and condition of the Patriarchate is in no way proportionate to the importance of the Patriarch in the church world . . . Many of the Orthodox churches in Istanbul were converted into mosques. A number of the more historic ones are now museums. Among these is St. Sophia, built in the 6th century . . . ."

Gone are forever the days when over half a million Greek Orthodox lived in Turkey—most of them in Constantinople, some attending the famous School *Megali tou Genous Scholi*, the University of the Greek nation. The remnants of the fabulous heritage are still there and it is not either their number or the condition in which they are preserved that can compel people to forget history and tradition or accept their total disappearance. However, in this ingrate world of ours both power and radiance seem to be important factors of influence.

Does this mean that the mission of the Ecumenical Patriarchate is coming to an end? Nobody is either eager or in a position to answer the tragic question in one or another way. But the unfortunate turning point cannot be ignored and the thought about the present and future influence of the Ecumenical Patriarchate on other churches and on Orthodox all over the world is only natural.

There has been some discussion in connection with the dependence of the Greek Orthodox Church of America on the Ecumenical Patriarchate of Constantinople and the possibility of the Church becoming autonomous.

The late Panos Peclaris, writing in the *Argonaut* magazine (Athens, 1958), said that "The view supported by some priests as well as some laymen that the Greek Orthodox Church of North and South America should be granted autonomy carries the very sperm of the idea of lowering the Church to the same level of the numerous so-called 'churches,' the existence of which is due to means and goals hardly related to Christianity. If this were to happen it would be a heavy blow against the Ecumenical Patriarchate while at the same time the Greek Orthodox Church of America would be losing part of its historical and concrete prestige. The various American 'churches' would give anything to link themselves to a perennial and highly respected institution like the Ecumenical Patriarchate. Thus, these ideas of the Greek Archdiocese of North and South America getting away from the Throne are mere stupidities . . . The dependence of the Greek Orthodox Archdiocese of North and South America on the Ecumenical Patriarchate should be considered a privilege and its preservation should be a basic and vital aim of every Orthodox . . . Thus the argument in favor of the existence of an autonomous 'American' Orthodox Church being in harmony with the goals of the American community is absolutely erroneous . . ."

It should be pointed out that because of the very peculiar and precarous conditions under which the Ecumenical Patriarchate exists today, in Constantinople, the Patriarchate itself counts on the Greek Orthodox Church of America much more than it is realized. The financial support of the Greek Orthodox Archdiocese is badly needed in Constantinople. Its vigilance over the constant pressure exercised on the Patriarchate by the Turks is indispensable. The Greek Orthodox Archdiocese is for the Patriarchate a sort of "shield" of protection against any further deterioration of the situation in Turkey, which could lead to renewed pressure against the Patriarchate and the remaining Greek Orthodox.

The Greek Orthodox Archdiocese of North and South America had been collecting for several years funds with which to help the Ecumenical Patriarchate either to rebuild its present inadequate location at Fanar or preferably locate itself in a more desirable section of Constantinople. The tragic events of September 1955, during which Turkish hordes attacked ruthlessly Greek priests and destroyed Greek property brought the drive to a halt since it was not possible to know whether the Patriarchate could continue to remain in Constantinople. Indeed, the question has never been answered in a categorical manner.

A demarcation line should be drawn between the cherished tradition and today's reality. In regard to the eventual autonomy of the Greek Orthodox Archdiocese of America from the Ecumenical Patriarchate of Constantinople one must take into consideration that the Patriarchate has probably remained away from the reality of the American environment and as a consequence has not been receptive for reforms through which a dignified, stable place could be secured for the new Greek-American generations.

The Establishment of an Autocephalous Russian Orthodox Church in America

T HE existence in one and the same country of several parallel Orthodox jurisdictions—the Greek, the Russian, the Syrian, the Rumanian, the Albanian and others—was considered a "canonical abnormality" hampering the spiritual and social witness of Orthodoxy. It is with this idea in mind that a new, independent Russian Orthodox Church was formally established in America by the Holy Synod of the Moscow Patriarchate over some strong objections.

From the Russian point of view it was hoped that the establishment of the new church will unite a divided Eastern Orthodoxy and all Orthodox Christians in this country of all national origins.

Upon the establishment of the new Church, Metropolitan Ireney, head of the Russian Orthodox Greek Catholic Church of America, better known as the Metropolia, issued an encyclical letter urging churchgoers to promote a "gentle unity" among Orthodox Christians in America.

There were three branches of Russian Orthodoxy in the country; the largest, the Russian Orthodox Greek Catholic Church in America with 700,000 members. Next were the Russian Orthodox Catholic Church in America, Patriarchal Exarchate, with some 160,000 members and the Russian Church outside Russia with about 60,000 members. Under the agreement with the Patriarchate of Moscow for the establishment of the new Church the Patriarchal Exarchate was dissolved.

The composition of the Russian Orthodox Church in America, including all its subdivisions, derives from the type of community that developed within the United States as a minority Church. It followed the purpose of surviving rather than teaching or recruiting believers. The same purpose was originally adopted by the Greek Orthodox Church in America.

Russian Orthodox missionaries came to America in 1792. They established work in Alaska and gradually moved down to the West Coast to form a station known today as Fort Ross, California. A diocese under the Church of Moscow was established in 1840 in America. From that time until the early 20th century, the jurisdiction of Moscow was recognized in North America.

The Russian Revolution of 1917-18 and World War I changed the situation. The Soviet domination in Russia made the relations of the Russian Orthodox in America with the Mother Church in Moscow precarious—if not impossible. In 1924, the Sobor (governing unit) proclaimed a temporary "self-government" and established the Metropolia.

The Russian Orthodox hoped that the establishment of an autocephalous "Orthodox Church of America" will provide American Orthodoxy as a whole a new opportunity. This did not mean, however, that the Russians were aiming at heading and governing the new American Orthodox Church.

Fr. John Meyendorf, who conducted the negotiations between the Moscow Patriarchate and the Russian Orthodox Church in America, writing in the magazine *The Orthodox Church* said: "Obviously there can be no question of making this unity (Orthodox unity) under the Russians. Autocephaly implies the end of eccleciastical colonialism: Church life in America must have no other goals than the progress of Orthodoxy in this country . . . It cannot serve particular interests."

The granting of independence to the Russian Orthodox Church in America by the Moscow Patriarchate—the Mother Church in an officially atheist country—raised the question as to whether there could be a political significance or implication in connection with the decision. Father Meyendorf, who is also a member of the World Council of Churches, said in this regard that "The acceptance of the Moscow independence does not mean in any way that we solidify ourselves with Soviet politics . . . In a way it is the opposite —we are free now."

Yet the question remains unanswered. Why was this freedom offered at a time when the existence of the Church in the Soviet Union is much more dangerous than it was even before, and there is no doubt, of course, that the Patriarchate of Moscow had the approval of the Soviet government in order to grant autocephalia to the Russian Orthodox Church in America?

The Ecumenical Patriarch, Athenagoras I, spiritual leader of Eastern Orthodox world, refused to recognize the new, independent Russian Orthodox Church of America. In a letter to the Patriarch of Moscow, Alexei, who died April 1970, Athenagoras, "first among equals" in the hierarchy, said that the Orthodox Church of America would not be enrolled in the Sacred Catalogue of the Holy Orthodox Autocephalous Churches and that the question of Orthodoxy's future in America should be decided in a Pan-Orthodox fashion.

The Patriarch also wrote that "We consider it superfluous and useless to enumerate in detail all the disastrous consequences that such a possible action by the Holy Russian Church might result in. For your Beatitude (the Patriarch of Moscow) well knows what an overthrow of our ecclesiastical order, and what a more general upheaval can come about when such proclamations of autocephality are made in violation of jurisdiction, spontaneously and unilaterally, on behalf of a Church, by anyone of the autocephalous Churches."

"Turning now to those Orthodox Churches in 'diaspora' in America," Athenagoras added, "which are subject to various old country jurisdictions, and which depend on them until there is a Pan-Orthodox resolving of the matters involved, it is obvious that the proclamation of the autocephality of anyone of these churches, if it is done in the manner now being planned with reference to the Metropolia, constitutes an action which is not only contrary to sacred canons which have been the order of our Orthodox Church for many centuries, but an action which, instead of furthering brotherly efforts for the re-establishment of regular relations, could become a source of problems for Orthodox in America. The results of these problems cannot avoid becoming, in a more general sense, the object of upsetting inter-Orthodox relations."

The 28th canon of the Council of Calcedon (451 A.D.) gives to the Church of Constantinople jurisdiction over territories beyond the limits of Christianity at that time. The granting of national Churches status, or independence by Constantinople, therefore, has canonical basis as well as precedent.

It was from Constantinople that the Russian Church received autocephality in the 16th century. The other national churches, such as the churches of Bulgaria, Rumania, Greece and Serbia, were given independent status, mostly during the past two centuries. Independence had characteristically come from the Ecumenical Patriarchate following a referendum of the other Orthodox Churches.

On the other hand, the Church of Moscow argued that it could give independence to the Metropolia on the basis of primacy of missionaries in America, but the argument does not seem to be shared by all other Orthodox Churches.

The Orthodox division in America seems to follow a typical pattern of national churches. However, the largest jurisdiction—the Greek Orthodox Archdiocese of North and South America—whether auto-cephalous or dependent from the Ecumenical Patriarchate favors a merged Western Synod under a spiritual authority deriving from divine rights established in the distant past by Constantinople.

Until matters are decided, one way or another—and in this con--nection one should wait for the Pan-Orthodox Council to convene sometime in the future—the establishment of a single American Orthodox Church uniting all Christian Orthodox in this country remains problematic. As long as a division which might create further problems exists, the Greek Orthodox Archdiocese of North and South America has to decide on how to protect the new Greek-American generations from showing an eventual preference for a more pragmatic Orthodoxy, away from the influence and the jurisdiction of churches outside America.

The establishment of the American Orthodox Church by the Russians should not be interpreted as a progressive move in harmony with the American environment. If such an interpretation were to be given then the Greek Orthodox Church in America might be labelled by these new generations as undecided, unrealistic in regard to its own position and to the necessity of adopting the necessary reforms.

The 20th Clergy-Laity Congress of the Greek Orthodox Archdiocese of North and South America

U P TO the late fifties the Greek Orthodox Church in America was influenced mostly by the older generation who, deeply anchored in the past, hardly envisaged the future of a Church which would be able to attract and retain the new generations. The Greek Archdiocese of North and South America was not in a position to assume a stronger leadership in questions pertaining to the identification of the religious and cultural Greek-American community. But gradually the new generations entered the scene and showed interest and concern about the future. These new generations were thinking—and even pressing—in terms of eventual changes which would make them feel more at ease within the American environment of which they are the genuine product.

It became imperative for the Church to study and possibly to revise its various activities. Doubts as to whether the Church was following the right attitude in view of so many changes and so many demands started to grow in the mind of the Church. Archbishop Iakovos expressed these doubts in his keynote address to the 20th Clergy-Laity Congress of the Greek Orthodox Archdiocese of North and South America held in New York City, between June 27 and July 4, 1970, when he asked: "Does our Church follow the road which will lead to its perpetuation, or should it chart a new course? Can it live unto itself, without dependency upon a Mother Church, or without interdependency upon other Orthodox Churches in America? If we should take into serious consideration the reality here, how many and what manner of readaptation should it undergo in order to be considered a serious factor in the creation of a religious life in America?"

During the Congress, and in the most dramatic move of its fifty year history in this country, the Greek-Orthodox Archdiocese of North and South America approved the use of vernacular languages in its services. No repudiation of Greek was involved in the action of the biennial clergy-laity Congress. The resolution, which also

230

called for a liturgical review, adopted unanimously, gave local parish priests, in consultation with bishops, the right to decide on the language question. The debate was lengthy and often emotional but the affirmative vote of 1000 delegates left little doubt as to how the Congress felt. Yet, the decision was interpreted in some circles as a "total abolishment" of the Greek language.

In 1964, the Clergy-Laity Congress held in Denver, Colorado, had approved the use of English in sermons, Gospel readings and a few prayers in the Sunday liturgy. Actually the decision of the 20th Congress in regard to the use of vernacular merely legalized a situation already existing in certain areas where the use of English was considered indispensable. But the "furor" created both in this country among Organizations and Federations and in Greece itself did not subside. A number of clarifications issued by the Greek-Orthodox Archdiocese of North and South America and two letters sent by the Ecumenical Patriarch of Constantinople—indeed couched in a rather Delphic manner—proved to be of no avail. The attacks against the Greek Orthodox Archdiocese and the decisions of the 20th Congress continued and often led to a distortion of certain facts.

The decision of the 20th Congress was based on a report of the Liturgical and Linguistic Committee (composed of forty-six priests and twenty-eight laymen) which submitted the following resolution:

> BE IT RESOLVED THAT THIS CONGRESS recognizing the great need for liturgical review and study receive with satisfaction the report of the appointment of a liturgical committee chaired by His Grace, Bishop Timotheos of Rodostolou, and recommends that staff and economic support be accorded it.

At the outset it should be clearly understood that nothing in this report is to be interpreted as a repudiation or denial of the utilization of the Greek language in the ecclesiastical services performed in the Greek Orthodox Archdiocese of North and South America. Officially since the Clergy-Laity Conference held in Denver (1964) there is authorization for only the most limited use of languages other than Greek in ecclesiastical services. The committee in its deliberations, however, ascertained that languages other than Greek are in fact being used in various parishes throughout the Archdiocesan District to meet specific local situations. The committee determined that the use of languages other than Greek has occured because of the needs of the communicants and the need to make Greek Orthodoxy relevant to 20th Century man.

Therefore, the committee respectfully reports as follows:

WHEREAS language is an indispensable tool for the teaching and understanding and practice of the Faith;

WHEREAS the peoples of this Archdiocese speak a number of vernacular languages: Greek, English, Spanish, French, or Portuguese;

WHEREAS we conceived it important and in the Orthodox tradition that the teaching, liturgies and mysteries of the Church be transmitted to the people in their own vernacular language;

BE IT RESOLVED that this Congress recommends that the Archdiocese permit the use of the vernacular language as needed in church services in accordance with the judgment of the parish priest in consultation with his bishop;

BE IT FURTHER RESOLVED THAT in those instances of need for further consultation the matter shall be referred to the Archbishop.

It is recommended that the Archdiocese, through the proper body, assemble various church musicians for arranging and revising the Liturgical music for our Church, for use in the vernacular.

Following the continuation of the attacks against the decisions of the 20th Clergy-Laity Congress, the Greek Orthodox Archdiocese issued a communication in which it clarified that:

1) The resolution by which the Archdiocese is asked to permit the vernacular in the Liturgy wherever and whenever necessary, does not mean that Greek is replaced by any other language if the congregation understands Greek. The resolution concerns Orthodox congregations who do neither understand nor speak Greek; and by vernacular, Greek, English, French, Spanish, or Portuguese is meant, as the case may be.

2) No Liturgical changes have been decided nor are to be decided in the foreseable future. A study of our liturgical texts is in process not only here, but in Europe as well, even in Greece. In fact, our liturgical texts will be on the agenda of the Orthodox Synod expected to begin its deliberations in 1973.

3) The English translation of the Liturgy on which the Archdiocese's Liturgical Commission is working, constitutes no new development. It merely aims at providing a truer and better English rendering and consequently at superseding the dozen or

more translations now used in various communities partly in ceremony and partly for following the ceremony by members not understanding Greek.

In so far as the issue of a certain measure of autonomy to be granted to the Greek Orthodox Church in America, in an announcement of the Archdiocesan Council it was stated that:

> The 20th Clergy-Laity Congress seriously occupied itself with the Topic: 'What is the future of our Church under existing and newly arising conditions?,' and commissioned the Archbishop to submit a pertinent memorandum to His All-Holiness the Ecumenical Patriarch, and to the Holy Synod of the Ecumenical Throne, which would analyze the reasons for requesting the privileges of a measure of autonomy, but would in no way ask for independence or autocephaly for our Church, or for the breaking off our ties with the Mother Church of Constantinople.

In his keynote address to the 20th Clergy-Laity Congress Archbishop Iakovos said that: "It is a fact that our Church is being led, sooner or later, to a condition of autonomy, in the example of every American Church. The conditions prevailing in this land and in the countries which our Archdiocese encompasses, demand some type of autonomy. The needs cannot be met and appreciated from afar. The growing responsibility placed upon the Archdiocese does not permit it to remain unresponsive or deny the strength which comes from the opinion of its clergy and laity in determining the decisions which would serve its future."

In regard to the decisions of the 20th Clergy-Laity Congress and to the created undesired situation that followed the Congress, the Ecumenical Patriarch sent two messages, to which various interpretations were given.

In His message of September 12, 1970, Athenagoras said that "The more than a thousand delegates of the Parishes voted brilliant and praiseworthy resolutions on vital community, educational, social and economic problems that occupy the faithful in the blessed land of America. The resolutions, as well, indicate the means by which will be maintained the immortal language of our fathers sanctified by the fact that this is the language in which were written the Holy books of the New Testament, that hand down to us the words and acts of Our Savior. Also, the resolutions indicate the means by which the valuable legacy of our familial and ecclesiastical traditions will be maintained. In view of such resolutions we cannot but feel exceptionally moved and strengthened in the pride we take in you." (The message was addressed to the Reverend Clergy, the members of the Parish Councils, to the Archdiocesan Organizations and Societies and to the Christian of the Greek Orthodox Archdiocese of North and South America.)

Referring specifically to the question of the Greek language, the Ecumenical Patriarch said: "We woul like to believe, however, that the turmoil caused was certainly the result of a simple misunderstanding, because there can be no one among you who can have an opinion different than that the Greek language is and will forever remain the basic and pre-eminent liturgical language of the Greek Orthodox Archdiocese of America . . ."

Part of the Greek-American press refused to accept the view that it was all a "misunderstanding" and as a matter of fact interpreted the Patriarchal message as a clear repudiation of the decisions reached by the 20th Clergy-Laity Congress regarding the question of language. On the other hand, the Greek Orthodox Church thought that the Patriarchal message "in essence contains a paternal appeal . . . for the restoration of the disturbed peace and tranquillity in the hearts of some of our people, arising from rumors that the usage of the Greek language in our services will be abolished."

It is interesting to mention here that during the Congress and speaking about the present and future system of education, Mr. Emmanuel Hatziemmanuel, of the Department of Education of the Greek Orthodox Archdiocese of North and South America in his address had this to say in connection with the Greek language:

> Effective teaching of the Greek language is not only an obligation on our part to past, present and future generations of Greek ancestry, but a privilege to teach it and a privilege to learn it on the part of our children. This kind of etiology should at all times guide our approach to the question of the Greek language and should animate and drive those who have the honor and sacred obligation to teach it. The Greek language is our Church language, and though the form of the latter is much more ancient than spoken Greek, children with a sound footing in modern Greek will benefit in worship.

Such statements can hardly justify the contention that a campaign is underway to abolish the Greek language. Nor is this a message that will determine with the utmost precision what must be done for the perpetuation of Orthodoxy in America and the continuation of hellenic "awareness" among the future Greek-American generations but rather the specific requirements within the environment in which this future is shaped.

In this connection the role of the Church is to try to anticipate this future and be prepared for it with the firm conviction that a church does not belong only to the past but must find its right place—a place dictated by reality.

As to the question of the language which has created such a controversy the adoption of a bilingual system—Greek and vernacular—of religious communication with all believers might provide a solution in harmony with the needs and demands of all Greek Orthodox in America.

Some Closing Remarks

PREDICTIONS about the future of Hellenism in America can be dangerous and fallacious—especially when one is fully aware that when attempting to foresee the future one realizes that historical evolution is an unpredictable adversary.

One thing, however, is certain: it would be a tragic mistake if the future of Hellenism in America was to be seen as a contest between Americanization and Hellenization. No pressure from whatever source can mold the future which, above all, is subjected to the power of evolution. I believe that both the Greek Orthodox Church in America and Greece itself should feel satisfied if the Greek-American generations to come can be inspired by an Hellenic awareness—a proud feeling of Philhellenism. No one can fight indefinitely against the pace of historical evolution.

The new Greek-American generations represent an entirely different aspect of Hellenic presence in the United States. As time goes by Americanization follows its normal, logical course. There is no ethnic group in America which has finally avoided the inevitable assimilation. Some battles are still fought, but they are rather delaying actions. The new Greek-American generations cannot be an exception to the rule. They are gradually drifting away from the full influence inherited from their parents or grandparents. They go to the Greek Orthodox Church. Yet, some Greek-Americans attend churches of other denominations. The best one could expect of them is to develop and retain a feeling of justified pride for the ancestry.

The new Greek-American generations might lose their spiritual link with Greece if national identification with Greece was to be imposed upon them as a duty to their parents or an obligation to their origin. Nobody seems to take into consideration their primary obligations to the United States. To the Irish-Americans, the French-Americans or the German-Americans and to so many others, their respective countries of origin are no less glorious than Greece is to the Greek-Americans. Yet, their gradual and unavoidable

Americanization has not been halted.

The argument offered that, after all, the Greeks of Turkey and of Egypt have succeeded, through the ages, in retaining their absolute national identification with Greece and that, therefore the Greek-Americans of the future should do likewise, does not stand to reason. Both in Turkey and in Egypt, the Greeks were at all time the predominant influential force and, moreover, the absorbing potential of these two countries was, indeed, non-existing. Especially in Turkey, the Greeks lived in a hostile environment and the necessity to maintain a defensive attitude against pressures and abuses galvanized their "Greekness." Most parts of Turkey where they resided, and more particularly Constantinople, belonged to Greece. They felt and behaved as though they were under foreign occupation. In Turkey and in Egypt, the Greeks did not face any spiritual or intellectual competition. To the contrary they communicated their own intellectual superiority to the natives. The exact opposite is true insofar as America is concerned: the spiritual and intellectual influence of the environment is extremely effective —the environment is friendly and the future promising.

The United States has offered hospitality, freedom, opportunities and prosperity in order to achieve one day a genuine, uniform national entity. Efforts or tendencies at preventing eventually the realization of this natural phenomenon cannot be expected to be tolerated by the American nation as a whole.

Those who still refuse to recognize and accept historical evolution must realize that the future of Hellenism in America lies in a selection between total disappearance and the survival of Greek consciousness among the future Greek-American generations.

The perpetuation of Hellenic awareness can be secured only through a realistic approach dictated by the necessities imposed by reality and not by any hasty, superficial, miscalculated pressure upon the present and future Greek-Americans. It must be emphasized, time and again, that American born citizens of Greek ancestry represent today's Hellenism in America. It is a new, different brand of Hellenism, which should not be compared or confused with the first Greek immigrants and which demands to be considered as such.

The new immigrants coming from Greece are actually taking the place of the first immigrants; they, too, are facing problems of adjustment though they are not subjected to the same difficulties and obstacles encountered by their predecessors.

The nature of the contact between the future Greek-American generations and Greece itself depends to a large extent upon the various Greek Governments. They should not consider the Greek-Americans or, as a matter of fact, the Greeks of the Diaspora, as a "problem" which must be resolved. Actually, there is no "problem" whatsoever.

In a conversation with this writer Archbishop Iakovos said that "Greece—and its Governments, present and future—should realize that the Americans of Greek descent coming into closer contact with the Greeks of Greece would like to find that there are similarities between them—similarities of democratic thinking. Any lack of interest on the part of Greece in regard to the religious, political, democratic and cultural sensitivity of the Greek-American generations would, without any doubt, lead to a fatal suspension of any relationship."

However, this relationship should come under certain rules and regulations as far as Greece is concerned. It must be understood that the child or the grandchild of a Greek immigrant is an American citizen. What should be expected of him is the reaction of an American conscious of his origin.

I sincerely hope the day will come for all those concerned with the problem to see things as they are and not as they would like them to be. If, and when, this day will come the question of the perpetuation of Hellenism in America—the hellenic presence in the United States—will be better understood and placed in its right perspective on both sides of the Atlantic.

BIBLIOGRAPHY

Andreadis, Arist. *Argonaut* magazine (1961)

Bennet, Rosemary and Stephen Vincent. *A Book of Americans* (1933)

Burgess, Thomas. *Greeks in America*

Constant, Theodore. *Employment and Business of the Greeks in the United States* (1945)

Dahl, Robert. *Time* (December, 1966)

Emmanuel, Philippos. *Course of Study* (1958)

Everett, Edward. *North American Review* (1823)

Fairchild, Henry Pratt. *Greek Immigration in the United States*

Giannacoulis, Theodore. *Introduction to the History of the Greek-Americans*

Goudas, Athanasios. *Vioi Paralliloi Andron tis Epanastaseos* (1875)

Hutchinson, A.P. *Immigrants and their Children—1850-1950* (1956)

Javaras, Paul. "New Tendencies in the Thinking of the Greeks in America," *Greek Review* (December, 1926)

Kollias, Sifis. *Demetrios Callimachos—Mia Artia Agonistiki Syneidisis* (1945)

Kourides, Peter. *The Evolution of the Greek Orthodox Church in the United States and its Present Problems*

Lacey, Thomas. *Our Greek Immigrants*

Lonn, Ela. *Foreigners in the Union Army and Navy* (1951)

Louros, Nikos. *Argonaut* magazine (1958)

Malafouris, Babis. *Oi Ellines tis Amerikis* (1948)

Manolis, Paul G. *Orthodox Observer* (May, 1966)

Menzies, Archibald. *Small Pamphlet* (1763)

Nahirny, Vladimir C. and Fishman J.A. "American Immigrant Groups: Ethnic Identification and the Problem of Generations," *Sociological Review* (1965)

Lowry, Nelson. "Speaking of Tongues," *American Journal of Sociology* (1948)

Pamboukis, Panos. *Apodimos Ellinismos* (1961)

Panagopoulos, E.P. *New Smyrna—An Eighteenth Century Odyssey*

Papas, Aris T. *The Personality of Greek-Americans* (1964)

Patrinakos, Nic. D. *The Individual and the Orthodox Church*

Peclaris, Panos. *The Hellenic Review* (April, 1963)

Perros, George. *Officers of Greek Descent in the Union Navy 1861-1865*

Price, C.A. *Immigration and Groups Settlement*

Purchas, Samuel. *Pilgrims*

Riesman, David. "Some Observations Regarding Marginality," *Phylon* (1951)

Saloutos, Theodore. *The Greeks in the United States* (1964)

—,— . *They Remember Greece* (1956)

Sandburg, Carl. *Abrahaam Lincoln: The Prairie Years and the War Years*

Taylor, Alex. *Tutching's California Magazine* (1859)

Tuckerman, Charles K. *Magazine of American History* (1887)

Valaoras, Vassilios. *Ellinismos ton Inomenon Politeion* (1933)

Vlachos, Evangelos. *The Assimilation of the Greek in the United States* (1968)

Vournas, George C. *Congressional Record Proceedings and Debates of the 86th Congress*

Wade, Richard. *Time* (1966)

Warner, Lloyd. *The Social System of American Ethnic Groups* (1945)

Zolotas, Xenophon. *Immigration and Economic Development* (1966)

Zoustis, Vasssilios. *O Ellinismos tis Amerikis kai i Drasis tou-I Istoria tis Ellinikis Arhiepiskopis Voriou kai Notiou Amerikis* (1944)

Ziogas, Elias. *Argonaut* magazine

ARCHIVES, CONGRESSIONAL DOCUMENTS, ETC.

Washington National Archives

North American Review

Columbia Encyclopedia

The Florida Historical Quarterly

Archives of Florence and Venice, published in Italian by Professor Spyridon P. Lambrou

American Historical Review

New York Commercial Advertiser

Congressional documents related to the 1821 Greek War of Independence

Annals of the United States Congress

Washington Historical Quarterly

The National Cyclopaedia of American Biography

Dictionary of American Biography

Reports of U.S. Legation in Athens, 1904

Annual Reports of the Commissioner General of Immigration

The Washington Post, 1904

Report of the President of the Foreign Relations Committee of the United States Senate, 1909

Archives of the City of New Orleans

California newspaper (January, 1917)

Argonaut magazine

Un Report Determination and Consequences of Population trends 1953

Hellenic Review-New York, 1960